GHOST
TOWNS
OF
KANSAS

GHOST
TOWNS
OF
KANSAS
A Traveler's Guide

DANIEL FITZGERALD

University Press of Kansas

Published by the University Press of Kansas
(Lawrence, Kansas 66049), which was organized
by the Kansas Board of Regents and is operated
and funded by Emporia State University, Fort
Hays State University, Kansas State University,
Pittsburg State University, the University of
Kansas, and Wichita State University

Library of Congress Cataloging-in-Publication Data

Fitzgerald, Daniel.
Ghost towns of Kansas: a traveler's guide /
Daniel Fitzgerald.   p.   cm.
Bibliography: p.
Includes index.
ISBN 0-7006-0367-0 (alk. paper).
ISBN 0-7006-0368-9 (pbk.)
1. Cities and towns, Ruined, extinct, etc.—Kansas
—Guide-books. 2. Kansas—Description and
travel—1981- —Guide-books. 3. Kansas—History,
Local. I. Title.
F679.3.F58 1988
917.81'0433—dc19
88-26

Printed in the United States of America
10 9 8 7 6

CONTENTS

1595

FOREWORD

When I first came to work at the Kansas State Historical Society nearly thirty years ago, I was shown a shelf filled with about forty clothbound, loose-leaf notebooks. "That's our dead-town list," I was told, and the matter was dropped. Curiosity got the better of me—I lost no time in examining the dead-town list, and the more I studied it the more fascinated I became. As the years passed and I did more research into Kansas history, the dead-town list became invaluable as a primary source.

The list contains the names of about 6,000 communities that either never saw the light of day or, if they did exist, are no longer around. Had these towns been built and survived, they—combined with the incorporated towns in Kansas today—would have resulted in a density of one town for every twelve square miles. One could not have walked, ridden, or driven more than seven miles in any direction without encountering another community. These dead towns are prime examples of major entrepreneurial activity in Kansas from 1854 to about 1890. Potential promoters and investors perceived town building as a sure fire capital venture designed to make them rich almost overnight.

That such a condition existed is not surprising when one remembers that when Kansas Territory was opened to white settlement on May 30, 1854, there were only a few non-Indian settlements within its boundaries. Caucasian residence was limited to military posts, Indian missions operated by a variety of religious persuasions, and government-operated or -licensed centers such as trading posts. Before Kansas Territory was created, land was reserved for its Indian occupants; white settlement was, in theory, prohibited. What a magnificent opportunity, then, when these more than 80 million "uninhabited" acres suddenly became available. In that part of Kansas closest to Missouri, towns sprang up virtually overnight, and as modes of transportation and settlement pushed west, town building traveled along.

As in any business venture not all towns succeeded in making their promoters wealthy, and some towns never progressed beyond the planning stage. Furthermore, many towns that were established soon died for a variety of reasons. A good example of success and failure, side by side, are the cities of Atchison and Sumner.

The Atchison Town Company was formed in Missouri on July 27, 1854, and the first sale of town lots took place on September 21. By February

3, 1855, the town had its own newspaper, the *Squatter Sovereign*. Atchison was a center of proslavery activity, and free-staters were not welcome. John P. Wheeler, an ardent abolitionist, decided that a free-state town in the vicinity would prosper, and he laid out the town of Sumner some two or three miles down the river. As part of his town promotion Wheeler issued a colored lithograph depicting Sumner's advantages and sent copies back East to possible investors and settlers. John James Ingalls, later U.S. senator from Kansas (1873–1891), was one of many lured by what he later called "that chromatic triumph of lithographed mendacity."[1]

The Wheeler lithograph depicted a bustling river city boasting a variety of cultural activities. What Ingalls actually saw when he arrived on October 5, 1858, was quite different. He wrote home to his father in Massachusetts that he had just landed "in the Promised Land, supposed to be flowing with milk and honey. . . . There are no churches in the place, instead of four, as was represented to me. No respectable residences; no society; no women except a few woebegone, desolate-looking old creatures; no mechanical activity. . . . no schools, no children; nothing but the total reverse of the picture which was presented to me."[2]

At one time Sumner's population was much larger than Atchison's, but as the latter turned to free-state proclivity the citizens of Sumner, including Ingalls, drifted north. In June 1860 a tornado all but leveled Sumner, and it was never built back. Today little remains of its early dreams.

This process was repeated over and over again for the next thirty years or so. As railroads built west from the Missouri River, towns sprang up along their supposed and actual routes. Everest and Effingham were named for persons associated with the central branch of the Union Pacific, as were Wetmore, Goff, Corning, and Greenleaf. Downs commemorates William F. Downs, general superintendent of the Missouri Pacific. Vining, Moran, Roper, Amiot, Fanning, Leonardville, Kelso, and Skiddy are all associated with railroads. Perry on the Union Pacific was named after the railroad's president, John D. Perry. The Santa Fe often named its towns for officers of the company—for example, Coolidge, Spivey, Lakin, Nickerson, Hunnewell, Cheney, and Strong City.

Sometimes town promoters missed the boat when the railroad was routed in a more advantageous direction than that originally planned. If a railroad did bypass a fledgling town for another townsite, proprietors would often move their buildings to the new location. Thus towns that erupted on the plains overnight could disappear just as quickly. One can picture the scene presented by large frame buildings moving across the prairie to the railroad much as a tourist would travel to the depot.

Many a Kansas town died because it lost or never attained the county seat. Fights among rival towns were common as western Kansas counties were being organized. Sometimes noted gunfighters—such as Bill Tilghman and Jim Masterson, Bat's brother—were employed to ensure the interests of a particular town, and on occasion bloodshed ensued as records were purloined from one courthouse and taken to another. Losing the county seat often meant death for a town.

Newspapers were extremely important to newborn communities. Efficient town companies and promoters saw to it that a newspaper was one of the first businesses established. The object of the press was not so much to inform the public of local and national happenings as to "boom" the town. Just as Wheeler took liberties with his lithographic description of Sumner, so did the editors of many newspapers. Trail City, which built on the border of Kansas and Colorado in 1885, advertised that the town was "beautifully located on the Arkansas river at the intersection of the Santa Fe railroad with the Great National Cattle Trail . . . presenting the most Enchanting Scenery, surrounded by verdant hills, in full view of Pike's Peak and the Rocky Mountains."[3] Drawings often showed factories belching black smoke into the clear Kansas air as a sign of progress. Others turned the Great American Desert into lushfarmlands. Clearly the land-seeking pioneer was hard put to know in which paradise to settle.

Towns are still created in Kansas today, but the founders' motives are different. Development of an industry in an out-of-the-way location caused some activity in the first two or three decades of the twentieth century. Many new towns assumed the names of old sites that were flooded to create federal reservoirs.

The opportunity to become wealthy through town building no longer exists in Kansas, which perhaps is fortunate. The possibility of dying still haunts rural communities as businesses and residents move to nearby larger towns, thanks to the mobility provided by the automobile. The era of town boom or bust is a fascinating period of American history that has not been extensively explored. The pages that follow provide an enjoyable introduction to an often overlooked and unappreciated epoch in our past.

Joseph W. Snell
Executive Director,
Kansas State Historical Society
Topeka, Kansas

PREFACE

Horace Greeley once stated, "It takes three log houses to make a city in Kansas, but they begin calling it a city as soon as they have staked out the lots."[1] The history of the 6,000 extinct geographical locations, or "ghost towns," that were born, prospered, and died in the history of the state bears out this statement. In the following vignettes of Kansas ghost towns, it will also become apparent that the existence of "three log houses" was significant enough to change the course of history.

Lost communities made a lasting impression on me while I was traveling in Colorado years ago. After visiting towns such as Black Hawk and Central City, I became enamored of—if not obsessed with—the boom and collapse of frontier communities in the early development of the West. Much to my surprise, I then found these boom-and-bust communities to be as prevalent in Kansas as in the old mining sections of Colorado. What began as a personal adventure became a three-volume set of books entitled *Ghost Towns of Kansas*, which I published between 1976 and 1982.

In writing this volume on Kansas ghost towns, I have reevaluated those earlier works in order to produce this one coherent whole. I sifted through those ghost town histories to find seventy-nine that I consider unique or singularly important, and their stories appear here in completely rewritten form. I also added twenty new ghost town histories. This book has been divided into nine sections corresponding to regions of the state; within each section, the towns are mostly arranged from east to west and are located on the map of the section.

Ghost towns in Kansas are quite different from those in many other western states. Kansans have always found a use for lumber and brick from deserted buildings; as a result, little remains of many of the communities discussed in this book. The sites of many old towns have been plowed or used as pasture by farmers. More often than not, all that is left of a Kansas ghost town is dust and tumbleweeds; imagination becomes the key.

My definition of a Kansas ghost town is a town that has disappeared completely or is only a shadowy remnant of what it once was. Some of these communities still have life, although nothing to compare with the prosperity they enjoyed in their heyday. Too small for more than a post office and a few stores, they still have spirit and hope for a brighter future. I included a few sites that were not towns but were either significant temporary campsites or stage stations established along major trails. Two examples,

Alcove Springs and Henshaw Station, were important local points of interest but never developed into full-blown communities. They will give the reader a different, if not unique, perception of the settlement and development of early sites in Kansas that never materialized into anything substantial after they ceased to perform a particular function.

I hope readers will enjoy the following vignettes of some of the more colorful Kansas ghost towns. As you tour the sites of these towns, I also hope you will appreciate the subtle beauty Kansas reveals to those who take the time to experience it—from the chat piles of southeast Kansas against a late summer sunset to the green lushness of the Flint Hills against the backdrop of a huge thunderhead. A final note: Please remember that the sites of many of these towns are now private property, and permission should be obtained before visiting them.

Daniel Fitzgerald

ACKNOWLEDGMENTS

This volume is the culmination of over twelve years' work. In that time, help has come from many quarters. A number of individuals, however, deserve special mention.

Many staff members of the Kansas State Historical Society helped me get started and have kept me going through the years. They include Joseph Snell, Robert Richmond, Jack Traylor, Gene Decker, Terry Harmon, Portia Allbert, Nancy Sherbert, Thomas Norris, Pat Michaelis, Art DeBacker, Connie Menninger, Sara Judge, John Lynch, Jane Journot, and Robert Keckeisen.

Several professors in the History Department at the University of Kansas tolerated my lengthy class papers and helped to improve my writing style. They include Rita Napier, Don McCoy, William Stitt Robinson, Robert Oppenheimer, and Ray Hiner. They will never know how much I appreciated their help.

Relatives, friends, and colleagues in the field of history have been constant sources of assistance. They include my wife, Gwen; my parents, Calvin and Mary Fitzgerald; Bradley Trimble, who also conceived the idea of a book on Kansas ghost towns; Gene DeGruson; Mike Printz; Dr. Jack Deeter; Cory Barron; and, of course, Nyle Miller, who always had a new town for me to research just when I thought the well was running dry.

A book is rarely the work of one person alone. *Ghost Towns of Kansas: A Traveler's Guide* has benefited more than most books from the contributions of many people behind the scenes. In my own way, I thank each of the people mentioned here for being there with ideas when I truly needed them. This book is dedicated to them.

Daniel Fitzgerald

The Regions of Kansas

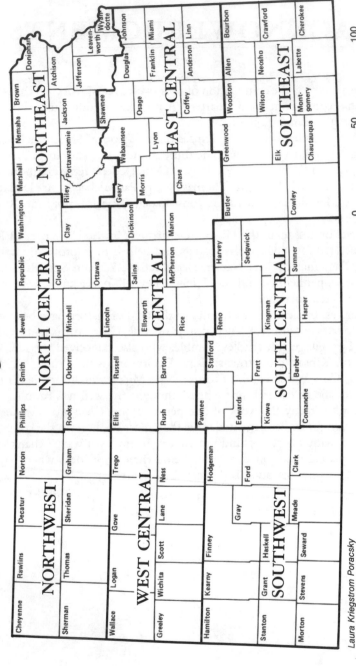

Laura Kriegstrom Poracsky

Scale in Miles

0   50   100

1

NORTHEAST KANSAS

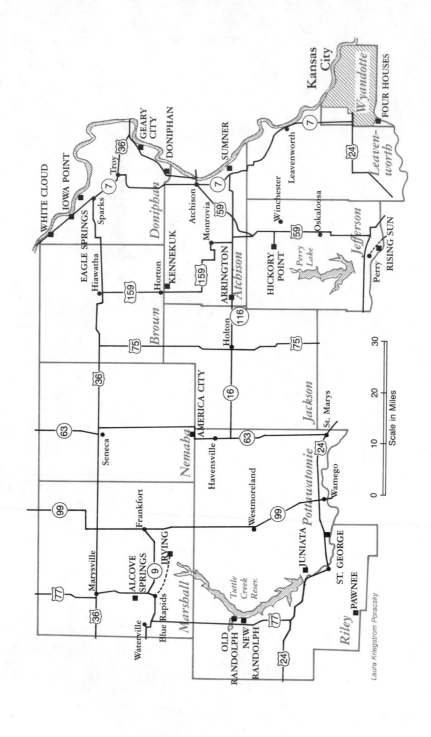

Laura Kriegstrom Poracsky

WHITE CLOUD
Doniphan County

Today Kansas Highway 7 winds its way along the Missouri River and the bluffs region in extreme northeast Kansas, meandering through a quiet village nestled among the high hills. At first glance this sleepy little burg hardly seems worth a stop, but if we can turn the clock back to the 1850s, the view becomes quite different. Steamboats are docked along the levee, and the people are excited and busy. The general stores and saloons beckon the wayfarer to come in and have a mint julep. Huge French-style mansions above and below Main Street glow with a New Orleans atmosphere, and southern belles and country gentlemen sit on shaded verandas passing the day in quiet conversation while the people around them move at a rapid pace. This was the White Cloud of yesterday, a rich and distinguished city—the last trace of culture and civilization the emigrants saw before they departed for the "wild and woolly" West.

Indians had lived in the area for centuries. Rising unnaturally from the landscape surrounding the townsite are strange mounds, remnants of a sedentary, agricultural civilization that archaeologists call the Kansas City Hopewell Complex. The influence of this civilization extended as far north as the White Cloud locale sometime in the first century A.D. Many mounds have been found along the Missouri River, and Indian artifacts still litter the bluffs.[1]

White settlers began arriving in northeast Kansas after the Kansas-Nebraska Act was passed in 1854. In early 1856 the White Cloud Town Company was formed by a number of free-state men: J. H. Utt, J. Foley, C. Dorland, H. W. Peters, and Enoch Spaulding. Their first attempts to secure land from the local Iowa, Sac, and Fox Indians were futile, as the Indians were not interested in selling any of their reserve. White Cloud was, however, able to grab the title of county seat out of the hands of Bellemont residents late in 1856, and it remained the county seat for a number of years. In the spring of 1857, when other river towns were already thriving, the White Cloud Town Company finally succeeded in buying land from the Indians by offering additional incentives and increasing the purchase price.

On July 4, 1857, a big celebration was held in White Cloud to promote the town and sell lots. Crowds of settlers had been gathering in town all summer, and more people were brought in on three large steamboats from as far away as St. Louis and Council Bluffs for the Independence Day festivities. The day became one of the town's most successful: More than $24,000 worth of lots were sold.

The town company chartered two boats, the "Watossa" and the "Morning Star" . . . [and] engaged the St. Joseph brass band to provide music for a "grand ball" at night on the "Morning Star." They brought in a 24 pound "field piece" to provide the necessary noise. As the size of the promised crowd increased the committee on foods added to the beeves, sheep, pigs, and fowl held in readiness for cooking. . . .

"Business before" was the motto of the town company. For 1 ½ hours they sold lots. Then a procession formed, and the band led the way to a grove below the sawmill where everyone partook of the barbecue of bread and meat . . . in old Kentucky style. . . . At night two dances completed the program, one on the "Morning Star" and another in the room under the office of the *Kansas Chief*. . . . The boats waited until morning to leave.

Sol Miller . . . estimated the attendance at 2,000.[2]

After the land sales and excitement had died down in White Cloud, building began in earnest. The first businesses established were lumberyards, and soon White Cloud was manufacturing more than twice as much lumber as any other town on the Missouri River. The Beeler & Sons lumber company, located on the levee, had four sawmills operating at full capacity.

In 1857 the White Cloud Town Company was reorganized, with thirty trustees. The town company offered a free lot to any businessman who would agree to build on it immediately. Judge Michael Byrd built the first general store in town, but in 1858 this building was torn down and replaced by a planing mill. Dr. J. R. Gatling, secretary of the town company and inventor of the Gatling gun, opened a merchandise store, but at the outbreak of the Civil War in 1861 he left White Cloud and never returned.

Among White Cloud's first dignitaries was the editor of the town's *Kansas Chief*, journalist Sol Miller, whose fame as a writer and historian soon spread across the state. A loyal Republican, Miller was also independent, fearless, and blunt; he was respected even by those who opposed or hated him (even though at times his writing was in bad taste or even obscene). He wrote his editorials without regard for the prestige or power of any man and thus became one of the most influential and controversial journalists in Kansas.[3]

A large building was erected to house his newspaper, the *Kansas Chief*. The lower story was occupied by Ben Raffner's general store and the upper story by Sol Miller and his printing press. On the day the newspaper office opened, Miller was away on business. When he returned he found the type cases smashed and turned over and the type scattered all over the floor. This setback was but one of many Miller had to overcome as a con-

White Cloud was a major lumber producer for the region. This sketch appeared in Frank Leslie's Illustrated Newspaper *of June 5, 1867, with the caption: "Shipping Ties for the Union Pacific Railroad at White Cloud."*

sequence of his outspokenness and disregard for the sensibilities of many influential White Cloud businessmen and residents.[4]

Sol Miller's most colorful journalistic debate was with Thomas J. Key, editor of the *Doniphan Constitutionalist*. The two men became adversaries and exchanged insults in each issue of their respective newspapers. For example, Miller wrote on August 20, 1857, of Keys, a delegate to the constitutional convention, "It is said, but we hardly believe it, that he every morning sticks his head into an empty flour barrel, and yells at the top of his voice, 'Honorable THOMAS J. KEY!' just to hear how it sounds; and that he has all the little boys hired, with candy, to exclaim, when he walks down the street, 'There goes *Honorable* THOMAS J. KEY!' " Key responded on October 7: "We would gently hint to the cross-eyed, crank-sided, peaked and long razor-nosed, blue-mouthed, nigger-lipped, white-eyed, soft-headed, long-eared, crane-necked, blobber-lipped, squeaky-voiced, empty-headed, snaggle-toothed, filthy-mouthed, box-ankled, pigeon-toed, reel-footed, splay-footed, ignoble, Black Republican, abolition editor, to attend to his own affairs or we will pitch into him in earnest."

The first doctor in White Cloud was Thomas C. Shreve, brother of Capt. Henry Shreve, the founder of Shreveport, Louisiana. In the 1850s, when fever and ague were common ailments, Dr. Shreve always came to the aid of the suffering settlers. He was instrumental in bringing Quaker missionaries to this section of Kansas, and they not only induced other Quaker families to settle in White Cloud but also taught English and Christianity to the local Indians. These early missionaries greatly influenced the Iowa, Sac, and Fox Indians, who not only attended a nearby mission school but also became sedentary farmers. In 1857 Dr. Shreve built a huge southern-style mansion and had all his family's belongings—including a quilt made in 1820, a dozen fiddle-back chairs, and a treasured letter from George Washington—brought by steamboat up the Missouri River.[5]

On April 1, 1858, an Ohioan named Joshua Taylor purchased a small side-wheel steamer with the intention of establishing a ferry at White Cloud. When he arrived on June 3, he was greeted on the levee by an enthusiastic crowd and the firing of a cannon. Taylor formed a partnership with J. W. Moore, and they operated their boat, the *White Cloud*, until the spring of 1862, when they sold it to Ozias Bailey. Bailey ran the ferry for several years until the boat was wrecked and became unfit for further service.[6]

The two years before Kansas statehood were the "grand" years in White Cloud's history. A subtle French influence in architecture gave White Cloud the appearance of a typical southern community, and life was active and exciting. Some businessmen in White Cloud made quick fortunes before the Civil War, and their personal tastes were expressed in their elegant homes. The southerners, the French, the emigrants, and the Indians all came to trade in this bustling city.

White Cloud was a southern community because the steamboat trade was strictly oriented to the south. Most steamboat owners were southerners; most goods shipped by steamboat from White Cloud went from St. Louis south to New Orleans and the Gulf of Mexico. Thus business interests benefited from White Cloud's initial "southern orientation" and its establishment by several southern businessmen. This southern influence, however, apparently did not carry over into the political viewpoint of the community. Several free-state men were also involved in the founding of White Cloud, and consequently the community was never a strong advocate of slavery, although it did exist. Records in the Doniphan County Register of Deeds office show that on April 21, 1857, the following slaves were sold by Walter O. Bannon to Giles A. Briggs: one black woman named Sarah, a child named James, and a black man named Ar-

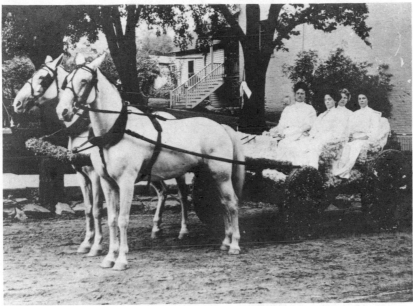

White Cloud residents held a street fair every year. Here a decorated carriage holds four ladies dressed in their finest clothes, posing for the photographer around 1890.

thur. The consideration of the sale was the release by Mrs. Briggs of her interest in land she owned in Missouri.

With the coming of the Civil War, White Cloud's romantic era came to an end, and during the war, White Cloud's residents were continually threatened by southern sympathizers from Missouri. On one occasion Daniel Todd and his family of six were kidnapped and taken across the Missouri River, but Todd managed to escape and joined the Union army. After the war he returned to White Cloud with his family and lived there for many years.

On May 3, 1863, at about 4:00 in the afternoon, a destructive hailstorm that lasted for more than a half hour hit the town. Many sheep, calves, chickens, and dogs were killed, and most of the larger livestock were seriously battered by the hail. Some of the townspeople were hurt; indeed, one man received fatal injuries when he attempted to save his wife, who had been knocked to the ground by the hailstones. Roofs were damaged, and innumerable windows were shattered.[7]

Despite these setbacks, the town prospered. In the same decade White

*White Cloud declined rapidly during the 1930s. This view shows Main Street, the river,
and the old steamboat warehouse on a quiet summer afternoon circa 1930.*

Cloud was officially incorporated, a mayor was elected, and many more
buildings were constructed. The first frame schoolhouse on the northwest
side of town was struck by lightning and had to be abandoned, but a brick
school was erected west of Main Street. Another large schoolhouse with
four classrooms was completed in February 1872 at a cost of $11,000.[8]

In 1870 a railroad—the Atchison & Nebraska—finally came to White
Cloud, thereby enabling the town to compete with several area communities that already had the advantage of a railroad link. In an 1873 advertising brochure printed by the railroad, White Cloud was noted as an
"energetic city—many manufacturing interests are represented, as well as
every branch of mercantile business." The population was listed as 2,000,
and businesses included "four general stores, two grocery stores, three drug
stores, one hardware store, two restaurants, two hotels, one livery stable,
one barber shop, one grist mill, one sawmill, two boot and shoe shops,
two blacksmith shops, one jewelry store, one billiard hall, one harness shop,
one wagon shop, one meat market, one printing office, one millinery store,
two carpenters, two lawyers, four physicians, three painters, and three
plasterers."[9]

The town's newspaper business was irregular during the 1870s. Sol Miller's
Kansas Chief moved to Troy in 1873. Another newspaper, the *White Cloud
Review*, strongly Republican in sentiment, was established by C. H. Holton

The Alex Poulet mansion remains a symbol of White Cloud's former elegance. Purchased for back taxes several years ago, it is now charmingly restored and is on the National Register of Historic Places.

& Company in 1880, but it lasted only one year before it ran into financial trouble.[10]

In the 1880s White Cloud began a slow decline, which was not noticeable at first. A business closed or burned down and was not replaced; one by one, families moved away to other towns. The Atchison & Nebraska Railroad stopped in town less often as the years went by, and the citizens began to take their business to Troy whenever possible. The effect of losing the county seat to Troy two decades earlier was a major factor in the town's economic slump. The boom days at White Cloud were nearly over. Even the beautiful mansions began to fall into disrepair, and before long the faded charm of the romantic age had disappeared.

In the early 1900s White Cloud became known as the place where "piggy banks" originated. A ten-year-old boy named Wilbur Chapman sold a prized pig to raise money for a boy in a leper colony, and his generosity gained national attention. It fostered the "piggy bank movement," and small banks in the shape of pigs were sold all over the country.

Yet White Cloud continued to decline. Currently the town is only a shadow of its former self, although a few nice houses and buildings still exist from the town's boom days , when it was called the queen of the Kansas steamboat towns. Directly west of Main Street is the old brick schoolhouse, now the town museum, and north of Main Street stands the loveliest structure in town, the Poulet Mansion, home of Alex Poulet, a Frenchman who lived in New Orleans and Iowa Point before moving to White Cloud after the Civil War. There he opened a hardware store, a general merchandise store, and a bank and became one of the town's most prominent citizens."[11]

Poulet's former home is a rectangular three-story Renaissance-style mansion built of red brick with a tower over the main entrance. Only two stories are visible from the front because of the sloping site, but the back view exposes all three floors and two long balconies adorned with iron railings.[12] When walking through the rooms of the mansion, which is now a private residence, one can almost hear the noise of the wagons on Main Street, the cries of the workers on the levee, the whistle of the steamboats, and the laughter of the southern belles as they are entertained by suave cavaliers. One glance out the window, however, at the abandoned buildings and the silent streets, and the romantic spell is broken. White Cloud becomes just another ghost town battling to survive.

White Cloud can be reached by taking U.S. Highway 36 west from Troy to the junction with state Highway 7 at the town of Sparks. Take Highway 7 and follow the signs north to White Cloud.

IOWA POINT
Doniphan County

Iowa Point, first settled in 1854, was located on the property of Reverend Samuel Irvin, who received the land from the U.S. government in payment for his missionary activities at the nearby Iowa, Sac, and Fox Indian mission. In 1855, Harvey W. Forman and John S. Pemberton platted the town and advertised lots in the local newspapers. Eager buyers arrived by the hundreds on steamboats from St. Joseph, Weston, and Westport Landing in Missouri, and Iowa Point boomed almost overnight.

The first buildings in town included a hotel, steamboat warehouse, general store, blacksmith shop, drugstore, meat market, sawmill, flour mill, and post office.[1] By 1857 Iowa Point, with a population estimated at 3,000, was the second largest town on the Missouri River after Leavenworth and had surpassed Atchison as a wholesale center.[2]

This view shows one of Iowa Point's early businesses around the turn of the century. Today this building has disappeared, leaving only a vacant lot.

The town was a major shipping point between Fort Leavenworth and Omaha, Nebraska. From one to five steamers docked there daily during the active seasons, and many families heading for claims in other counties disembarked at Iowa Point before heading west. Among those doing the most business were the many "Forty-niners" returning from the gold fields of California, who deposited their sacks of gold dust with the businessmen for safekeeping until they could board the next steamboat heading east.

Some of the town's financial success was due to publicity by the newspaper, the *Iowa Point Weekly Inquirer.* One of its many advertisers was Winkler's Saloon, where "cocktails and mint juleps are shaken up and stirred with pure crushed sugar to suit the fancy or taste of the customer." There were ads promoting trade with steamboats with such unlikely names as the *Watossa, Florence, Sioux City, St. Joseph & Sioux City, John Warner, T. J. McGill,* and *Mansfield.*

In the spring of 1857 local businessmen were taking in $1,000 a day, much of it in gold, which was so common that other types of currency were almost obsolete. In 1858, after a large brick hotel had been built and a steam ferryboat had begun operations on the Missouri, Iowa Point was at the height of its short-lived prosperity.[3]

Early in 1859 an economic recession, caused by the delayed arrival of the Panic of 1857, affected the community. The Iowa, Sac, and Fox Agency, a major source of revenue to the town, was moved several miles away; in addition, much of the town's prosperity was artificial, based on money from outside investors who had purchased lots with no intention of moving there. During the inflationary years of 1856 and 1857, these investors made handsome profits buying and selling lots, but they all lost money after it was suddenly in short supply as a result of the Panic of 1857. When Missouri's major bank, the Bank of Missouri, failed, many investors with investments in Iowa Point went bankrupt. At the same time the hotel burned down, the ferryboat sank, and the newspaper suspended business.

Iowa Point was divided over the slavery issue. During the territorial election in 1858, two men were seriously injured in a fight between proslavery men and free-state sympathizers. Later that year, the sheriff arrested a free-state man and charged him with horse stealing. The next night a mob of proslavery men attempted to abduct him from the jail and hang him. The prisoner grabbed a knife from his assailants and fought them off until the sheriff arrived. In the fray, one man was seriously wounded, and to avoid further trouble, the sheriff promptly ordered the prisoner to leave town.

At the outbreak of the Civil War, the town's population was evenly divided between northern and southern sympathies. Some of the northern sympathizers hastened to join the Union army, but those who stayed behind declared a war of their own. The town virtually went up in smoke. One night a southern sympathizer would carry a torch; the next night a free-state man would ignite a building. One fire in 1862 burned all the houses on one side of Main Street. Free-state citizens, fearing a Confederate invasion from across the river, organized a company of militia under the command of Capt. C. J. Beeler. In 1862 a threat of attack from the opposite bank of the Missouri River caused Captain Beeler to call in a company of the 8th Kansas Infantry. The enemy never appeared, but the danger of a possible invasion continued for three more years.

Soldiers returning from the war found a town nearly depleted of business; by 1870 Iowa Point had a population of about 500.[4] The decline continued. In 1933 the post office was closed, and today only a few houses remain on the site.

You can reach Iowa Point easily by taking U.S. Highway 36 west from Troy to the junction with state Highway 7 at the town of Sparks. Take

The Pemberton home, built in the 1850s, was one of the finest residences in Iowa Point. This structure, which shows architectural influences from the Old South, no longer stands.

Highway 7 north to Iowa Point. The ghost town sits immediately to the west of the highway and is clearly visible.

EAGLE SPRINGS
Doniphan County

More than 200 years before the coming of the white man, Indian medicine men supposedly discovered the healing properties of the water at what became Eagle Springs and performed many miraculous cures. One of the springs—believed to be the fountain of youth—was sacred to the Kansa Indians.[1] In 1880 Prior Plank purchased the springs site and employed chemists to analyze the water. The results justified his belief in the springs' medicinal properties, and in 1883 he built two large hotels and created a health resort for the cure of "real and imaginary ailments."[2] He named the site Eagle Springs because of the many eagles he had seen circling the area. Plank and Peter Weidemeier captured one of the eagles and took it to Nat Bailey, the Doniphan County sheriff, who placed it in a large cage in the courthouse yard. The eagle eventually became part of a publicity scheme for the springs.

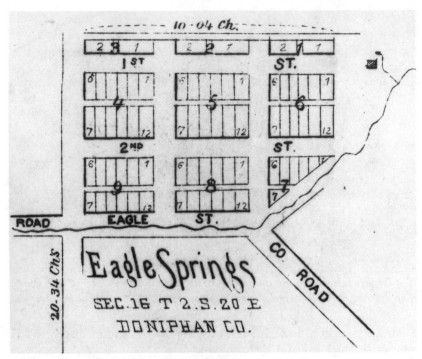

A plat of Eagle Springs, 1886. The little community was focused around the resort and mineral springs, which drew thousands of visitors every weekend.

Eagle Springs became increasingly popular. On Sundays sightseers came in vehicles of every make and description. The Burlington & Missouri River Railroad established a station and ran excursion trains from all points within fifty miles. The people hunted for Indian arrowheads, drank the springs water, and had a good time climbing the hills. One popular "wonder" nearby was an old mound dating back to the Kansas City Hopewell mound-building culture.

Eagle Springs had everything a resort needed: a romantic past, a wealth of natural beauty, pure cool air, and medicinal waters. But financial success was elusive. Prior Plank did not have enough capital to carry out his plans fully, and even though people came by the hundreds, they did not leave much money in Eagle Springs.[3] By the late 1880s the health resort and the two hotels had been forced to close as the number of visitors dwindled to only a few people on the weekends. George J. Remsburg, a local historian, attributed the failure of this "romantic spot" to lack of advertising.

Several attempts were made to restore interest in the area. In 1895 a minister from Chicago held a chautauqua there, and his tent meetings were attended by many people. Plans were made to build a Union church on the site, but the proposal failed due to lack of financial backing.[4] In the early 1900s the springs were closed to the public after several local judges built country homes near them. It was not until 1922 that the resort was revived when Dr. W. W. Simonson of Fort Worth, Texas, came to Eagle Springs and began renovating one of the old hotels, which he liked to call the Drugless Sanitarium. The inn was remodeled along colonial lines, and a complete system of mineral baths was installed. People started coming to Eagle Springs again. Unfortunately, the sanitarium failed during the depression of the 1930s.[5] Today the resort is in ruins; only the springs and a large swimming pool remain. At one point local residents attempted to redevelop the area, but they failed because of the perennial problem of Eagle Springs—lack of funds.[6]

Eagle Springs is now private property. To get to the vicinity, take U.S. Highway 36 west from Troy to the junction with state Highway 7 at the town of Sparks. Take Highway 7 north about two miles and turn northeast on a dead-end dirt road. After crossing a bridge, drive to the end of the dirt road. This route is the closest publicly accessible one to the springs site.

GEARY CITY
Doniphan County

On March 23, 1856, seven men from Leavenworth surveyed and organized a new town on the Missouri River, upstream from Doniphan. The men named the community Geary City in honor of John W. Geary, the territorial governor.[1]

At first Geary City seemed destined to become one of the largest river towns in northeast Kansas. Settlers arrived daily and purchased lots. The first business building constructed was a hotel, and it was followed by several stores and a newspaper, the *Geary City Era*, a lively paper edited and jointly owned by Joseph Thompson, Earl Marble, and Edwin Grant. The three editors had different political opinions, and as a result the paper did not favor any particular group. However, the *Era* was discontinued in the summer of 1858.

Geary City had a number of distinguished citizens during the late 1850s, including Robert J. Porter, who was a long-time treasurer of Doniphan County, the sheriff, and a member of the convention that framed the state constitution.[2] J. L. Roundy was the proprietor of a furniture store at Geary

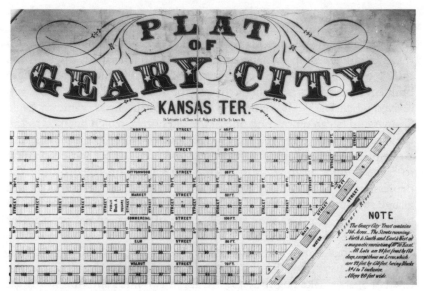

*A plat of Geary City as it optimistically appeared in 1856. The town in reality was a
haphazard collection of buildings near the Missouri River. However, plats such as this
one helped to entice prospective buyers.*

City in 1857, James McCahon was the first lawyer in town, and Dr. Franklin
Grube, a man who had traveled extensively both in Europe and in Africa,
was the first doctor.

After a brief period of prosperity Geary City suffered from a serious financial depression known as the Panic of 1857. Businesses failed, and there was
a rapid decline in river commerce and trade. As a result, the town was nearly
abandoned by the 1860s.[3]

During the Civil War proslavery men, or "border ruffians," were a problem in this area of Kansas. They attacked farms and communities on both
sides of the river, killing and robbing innocent people. One of them, a
man known only as Chandler, attempted to spread destruction and fear
among the settlers in the Doniphan area, but he met with little success
and was shot and killed at Geary City in 1862. His last resting place is in
an unmarked grave on a high hill just south of the townsite.[4]

Geary City was temporarily saved from oblivion in 1870 when the Atchison & Nebraska Railroad was built from Doniphan and Geary City to
Wathena, which is about six miles west of Elwood (St. Joseph). However,
the track was abandoned after a few years, and Geary City was left isolated

again. By 1907 nothing remained of the town except a store and a church. Today, other than an occasional foundation stone and a few pieces of glass, the town has completely disappeared.[5]

Geary City can be reached by taking a gravel road northeast from Doniphan until it junctions with another gravel road at Brush Creek. The traveler will be at the site of the town, although most of it is now private property.

DONIPHAN
Doniphan County

The history of the Doniphan townsite dates back to 1675 when it was first occupied by the Kansa Indians. Capt. Etienne de Bourgmont, a French explorer, visited the Indian village in 1723 and 1724, and he wrote in his journal that the village contained at least 150 lodges.[1] In 1775 the tribe moved to other sites along the Kansas River to avoid conflicts with the encroaching Iowas and Sacs, who were well stocked with firearms traded from the French. Artifacts of Kansa culture are plentiful in the area.[2]

The region remained largely uninhabited by whites after 1775 until Joseph Utt, a Kickapoo Indian agent, arrived and opened a trading post in 1852.[3] James F. Forman arrived late that same year and built a store from the lumber of the wrecked steamboat *Pontiac*, which had partially sunk in the Missouri River.[4]

In 1854 the Doniphan Town Company was organized in St. Joseph, and Forman was appointed to survey the townsite.[5] The name Doniphan was chosen in honor of Alexander W. Doniphan, a hero in the Mexican War. Doniphan was touted as the foremost town on the Missouri River because of its excellent rock-bound steamboat landing, and consequently, in the first town lot sale, held on April 15, 1855, one lot sold for $2,000.[6] Indeed, in 1858 it was noted that "Smith's bar lies one mile above the town and extends completely across the river which makes Doniphan the head of navigation for heavy-draught steamers."[7]

Doniphan's importance as a steamboat town transformed the community into one of the largest towns on the upper Missouri River in the 1850s, and along the wharf two warehouses were erected that could hold cargo from at least fifteen steamboats at one time. One Doniphan resident later recalled that he had seen as many as twenty boats come up the river in a single day and that "on many days three and four boats would be unloading at the same time on the wharf."[8] In addition to other steamboat traffic, the town was an important shipping point for grain being

The Denver *stopped at ports such as Doniphan while taking passengers and goods up and down the Missouri River. This view was probably taken in the early 1860s.*

transported to eastern markets. The first grain elevator in Kansas was built at Doniphan by Adam Brenner, who also founded the Brenner Vineyards near Doniphan in 1865.[9]

The Doniphan House Hotel was constructed during the winter of 1855 by Barney O. Driscoll.[10] Unfortunately, on the day of the hotel's grand opening a blizzard struck the town and the temperature dropped so low during the night that a guest named Eugene Hantz died of frostbite in one of the hotel rooms.[11] In 1857 the St. Charles Hotel was built, and it had forty rooms, a large lobby, a spacious dining room, and a large barroom.[12]

Seven newspapers were founded between 1855 and 1881. Most of them were discontinued so quickly that they were forgotten, but two newspapers are especially noteworthy. In 1855 the first issue of the *Kansas Constitutionalist* was published, but it lacked financial support and failed by 1857.[13] Early in 1858 James Redpath published the *Crusader of Freedom,* a radical Republican newspaper that was intended to be a personal soapbox for the Kansas abolitionist leader, James H. Lane. However, in May 1858 Redpath and Lane quarreled, and the newspaper was discontinued.

During the 1850s proslavery advocates from Atchison and St. Joseph came to Doniphan to promote their cause. On one election day, more than 100

An interior view of St. John's Catholic Church at Doniphan, circa 1890.

South Carolinians came hoping to influence the Doniphan voters into making Kansas a slave state, but the citizens of the town were staunch northern sympathizers and refused to change their politics, which aggravated the men from the South.[14] Miraculously, none of the encounters between the two factions ever resulted in bloodshed.[15]

In 1857 a branch of the Kansas Valley Bank of Leavenworth was built in Doniphan, and the U.S. government located a land office there, causing a major business boom. James Redpath's book, *Handbook of Kansas,* described the town during this period: "We say to the immigrant, Go to Doniphan. It is destined to be the great emporium of the Upper Missouri. The population is more than 2,000."[16]

Doniphan could have been a great emporium, but economic conditions dictated otherwise. By the summer of 1858 the land office had been moved to Kickapoo, and the Panic of 1857 and the resultant depression were beginning to affect the new communities in the Midwest, forcing businesses to close their doors.[17] As Atchison became the dominant community in the region by attracting much of the emigrant trade, Doniphan continued to decline through the 1860s.

The steamboat trade, Doniphan's vital link to eastern markets, also began to decline with the coming of the more efficient railroad in 1859. The town needed to attract a railroad to continue growing, but unfortunately Doniphan did not obtain a railroad link for several years.

In 1870 the Atchison & Nebraska Railroad was built through the town, but in 1881 a major flood along the Missouri River washed away the road-bed. When the tracks were relaid they were moved farther west to avoid any more flood problems, and Doniphan was without a railroad and without any major source of income.[18]

During the 1870s the Brenner Vineyards, consisting of over 100 acres and producing millions of gallons of wine, still provided jobs for dozens of workers in the area. But the coming of prohibition in 1880 meant the end of the Brenner wine industry and unemployment for the workers.[19]

Doniphan became a quiet agricultural community after the Brenner Vineyards closed their doors. Townspeople went to Atchison to shop, and an improved dirt road became Doniphan's only connection to the outside world. The population of the town continued to decline for the next 100 years, and other businesses closed down with no hope of reopening.

Today Doniphan is almost completely gone except for the ruins of a general store, some winery buildings, and an old school. However, for those who would like to relive, in a small way, the romantic era of the steam-boats, however, the streets of Doniphan are a good place to visit. Doniphan can be reached by taking the scenic Missouri River road north from Independence Park in Atchison. Stay on the road for several miles until coming to Doniphan. Several buildings stand on both sides of the road and are easily accessible.

SUMNER
Atchison County

Sumner was located along the Missouri River three miles south of Atchison. Its founder was John P. Wheeler, a twenty-one-year-old surveyor who came west to establish a town in the newly organized territory of Kansas. In the mid-1850s free-state sympathizers were not welcome in the proslavery town of Atchison, and since Wheeler strongly favored the free-state cause, he was determined to build a town where abolitionists would be welcome.

Sumner's advantageous location was on what was known as the Grand Detour of the Missouri River, where the river shifted the farthest west along the Kansas-Missouri border. The town was built on and around the high bluffs, and the site was covered by a dense forest, but in spite of this rug-

This lithograph of Sumner, made in 1856, shows a prosperous port city. In reality, Sumner bore little resemblance to this fanciful drawing. Produced in order to promote investors, it brought future Senator John J. Ingalls to Kansas two years later.

ged location, the community prospered and grew. The town's official motto was Pro lege et grege, meaning "for the law and for the people."[1]

In 1856 Wheeler had a detailed color lithograph made of Sumner that depicted the city as having stately buildings, imposing schools and colleges, church spires that "pierced the clouds," elegant hotels and theaters, a river filled with steamboats, and levees lined with barrels of merchandise. In reality Sumner was not nearly that elaborate. Some of the townspeople could not even afford windows for their cabins, let alone financially support luxuries such as colleges and church spires. Nonetheless, Sumner was rather impressive for an early Kansas territorial community and for a time was home for quite a few prominent Kansans.

When the steamboat *Duncan S. Carter* docked at Sumner on October 24, 1858, a young college graduate named John James Ingalls was on board. He was fascinated by Wheeler's impressive lithograph of Sumner and had decided to see the city for himself. Ingalls stayed in Sumner for several years, but when the town began to decline, he moved to Atchison, taking with him the town's official seal—and the key to his hotel room. Ingalls later became one of the state's most outstanding senators.[2]

Albert D. Richardson, the noted author, journalist, and nominee for governor, lived at Sumner in the 1850s. His book, *Beyond the Mississippi* (1867), is a fascinating account of life in the West, and it immortalized Sumner in print.[3] Minnie Hauk, who was nine years old when she lived at Sumner, became a renowned prima donna and charmed two continents with her beautiful voice. Sumner was also the town where Mayor Jonathan Lang, also known as "Shang," the hero of Ingalls's "Catfish Aristocracy," lived and died. (After his companions had left, Shang stayed in Sumner until every house was abandoned. Soon after his death, lightning struck his old cabin and destroyed it.)

By 1858 Sumner had 2,000 people, which was 500 more than the population of Atchison, and several prominent businesses, including a hotel built by Samuel Hollister and a wagon and implement factory operated by Walter A. Wood.

At first the townspeople believed that Sumner would eventually become the county seat of Atchison County. Wheeler, president of the Sumner Town Company, was a member of the Kansas territorial legislature, and he pushed a bill through the House proclaiming Sumner the county seat, but legislative members from Atchison succeeded in defeating the bill in the Senate. In October 1858 an election was held to settle the question of which town would be the county seat, and Atchison was chosen. During the same year, Atchison changed its political climate from proslavery to antislavery. The change was positive and popular, and it secured Atchison's economic standing in the region.[4]

By the time the Civil War broke out, Atchison was attracting the largest share of local trade, and a number of residents and businessmen from Sumner moved there. Atchison also secured the first railroad in the area, which caused even more of the citizens of Sumner to move to Atchison. Houses in Sumner were torn down, the lumber was carted away, and foundation stones were dug up and moved. Successive heavy rains washed away the streets, and the forest once again began to cover the site. In June 1860 the few remaining buildings were either destroyed or badly damaged by a tornado. What economic collapse could not steal from the town, the elements finally took away.

The last remnant of Sumner was, not a building, but a road. In order to make it easier for the wagons to navigate up the bank from the wharf, a 60 percent cut had been made through one of the bluffs. The *Sumner Gazette* noted in 1859 that the laborers and teams who worked on the road were brought in from St. Louis and that $20,000 had been spent in grading the roadway, which was named Washington Avenue. This grade, though choked with timber, was the last visible trace of the community.[5]

On a clear moonlit night, the legendary ghost of Jonathan Lang still wanders across the Sumner townsite looking for the people who left him behind. Perhaps he is still waiting for the steamboats to dock at the wharf, or for the stagecoach from St. Joseph that is 100 years late. Not too far up the river, the whistle of a locomotive crossing the bridge at Atchison breaks the ghostly silence. Jonathan Lang will no doubt continue to watch for his companions to return, but Sumner is not likely to reappear.

Access to the Sumner townsite is virtually impossible except by boat down river from Atchison. The site is now overgrown with trees and is private property.

FOUR HOUSES
Wyandotte County

Four Houses was the earliest trading post of record on the Kansas River and the first nineteenth century fur "depot" in Kansas; the little that is known about it was recorded in the journals of Kansas and Missouri traders and explorers. It was built by Sara and Francis Chouteau, and after the flood of 1826 destroyed the family's Randolph Bluffs post on the Missouri River, other members of the Chouteau family took up residence at Four Houses.

Even the exact location of Four Houses has often been questioned, but a fairly reliable map of the 1830s shows "4 houses" at the mouth of a small stream, now Cedar Creek, which enters the Kansas River some two and a half miles east of DeSoto in Johnson County. By land this was about twenty miles from the mouth of the Kansas River. The name "4 houses" on the map is written on the south side of the river, which gives the impression that the post was situated on the south bank, but John McCoy wrote in an article in the *Kansas City* (Mo.) *Journal*, January 2, 1879, "In 1822 Col. Francis G. Chouteau established a trading post on the north bank of the Kansas River one mile above the mouth of Cedar Creek, near the Pacific Railroad station of Lenape."[1]

Apparently the Four Houses post continued to serve as the Chouteaus' base of operations until late 1828 when they built a post at a new location about twelve miles from the mouth of the Kansas River, or eight miles farther east.[2] No surface remains or relics marking this trading post site have been found, probably because several floods, including the devastating flood of 1844, have obliterated the site. If any relics could be found, a number of questions could be answered concerning the size and exact location of the Four Houses trading post.

RISING SUN
Jefferson County

The town of Rising Sun was founded in 1857 by Joseph Haddox on the north bank of the Kansas River near a ferry landing and just across the river from Lecompton, the territorial capital.[1] Haddox was elected president of the town company, and William B. Almond, William J. Norris, Henry C. Cockeril, Thomas Cockeril, and William G. Mathias were appointed trustees.[2]

The *Lecompton National Democrat* of January 7, 1858, had this to say about the town of Rising Sun:

> Situated . . . on the bank of the river in the . . . valley of rich and beautiful timbered land known as the Kaw Valley through which the Missouri Pacific R.R. is destined to run, it must, . . . become a place of importance. . . .
>
>   There is now a successful operation in Rising Sun, two steam sawmills which saw from 3,000 to 4,000 feet of lumber every day. A church is being built which will be completed before spring. . . . A schoolhouse has also been erected in which a competent teacher is now engaged. Two public buildings will also be erected in a short time.

Some sources claim that Rising Sun was a rival town to Lecompton, but actually Rising Sun was one of Lecompton's "satellite" communities because many of its residents worked in Lecompton, a town too powerful in 1858 to have a major rival across the river.

The citizens of Lecompton did cross over the river to Rising Sun for their entertainment since whiskey, gambling, and prostitutes were readily available there, and these particular pleasures gave Rising Sun a bad image. A later commentator observed that Rising Sun was "somewhat ragged in morals, boisterous in proclaiming her opinion, and exacting in law, providing always, that the law met the exaction of public approval—if not, a speedy trial, a stout rope and a nearby oak settled all disputes."[3] The same commentator also recalled and discussed one account of this method of settling disputes made by a resident of Rising Sun in 1858:

As I looked from my north door one bright summer morning I was a little startled to see the bodies of four men hanging from a limb of an oak, and in a few days afterward two more bodies hung from the same limb. This on its face would look shocking, indeed; but we know every picture has . . . a reverse side, and so in this case, . . . we see that these men had been caught red-handed in stealing horses and cattle from that section of the country. They had no jails in which to imprison these thieves, and then as now the courts were too weighed with brains, too slothlike in prosecuting evil doers; so self-preservation dictated the law of Lynch.[4]

Was the town as rough as this and other accounts indicate? There is no satisfactory answer because too little was recorded about the town while it existed.

Rising Sun profited from river trade during the late 1850s and 1860s. In 1857 Jerome Kunkel began operating a ferry where Rising Sun was established, and this venture helped the town become a major business point on the river. In 1861 a state road was constructed from Rising Sun to Grasshopper Falls (Valley Falls) on the west side of the Delaware River, which brought added business to the community.[5]

Lecompton's decline in power, which led to a downward trend in the economy at Rising Sun, began when Topeka became the state capital in 1861. The Kansas Pacific Railroad built through the area in 1865, but it missed Rising Sun by a mile. Without the railroad, the community did not stand a chance for permanence, and with the decline of Lecompton across the river, hard times finally hit the little town. By 1870 all of Lecompton's "satellites" had disappeared—the town of Douglas to the east, several small townsites to the west, and Rising Sun to the north. All the buildings in Rising Sun were torn down or moved away, and the site is now a cultivated field. Its owners would probably say, "Rising Sun? Never heard of it."

Rising Sun, immediately north of Lecompton near the northern bank of the Kansas River, is on private property. Due to numerous floodings of the Kansas River during the nineteenth century, no foundations or surface remains mark the townsite.

HICKORY POINT
Jefferson County

The small quiet settlement of Hickory Point, five miles north of Oskaloosa, was the site of one of the most notable proslavery–free-state skirmishes ever fought on Kansas soil. The town was laid out in March 1855 and was located on the military road from Fort Leavenworth to Fort Riley and the stage route from Atchison to Topeka.[1] This combination meant the town developed a brisk trade with the emigrants heading west and with the soldiers on field expeditions.[2]

In 1856 the proslavery settlers were in the majority at Hickory Point, and at an election held in April these men took possession of the polls and greatly exaggerated the returns in their favor. After that event the free-state residents had little respect for the law in Hickory Point. Later in the spring, the situation between the two factions worsened, and the free-state settlers planned to drive the southern sympathizers out of the area. On Sunday, June 8, two proslavery men were driven out of town by the abolitionists. After this incident both factions organized into groups, and confrontations between them became more frequent.

The Battle of Hickory Point occurred three months later on September 14, 1856, and though it was called a "battle," in reality it was nothing more than a skirmish. When Gov. John W. Geary arrived in the territory, he issued a proclamation ordering all armed groups of men in the area to disband, but General James H. Lane, the noted free-state leader, did not immediately hear of the proclamation. He had just left Lawrence for the Holton area with a small band of men when he was met by dispatch riders from Osawkie. They informed him that southern sympathizers had just burned Grasshopper Falls (Valley Falls) and planned to burn other free-state towns. Since his assistance was requested, General Lane and his men marched to Osawkie, where he burned much of the town and drove away most of the proslavery sympathizers in the area. The next day Lane learned that a large party of proslavery men, armed for battle, was at Hickory Point, and he and his men marched to that community determined to either capture them or force them back to Missouri.

At Hickory Point General Lane found a hundred proslavery men assembled under the command of Capt. H. A. Lowe. Since the force was too fortified to be driven out, Lane sent a message to Lawrence asking for reinforcements and a cannon nicknamed the "Sacramento." This message, sent on Saturday, September 13, 1856, was received by Col. James A. Harvey. Following orders, he took the most direct route and arrived at Hickory Point about 10:00 A.M. on Sunday. In the meantime General Lane had been informed of Governor Geary's order to disband, and he started for Topeka expecting to meet Colonel Harvey's forces on the way. Harvey, however, had taken another route and missed Lane's company of men completely.

W. Breyman's sketch of the Battle of Hickory Point (1856) shows the three buildings that constituted the townsite under siege by free-state forces. Today, nothing remains of the town.

When Harvey and his forces arrived at Hickory Point, the proslavery men attempted to retreat but were intercepted and had to take refuge in the log cabins. Harvey ordered his men and wagons driven to within 300 yards of the buildings.[3] A proslavery witness, Dr. Albert Morrall, recounted the events at Hickory Point that day:

At Hickory Point, Harvey came down on us . . . with a cannon. I do not remember how many men he had, but it looked like he had three or four hundred. . . . When we saw them coming over the prairie dragging this cannon we divided into two parties. Twelve of us took possession of the blacksmith shop and the remainder went to the hotel. . . . Before we had accomplished this they fired the first shot from that cannon. It came through the shop and struck the butt of a gun. The gun was wrenched violently around, the barrel striking and breaking the leg of one of the men. . . . We then posted two men, one at each of the two corners of the shop toward the enemy to watch that cannon. When they [the enemy] started to touch the match to the cannon [the men] would notify us. Then we would all lie flat on the ground and the shot would go through the shop over our bodies. As soon as that passed over we would all jump up with our rifles, knock out the chinking from between the logs of the walls and shoot through the cracks.[4]

When the first shot from the cannon passed through the blacksmith shop, it killed one man, Charles Newhall. After firing about twenty more shots, Colonel Harvey found it impossible to dislodge Captain Lowe. He then ordered his men to back a wagon loaded with hay up to the blacksmith shop and set it on fire. A few of Lowe's men escaped through the smoke, but before long a man with a white flag came out of one of the houses and asked for a truce.

After some deliberation, the proslavery and free-state groups each agreed to give up raiding and plundering, and all nonresidents of each group agreed to leave the territory. A casualty count was taken: one proslavery man killed and four wounded; three free-state men wounded in the legs, one wounded in the head, and a young boy with a bullet through his lungs. The "Battle" of Hickory Point was over.[5]

Once he had the situation under control, Colonel Harvey and his men started back to Lawrence. Just five miles out of Hickory Point, they were all taken prisoner by a company of U.S. Dragoons and charged with disobeying Governor Geary's orders to disband and with attacking the proslavery men at Hickory Point. At the preliminary trials, eighty-eight of Harvey's men were found guilty of murder and fourteen were found guilty of "highway robbery," but many were released and others were placed on parole.[6] Colonel Harvey returned to Lawrence, although he had been advised by Governor Geary to leave the territory, and from that time on, relations between Harvey and Geary were strained.[7]

The settlers at Hickory Point were never bothered again by proslavery–free-state skirmishes, but when travel on both the stage route and the military road was discontinued, the small settlement was abandoned. Today the site is identified only by a Kansas State Historical marker along state Highway 59.

ARRINGTON
Atchison County

After the Kansas-Nebraska Act was passed in 1854 two settlers from Kentucky, Ransom Abner Van Winkle and Thomas Hooper, arrived in northeast Kansas and established a small sawmill in the valley of the Delaware River. When their business began to show a profit, Hooper wrote to his fiancée, Mary Arington, and asked her to join him. Not long after she arrived Hooper died, and in 1859 Miss Arington left for California—but not before the people had named the town after her.

After Hooper's death, Van Winkle abandoned the sawmill and used the building as a meeting hall and a school. In 1866 a stone schoolhouse was built near a site known locally as George Brenner's Cave. Van Winkle and R. C. Sweaney taught in the new school, and as one settler put it, "One of these teachers was not only a good instructor, but knew how to use tobacco. He could spit across the room through the key hole and never touch it."[1] In 1877 Julia Ward Howe, author of the "Battle Hymn of the Republic," came to Arington to live for a short time. She purchased some land and donated two acres to the town for another school. Until it was closed in the mid-1900s, the schoolhouse was still located on this same property.

In 1879 a post office was established in Arington, and it was the Post Office Department that changed the spelling of the town from Arington to Arrington. The first postmaster was Van Winkle, and the post office continued operating until the late 1960s.

In 1867 John Reider had opened a flour mill, powered by a water wheel, on the Delaware River. Seven years later Reider took a partner, W. H. Stockton, and together they enlarged the mill to two stories. This mill burned down on its first day in operation, and Reider and Stockton dissolved their partnership. Stockton still saw the need for a mill, and joined with Albert Ingler to build a stone mill in 1875. In 1879 Ingler drowned while crossing the river in his buggy, and Stockton sold the mill to D. S. Heneks. Heneks, together with his brother Joseph and son Noah, formed a corporation, and the mill became known as the Missouri Valley Roller Mill. The Heneks family operated the mill until 1896; they turned it over to a man named Wheeland, who ran the mill until it was sold to John W. Young in 1906; but by 1908 production had ended.[2]

An important factor in the growth of Arrington was its mineral spring. In the summer of 1881 D. S. Heneks became ill with dyspepsia, and since his well water was unfit for consumption, he decided to drink the water from a spring located along the east side of the river. The water tasted strange to Heneks, but he continued to drink it, and within a few weeks he had recovered from his illness. Later that summer some friends of the Heneks, who had just been to a health resort at Excelsior Springs, Missouri, came to Arrington for a visit. After sampling the water from the spring, they told Heneks the water tasted better than the water from the Missouri mineral springs.

The news soon spread, and in the fall of 1881, two enterprising businessmen from Holton obtained a ninety-nine-year lease on the property surrounding the spring. In March 1882 the Wright-Merle Analytical Chemists in St. Louis, Missouri, analyzed a sample of the water and sent

The roomy Arrington House Hotel as it looked around 1900 when the town was busy serving visitors at the Arrington Springs resort. When the resort lost its popular appeal, the town declined.

back the following report: "It is highly recommended for the following diseases: liver and kidney complaints, rheumatism, scrofula, gout, paralysis, dropsy, hemorrhoids, malarial complaints, chlorosis, amenorrhea, dysmenorrhea, laucorrhea, hysteria, and general debility."[3] A chemical breakdown of the water showed that it contained a high content of iron and magnesia carbonates.

The visitors who came to Arrington each summer to use the facilities at the mineral spring often exceeded the population of the town. In fact, another town was established in 1882 on the site of the spring called Arrington Mineral Springs or Arrington Springs Station.[4] According to one account of Arrington, "There are at present two first class hotels, three good restaurants, three boarding homes, three billiard halls, two large general merchandise establishments, one drug store, one grocery store, two livery stables, a blacksmith shop, barber shop, millinery store, and numerous carpenter shops."[5] There were also three saloons.

W. O. Lewis operated the Arrington House Hotel, and J. W. Beard ran the Beard Hotel; together they could provide lodging for eighty people. A group of men from Holton established a third hotel located in a park at the spring site, and over the next twenty years 300 cottages were constructed in the park, renting for $2.50 a week or $8.00 a month. Throughout the park there were swings, benches, and exercise bars for the visitors' benefit, and near the spring a large tent was erected for lyceums and band concerts that could seat up to 700 people. Visitors could rent rowboats for 25¢ an hour, and when the water was high and overflowed into the park, they all went boating and fishing. Also within the park there were bathhouses for ladies and gentlemen, as well as apartments, where refreshing warm and cold mineral water baths could be taken for a reasonable charge.

A great number of visitors claimed to have been cured of illnesses ranging from dropsy of the heart, kidney disease, paralysis, rheumatism, scrofula, St. Vitas dance, and nervous prostration, and two newspapers helped to spread the news of those claims. The *Arrington Times*, owned, published, and edited by W. A. Huff, and the *Arrington Argus*, published by T. W. Gardner, were both established in 1896, and both were filled with advertisements concerning rates and facilities at the park and the healthful properties of the spring.

The town continued to grow during the early 1900s, but in 1910 the tourist trade at the park and the spring began to dwindle, which created financial problems for the park and for the businessmen in Arrington. Shortly afterward a large portion of the town burned, and the mill and an adjacent dam were destroyed by the Delaware Drainage District for the purpose of flood control. In the "big fire of 1917" nearly half of the town was again burned and this time was never rebuilt. By the 1920s the tourists had stopped coming to the park and the spring, and that area eventually became farmland.

The town of Arrington itself dwindled but never died out completely, and its older residents remember the town's colorful Ransom Van Winkle, who is still spoken of as "Rip," "Uncle Van," and the "father of Arrington," inasmuch as he was the first postmaster, justice of the peace, school teacher, town trustee, county commissioner, and a Kansas state representative. His tombstone, long forgotten and hidden by brush, stands on a bluff overlooking the Delaware River.[6]

Only a few buildings are left in Arrington. One beautiful home has been restored; a small store continues to do business; and the foundations of another general store, a Baptist church, a livery stable, and the community center can still be seen. On a dirt road two miles north of the town lies an interesting old cemetery covered with weeds and gnarled trees in which one member of the infamous James Gang found his final resting place.

You can reach Arrington easily by taking state Highway 116 east from Holton about twelve miles. Several buildings and residences line both sides of the highway.

KENNEKUK
Atchison County

The town of Kennekuk, founded as a stage stop in 1858 and named after a Kickapoo Indian chief, was one of the earliest settlements in Atchison

County and the headquarters of the Kickapoo Agency. The agency was established as a mission school for the Kickapoo Indians, where children and other tribal members were taught Christianity, agriculture, and general studies pertaining to the "white man's way." Just before Chief Kennekuk died in 1856, he made a promise to those gathered around him that after three days he would rise up from the dead and speak to them. So for three days after his passing, more than forty Indians lingered around his body waiting for a resurrection that never happened. When these Indians finally dispersed and returned to their respective villages, they carried smallpox back with them, and the disease caused havoc among the Kickapoos.[1]

Kennekuk served at least three trails in the 1850s and 1860s: an overland freighting and stagecoach road from Atchison; a stagecoach and pony express trail from St. Joseph, Missouri; and a military road from Fort Leavenworth to Fort Riley.[2] When Kennekuk was a relay point for the stagecoaches, the stage drivers often boasted that only three minutes were needed to change teams, but sometimes it took long enough for the chilled passengers to go to the Kennekuk Hotel for a quick cup of hot coffee.[3]

During the 1850s when the wagon trains were heading west, the town was often jammed with people. As many as 3,000 oxen could be seen grazing on the nearby prairie, and almost as many Indians, soldiers, traders, and other transients would be camped around the town. These emigrants easily outnumbered the permanent residents in Kennekuk as there were never more than 100 people living in the town at any one time.[4]

A number of famous men visited Kennekuk in the 1850s and early 1860s. The most noted was Abraham Lincoln, who supposedly spent a night in the Kennekuk Hotel in 1859, a fact that was supported by his signature in the old hotel register. Years after his stay, the bedstead he allegedly slept in sold for an outrageous price, but the dispute as to whether or not Lincoln actually visited Kennekuk has never been settled.[5] Among the skeptics was George J. Remsburg, a local Kansas historian who firmly believed that "if Lincoln's signature adorned the old register of the Kennekuk tavern as some claim, it could have been forged by some wag who wanted to perpetrate a joke, or by some person who used the name of Lincoln as a means of concealing said person's identity."[6] Kennekuk and Horton residents, however, maintained that Lincoln was there, and one resident answered Remsburg's challenge: "I first arrived at Kennekuk in 1868, and it was a tradition at that time that Lincoln, Greeley, Fremont, and General Custer were the four outstanding notables who had stopped at [Kennekuk]. . . . Jennie Dollinds was there, and says she saw Lincoln herself, and remembers people talking about him being there after he had been elected president."[7]

The visits of other famous individuals have not been questioned. Samuel Clemens, better known as Mark Twain, stopped at Kennekuk in July 1861 on his way to Nevada where he experienced the adventures he related in his book *Roughing It*. Clemens highly praised the coffee at the Kennekuk Hotel, and he also noted that the owner's wife, Mrs. Tom Perry, was a fine cook and always had a steaming hot dinner ready when the stages arrived. Another visitor was Daniel Webster Wilder whose writing credits include *The Annals of Kansas* and a *Life of Shakespeare*. Wilder attended many of the dances held in the Kennekuk tavern and met his future wife in the Tom Perry home.[8] In 1859 John Brown passed through Kennekuk, pausing at the mission house and doffing his hat in approval of the work the mission was doing for the Kickapoos, and Albert D. Richardson included a short account of an event that occurred as he passed through Kennekuk in May 1860 in his book *Letters on the Pike's Peak Gold Region*.[9]

The pony express, which started at the Pike's Peak livery stable south of Patee Park in St. Joseph, was established in 1861, and Kennekuk was its first stop in Kansas. It was a short-lived experiment in mail service, but it added to the hustle and bustle of activity in Kennekuk during the Civil War years.

As the activity on the trails began to diminish after the Civil War and the railroad companies started to build in Kansas, Kennekuk's economy went from boom to bust. The fact that no railroad laid track through the community meant the town's heyday was over, and throughout the rest of the nineteenth century, Kennekuk was a small rural hamlet. One of the last big events in the town was the Fourth of July celebration of 1890, the largest in the community since the Civil War. One newspaper vividly described the holiday and included a description of the area at that time: "The Kennekuk grounds are two miles south of the old town in a beautiful grove on Mr. Thompson's land. The grove is four miles southeast of Horton, and carriages are constantly running between the two places, carrying hundreds of people and making the road a yellow cloud of dust. The best view you can get of Horton is from Kennekuk. The little stream and timber fill the valley below, and the bright town rises in a sprightly way on the hills beyond."[10]

But Kennekuk slowly disappeared. By the 1920s almost all of the old structures had fallen into disrepair, and the hotel was described in the *Topeka Capital*, August 13, 1922, as follows: "The leaning walls of a dilapidated structure, once a hotel near Horton, are about all that remain of the landmarks to back up the story of early history recorded in the minds of a few pioneers of this part of Kansas."

Some coins and other artifacts have been found on the townsite—a French five-franc piece dated 1828, an ox yoke, some wedding rings, brass stirrups, and a few buttons—but today the townsite is hard to find as most of the remains have disappeared. Like the chief it was named for, Kennekuk has not been resurrected from the dead. Both the town and the chief are peacefully sleeping and show no signs of awakening.

You can reach the site of Kennekuk by taking U.S. Highway 159 south from Horton. Immediately after crossing the Brown-Atchison County line, turn east on a gravel road and drive two miles.

AMERICA CITY
Nemaha County

America City was founded on February 14, 1857, by a group of prominent Atchison businessmen headed by Newcomb J. Ireland.[1] After inspecting the future townsite, Ireland returned to Atchison where he persuaded thirteen families of homesteaders to go back to the townsite with him. They loaded their belongings into their wagons and proceeded across the prairie to the banks of the Red Vermillion River. Once there they became the nucleus of the town of America City, which was projected to be a successful "sister city" of Atchison, a distinction the town never achieved.[2]

The location of the town was fifty miles west of Atchison on an overland trail known as the Parallel Road, and when county lines were organized in this region, America City was precisely on the Nemaha-Pottawatomie County line. The town was laid out on June 10, 1857, by Samuel Dickson, a general merchandise store owner and president of the America City Town Company.[3] That summer the settlers built a schoolhouse, a grocery store, and a Methodist church.[4] A post office was established in 1858.

America City was a successful town during its early years, primarily because of business from the overland freighters and stage lines that operated on the Parallel Road from Atchison west to Denver.[5] But the coming of the Kansas Central Railroad brought about a business and population decline in America City as tracks were laid on each side of the community, missing the town by several miles. Havensville, four miles south, and Corning, six miles north, became the prominent railroad points in the area. By the 1870s the Parallel Road no longer existed, and the railroads had taken over most of the freighting business.

By 1878 the only businesses in America City were three general stores, a hotel, harness and shoemaker, wagonmaker, physician, horse dealer, blacksmith shop, and the United Brethren Church. The population was

All that remains of America City is this school, now abandoned and used by a local farmer to store hay and farm implements.

only 100.[6] Still, the *Seneca Courier* of March 1, 1878, wrote, "the extension of the Kansas Central Railroad west from Leavenworth has hurt the prospects of the town as a trading point; but there is an excellent country surrounding America City, and the farmers and stock raisers are all of an enterprising kind, and will continue to prosper."

Despite that positive opinion, America City continued to decline, and by 1910 the population of the town was less than 30. The post office was closed in 1932, and that event and the depression of the 1930s hastened the town's demise. All that remains of America City today are the ruins of an old hotel building filled with broken furniture, an old stone house, a schoolhouse, and a church. The cemetery beside the church contains many graves of the first pioneers in this part of Kansas. To reach America City, take state Highway 63 north from Havensville. After crossing the Nemaha-Pottawatomie County line, turn left at the first junction with a dirt road, which places you at the townsite.

ST. GEORGE
Pottawatomie County

The founding of St. George, the oldest town in Pottawatomie County, was entirely accidental, and the sense of humor behind the naming of the community is an excellent example of what makes place-names so unique. In April 1855 a group of emigrants—George W. Gillespie and family, J. George Gillespie, and George Chapman and family—headed west from St. Joseph, Missouri, planning to go to California to look for gold. After several hard days on the road Mrs. Gillespie stated that she had traveled far enough, sat down, and refused to go any farther, so they camped on the banks of the Kansas River not far from Manhattan. The next day the group decided to homestead in Kansas Territory instead of going to California, and they founded the settlement of St. George. Why that name? All three male members of the party were named George, and since Mr. Chapman was considered a saint for tolerating his bossy better-half, they chose the name of St. George.[1]

Jacob Emmons was one of the earliest settlers in the area, and at one time he was the probate judge, lawyer, county commissioner, county clerk, and county surveyor—he literally held the county "in his pocket." When Emmons was unsure of the legal precedents for a particular case, he skillfully disguised his ignorance with splendid legal rhetoric that usually won his case whether his argument was pertinent or not.

George Gillespie, a postmaster at St. George, was also the town's justice of the peace, and the first couple he married paid him his fee with beans—legal tender in 1858. One of the first buildings in St. George was a two-story hotel and residence constructed for Augustine Becker, who, like Emmons, had many titles: cabinetmaker, justice of the peace, and postmaster. St. George was the county seat from 1857 to 1861, but no courthouse was built so county officials conducted the county's business in their homes. Becker's residence was considered the county's "unofficial courthouse," and many of the commissioners' meetings were held there.

For a brief time in 1857 regular steamboat service was attempted on the Kansas River between Kansas City and Fort Riley, and St. George was one of the ports. However, the river was too shallow and had too many sandbars to be navigable, so the operation was short-lived. The first steam and grist mill in the county was built at St. George in 1857, but it burned to the ground in 1858. St. George became a popular stop for overland travelers, and two large hotels, the Gillespie and the John Blood, were built to accommodate them.

The biggest drawback to the economy in St. George was the fact that the Fort Leavenworth to Fort Riley Military Road missed the town by two miles. This road, a major supply link and a principal artery of travel in the area during the territorial period, went through Louisville instead, a community that defeated St. George for the privilege of being the county

R. Benecke photo titled "The Mid-day Rest. Quail Shooting at St. George." Taken in the early 1870s, this view shows St. George in the background.

seat by only two or three votes in the election of 1861.[2] Louisville, however, eventually lost the county seat to Westmoreland.

In spite of no longer being the county seat, St. George still prospered, and five years later, the town got a railroad, the Kansas Pacific. On Independence Day 1866 the first passenger train rolled into St. George, and it was greeted by all the townspeople, who staged the biggest celebration the town had ever witnessed. After the depot was built in St. George, the trains stopped regularly for fuel and water, and St. George became a major railroad center and a distribution point for the territory north and east of the community.[3]

During the late 1860s and early 1870s, St. George had a population of 200, and businesses included a hardware store, drugstore, millinery shop, blacksmith shop, restaurant, brickyard, two hotels, and a real estate office. In 1879 most of the old townsite was vacated, and a new business district was built around the railroad. The community had placed all its faith in the "iron horse."[4]

St. George was a prosperous grain shipping point for several decades, but like many other communities that were dependent upon the railroad, it declined when the great era of the railroad came to an end. U.S. Highway 24 was built through the area, but it bypassed the main street in St. George by about two miles, causing many businesses in the downtown area to close.

A boarded-up depot in St. George. Obviously, the boom years of railroad passenger service are over.

Today St. George is still on the map and has a resident population, but the town is little more than an assorted collection of houses and a school. The railroad locomotives still go through the town, but they no longer stop. The cars on the highway skirt the townsite to the northwest, but most drivers are too rushed to slow down. Almost everyone has gone somewhere else, leaving the town a neglected relic of the railroad days. St. George is only two miles south and east of U.S. Highway 24 between Wamego and Manhattan. Follow the signs from either direction, which indicate the correct exit.

JUNIATA
Pottawatomie County

In 1853 the best known trail in what is now Pottawatomie County, the Fort Leavenworth to Fort Riley Military Road, crossed the Big Blue River and cut across the prairie through largely uninhabited territory.[1] A Virginian named Samuel Dyer operated a ferry on the Big Blue one mile below Rocky Ford near the location of Juniata, which was established in 1854 to benefit from the brisk trade brought by military expeditions and emigrants.[2] In 1854 the government built a bridge over the river at Juniata, but it washed away in a flood in 1856.[3]

On November 29, 1854, an election was held in Juniata to choose a territorial delegate to Congress.[4] It had been thought that Juniata was a proslavery town, but this election proved otherwise. Thirty-seven votes were cast in the district, and the voters failed to select a single candidate who favored slavery. Proslavery candidate John Whitfield received two votes; Free-State candidate John Wakefield, six votes; and the Democrat, R. P. Flenniken, twenty-nine votes.[5]

By December 1854 Juniata had a hotel, blacksmith shop, general store, jail, and a population of seventy.[6] George C. Willard described the new community in a letter of January 7, 1855: "A town site has been laid off here, and settlers are coming from nearly every state of the Union; about fifty families are here now. . . . Various tribes of roving Indians are scattered about us, but they are generally peaceable. . . . Provisions of all kinds are very dear here at this time. Potatoes and butter we do not get at all. Wages are pretty fair. Game is abundant—I have seen eight deer in one herd. . . . The river is filled with fish."[7]

On July 25, 1855, a post office was established in town, and Seth Child was appointed postmaster, but late in 1856 the post office was moved to another site across the river and renamed Tauromee.[8] This new post office, consisting of a pigeon-hole roll-top desk in the corner of a log cabin, was discontinued in 1858.[9]

Saloons sprang up both in Juniata and across the river in Tauromee. Samuel Dyer, the most prominent man in town, was described as an "old six-foot man of the Methodist Church South." He and his wife kept a hotel, a small store, and a home that was "one story high with three stories long."[10] In 1856 the quartermaster at nearby Fort Riley sent a new ferry boat to Juniata for Samuel Dyer to operate at the crossing where the bridge had stood.

In its early days Juniata showed promise of real growth, but by 1858 the town of Manhattan, five miles to the south, was a booming metropolis, and the rivalry between the two towns brought about the economic collapse of Juniata. Today hardly any remnants are left of the town. The old pilings of the Big Blue River bridge on the military road can still be seen if the river is not too high, and a few foundations and depressions where the buildings once stood can be found. The site of Juniata is not easily accessible and is private property. Inquire locally for permission and directions.

PAWNEE
Riley County

The small settlement of Pawnee, established in 1854 as a potential real estate investment, was the first territorial capital of Kansas, but because of its location and the sentiments of proslavery sympathizers, the community had only a slim chance of becoming the "Topeka" of its time.

Gov. Andrew Reeder, the first territorial governor of Kansas, had real estate investments in the new town, and in December 1854 he informed the Pawnee Town Company that he intended to meet with the legislature at Pawnee on July 2, 1855, provided that a suitable building could be made available. As soon as it became known that Pawnee might be the capital of Kansas, settlers began to arrive in droves and camped on the prairie. Money was invested, buildings were erected, business ventures were embarked upon, and house-raisings were frequent. The tiny city "grew hourly." Mrs. R. V. Hadden, a resident of Pawnee, wrote in her journal that in the spring of 1855 work began on the "Capitol Building," and this work continued through Sunday, July 1, when the carpenters finally finished the roof over the capitol in which the legislature was to officially convene the next day. The haste with which the two-story stone structure was built is indicated by the fact that a large hole in the west side of the upper story, which was used as a passageway to carry up stone and mortar, was never filled in. Also, carpenters forgot to nail down some of the floor boards, and when one end was stepped on, the other flew up. The desks were plain unpainted tables and the seats, old kegs and boxes.[1]

Several boarding houses and hotels in Pawnee were made ready for the legislators, but they largely ignored these accommodations. Most of them had a supply of tents, food, and cooking utensils with them so they could camp out, and the local hunters found a ready market for their buffalo, small game, and fish. The legislators arrived by horse, mule, wagon, and buckboard. The oldest member was fifty-five, the youngest twenty-three; nineteen were under thirty, and nine were under twenty-five. Only ten had lived in the territory more than a year; eight were abolitionists, thirty-one were southern sympathizers. The group included farmers, lawyers, doctors, and other professional men, either imbued with the "holy flame of patriotism" or animated by a determination to extend slavery. None of them were happy as Pawnee was not their choice for the state capital because it was too far from most of their homes and constituents.

Many other people came to Pawnee from out of town just to participate in the activities. Since the resident population was mostly free-state and the visitors were proslavery, neither party hesitated to loudly proclaim its opinion to the other. Fist fights were frequent.

On July 2, 1855, the legislative session began. The lower floor of the building was given to the House, and the Senate convened on the second story. Daniel Woodson, territorial secretary, called the roll of the House.

The first territorial capitol building at the old site of Pawnee is now restored as a historic property, owned by the state. Never fully completed, the original interior remains as rustic as when it was used by legislators for a few brief days in 1855.

John H. Stringfellow, editor of the Atchison *Squatter Sovereign,* was elected speaker of the House, and Reverend Thomas Johnson of Shawnee Mission was elected president of the Senate. The governor's message to the legislators dealt with such mundane matters as the boundaries of counties, the establishment of schools and courts, and his plans for taxation. He also touched upon the question of slavery in Kansas, but that issue had been settled in the minds of proslavery lawmakers long before the meeting of the legislature. As a result the governor's message was received with disrespect, and his wishes were openly ignored.

Oratory flowed from the delegates at the first stroke of the presiding officer's gavel, and the halls resounded with perorations demanding "justice for all," "southern rights," "the flag and the constitution," and a phrase that became familiar in the context of many addresses, "Kansas, the brightest star of all." The first act of the legislature was to declare an election that had been held in May null and void, hence ousting the free-state members elected at that time and reseating the proslavery men who had been thrown out. "You are lighting the watch fires of war," shouted the dispossessed minority, a prophecy that would be fulfilled six years later.

On July 4, 1855, a bill was passed transferring the seat of government from Pawnee to Shawnee Mission. Governor Reeder promptly vetoed this bill, but it was just as promptly passed over his veto. On July 6 the legislature adjourned to reconvene at Shawnee Mission on July 16.

With these proceedings concluded, the legislators hastily piled together their personal belongings, mounted their horses and mules or climbed aboard wagons and buckboards. As they traveled east across the prairie, they looked back without regret at the stone capitol, the deserted boarding houses, and the pathetic town that had blossomed on the plains, only to wither and die. Pawnee's five hectic days as the capital of Kansas were over, and Governor Reeder's influence was at an end. On July 28, 1855, Governor Reeder was removed from office and charged with purchasing Indian lands, speculating in town property, and endeavoring to influence the value of town lots in Pawnee by locating the seat of government there. Fearing that his life was in danger, Reeder left Kansas disguised as a woodcutter.[2] After the capitol building in Pawnee was cleared, the lower story was used as a combination carpenter shop and lodging place, and the upper story became a bachelors' club.

Pawnee had been laid out on land adjoining the Fort Riley Military Reservation, and the military road ran through the town, a fact that at first benefited the community. But in October 1855 the extension of the Fort Riley Military Reservation around the townsite caused a quick, forced exodus of residents. Of this occurrence, Mrs. R. V. Hadden of Pawnee wrote: "One day in September, as evening was approaching, a squad of mounted troops rode into Pawnee. They came to give official notice that the site of Pawnee had been taken for the use of the government, and all of its citizens must vacate their homes on or before the tenth of October."[3] When that date arrived, many residents were still in their houses. Sickness had prevented some from leaving; others simply had no place to go. No one believed they would be turned out immediately; they had faith the government would be lenient. But that faith was misplaced as troops came down from the fort, pulled the houses down, and Pawnee was in ruins.

The people had lost their worldly goods, and in a pitiful procession they trailed slowly away. Only the old capitol building was left. It was used as a storehouse by the military until 1877 when a windstorm ripped off the roof and damaged the interior. The Union Pacific Railroad built through the area in the 1870s, and since the old building stood just yards from the tracks, the travelers who looked from the train windows wondered about the ruin, "so eloquent of neglect and decay."

In 1900 the Kansas State Historical Society bought the Pawnee capitol building but had no money to spend for its preservation. In October 1907, Col. Samuel Woolard of Wichita began collecting funds to help restore the building, and he raised enough money to replace all the stones in the walls, square up the windows and doors, and fill the cracks in the building with cement. Thus, through Colonel Woolard's efforts, the old capitol building managed to weather a period of civic indifference.

In 1926 Gov. Ben Paulen called the attention of the legislature to the need of preserving the building, and the legislature appropriated $1,000 to strengthen and repair the walls and clean up the grounds. The Union Pacific Railroad became involved in the restoration and spent $20,000 renovating the building and grounds to their original appearance. A formal presentation of the building to the state of Kansas was made on August 1, 1928. Today the old capitol building stands completely restored. Although Pawnee's dreams of glory faded away, the town is memorialized forever in this old stone structure.[4] To visit the Pawnee capitol building, follow the signs on Interstate 70 immediately east of Junction City. The structure is only a couple of miles off the interstate.

"OLD" RANDOLPH
Riley County

The first town of Randolph in Riley County was one of the victims of the Tuttle Creek Reservoir, and the feelings of loss over the demise of the town still run deep. In an attempt to fight the decision of the U.S. Corps of Engineers, the citizens held mass-meetings at Randolph weekly; they put up huge billboard signs along the highways in the area; and they handed out political leaflets to anyone who would take them. In 1953 a documentary film entitled "The Tuttle Creek Story" asked the question, Should nine cities, 5,000 people, and 55,000 acres of fertile land be destroyed by "Big Dam Foolishness"? Despite the attention the dispute attracted, all the attempts to save the town were futile.

The history of Randolph dates back to 1855 when an early pioneer, Gardner Randolph, and his sons, daughters, son-in-law, and grandchildren settled in the Big Blue River valley near the mouth of Fancy Creek and laid claim to all the land within five miles of the creek.[1] Unfortunately, the laws governing the settlement of public lands in Kansas Territory stipulated that a settler could claim a quarter-section by preemption only if he lived on the claim for a year and improved it—then he could purchase it for $1.25 an acre. Since the Randolphs were unable to place someone on each quarter-section, they had no legal right to all of the land they had claimed.

Three men—Edward Secrest, Solomon Secrest, and Harry Shellenbaum—settled in the vicinity of Fancy Creek late in 1856, and in the spring of 1857, more settlers came to the valley. Gardner Randolph realized that laying out a town in the area would give him a stronger hold on his land, so he platted a town he called Randolph on paper. After a town company was organized, a surveyor was employed by Randolph to lay out the town, and a sixteen-by-eighteen-foot cabin was built in the center of the public square. Three other log buildings were built northwest of the cabin—a blacksmith shop, a private dwelling, and a church—because "three smokes and a blacksmith shop" officially constituted a town in early Kansas.

In 1858 J. K. Whitson and John Kress arrived from Indiana and decided to "claim-jump" the town of Randolph in the name of the abolitionist movement. They erected two cabins on the site, as required by the preemption law, which meant war to Gardner Randolph. He used force to make the Kress family move away, but Whitson refused to leave, and there were hard feelings between the two men for over a year. Finally they took their quarrel to the U.S. Land Office in Ogden (near Junction City) in 1859, and after two days of hearings the land agent rendered the decision that neither party had a legal claim; consequently the land reverted to its original open state. The agent reminded Randolph and Whitson that the first one to settle on the land would be declared the owner. Immediately both contenders rushed to their horses and rode off to Randolph twenty-seven miles away. Gardner Randolph followed the divide west of Mill Creek, but Whitson made a dash across hills and ravines, and when he reached the townsite he grabbed an ax and was cutting trees for a cabin when an exhausted Randolph arrived.

Whitson's first act as the new owner of Randolph was to change the name of the town to Waterville. Then he employed Daniel Mitchell of Ogden to resurvey the site; in return for his work, Mitchell was allowed to buy the six lots bordering the town square for the small sum of $50.

In 1861 Henry Condray and Whitson built the town's first sawmill and grist mill, which was known for turning out meal "slow but exceedingly fine." Condray built the first stone house in Randolph in 1863, and he purchased Gardner Randolph's interests in the town the following year. By the late 1860s the Fancy Creek valley had filled with settlers, and the town was becoming an important agricultural center.

By 1868 a new town, also called Waterville, had been built eighteen miles to the north. Randolph citizens believed that their town (still named Waterville by the state) would become eclipsed unless its name were changed,

On October 16, 1915, a Union Pacific train wreck occurred near Randolph. Everyone on board was either hurt or killed. Heavy rains, which caused part of the track and bridge to collapse, were responsible.

so they sent a petition to the state legislature to change the town's name back to Randolph. This request was granted on February 25, 1876. In the 1870s the town had a blacksmith shop, drugstore, furniture manufacturer, real estate office, livery stable, lumberyard, two doctor's offices, and a hotel operated by Miles Reed in the Henry Condray house.

On May 30, 1879, a tornado struck Randolph. Huge masses of black clouds mixed with lighter ones, and two funnels dipped to the ground and destroyed the corn cribs and stables of a settler on Walnut Creek west of Randolph. These two funnels remained on the ground, smashing everything in their path including houses, barns, stables, and trees. The funnels joined and became one large twister, and the residents of Randolph watched the storm's progress with a mixture of awe and fear. Some said it sounded like a thousand railroad trains. The funnel blew down the schoolhouse and destroyed the woods along the bottom of North Otter Creek, then it swung west and struck the home of Adam Schwein, killing an infant but sparing the mother who was holding the child. According to one eyewitness account, "The tornado came down the bluff from the southwest and . . . it tore up the ground for a space of about 30 yards wide as though it had been plowed or harrowed."[2] Many homes were damaged or destroyed, many people were injured, and several people were killed. Still, the town recovered.

In the mid-1880s the Blue River branch of the Union Pacific between

As construction began on Tuttle Creek Reservoir, "Big Dam Foolishness" was the watchword of many Randolph citizens who were forced to abandon their homes to the U.S. Army Corps of Engineers.

Manhattan and Lincoln, Nebraska, brought more business to the community, and "East Randolph" was built adjacent to the tracks near the depot.[3] Randolph was officially incorporated as a third-class city in January 1886. By 1910 the population of Randolph had risen to 575, and the town, an important grain shipping point along the railroad, had two more banks and an express and telegraph office.

On October 16, 1915, a tragic train wreck occurred near Randolph. Heavy rains had undermined the soil beneath the bridge over Fancy Creek, and when the Union Pacific's No. 18 crossed the bridge, it collapsed and plunged the train first into an embankment, then into the rough waters of the creek. Eleven of the fifty people on board were killed, and the others were injured.

Randolph survived the depression years, and by the end of World War II the town seemed to be looking forward to an upswing in both business and population. Prosperity for Gardner Randolph's town seemed just around the corner, but unfortunately, events dictated otherwise.

Floods in the Fancy Creek valley had become a way of life for Randolph citizens, but the 1951 flood was so devastating in this part of Kansas that the U.S. Army Corps of Engineers selected the Big Blue River as the site for a large dam. When the corps drew up plans for the Tuttle Creek Reservoir, one of the proposals included condemning the town of Randolph. When the citizens heard of this recommendation, they started the "Big Dam Foolishness" crusade and began to fight the proposed destruction of their community.

Alas, legally there was little the citizens of Randolph could do to prevent the U.S. Army Corps of Engineers from condemning businesses and homes and inundating the townsite. The government offered to move the town if 51 percent, or fifty-eight, of the property owners would purchase lots at the new site. Enough people agreed so eighty acres of land were purchased by the government two miles southwest of the old site, and residential lots and business sites were sold to the citizens of the old town.

When the relocation of the town began, some of the store owners became disgusted and vowed to move elsewhere, but for the most part, a feeling of unity prevailed among the residents, and many of them opened businesses in the new town. However, some of the older people remained unhappy about the move, and many people still have a deep-seated resentment toward the U.S. Army Corps of Engineers and Tuttle Creek Reservoir—old Randolph was their home and the new town only a "cheap imitation." Nonetheless, the citizens of old Randolph weathered many disasters, and new Randolph stands as a monument to the strength of those people.[4]

Today "Old" Randolph is accessible only to divers, as it lies under the waters of Tuttle Creek Reservoir immediately east of the present site of Randolph.

IRVING
Marshall County

In the autumn of 1859 a small group of residents of Lyons, Iowa, wished to resettle farther west, and they sent W. W. Jerome to Kansas to locate a suitable site for a new town. After he had traveled several hundred miles around the state, Jerome recommended the Big Blue River valley as an excellent place to homestead. When the colonists arrived, they decided to name their town Irving after Washington Irving, a popular nineteenth-century author.

Throughout its history the residents of the community suffered from disasters. The first setback, in the spring of 1860, was a severe drought that ruined crops and caused some farmers in the area to lose their land. In July fierce winds and thunderstorms blew down buildings, took roofs off houses, and destroyed the smokestack at the sawmill. These storms, with their lightning and wind, frightened many of the citizens in Irving, and that fall some of the colonists went back to Iowa. A few others moved to different areas of Kansas, but the majority of them stayed in Irving.[1]

In 1866 the community was invaded by grasshoppers; a "plague" so thick and heavy in the sky that it darkened the sun. When the grasshoppers left, the gardens had been totally eaten, the trees were barren as in the dead of winter, and the crops had been completely destroyed. There was another grasshopper invasion in 1875, but the proud people of Irving stood firm, replanted their crops, and took their chances with nature as they had in the past.[2]

In the early 1870s General J. C. Ward erected a grist mill, S. H. Warren opened a merchandise store in a small building that also housed the post office, and the Irving House—a hotel that was to pass through "many managements" during the 1870s—was constructed by J. F. Joy at a cost of $2,500.[3] In 1883, one author described Irving as it looked in 1878: "The town of Irving is located on the line of the Central Branch Railroad [later the Missouri Pacific], 90 miles from Atchison. Situated in the wide-spread valley of that winding stream, . . . the Blue, it unquestionably has a pleasant location. Irving has and always will have a good trade arising from . . . being located in one of the best settled and best cultivated portions of Marshall County."[4]

Perhaps the severest of Irving's disasters occurred in the afternoon of May 30, 1879, when two tornadoes destroyed most of the town, leaving nineteen dead and scores injured. (Until the Xenia, Ohio, twisters of 1974, no other town was ever hit by two tornadoes from two separate storm systems on the same day.) The air was dry and clear on the morning of May 30, but by mid-afternoon the weather had turned hot and sultry, and by 4:00 P.M., unknown to the residents of Irving, tornadoes had formed to the southwest in Riley County. After touching down there, a large funnel moved into Marshall County where it destroyed a schoolhouse and several homes and killed seven people before reaching Irving.

In the town itself, six died at the Gale residence, their clothing torn to shreds and stripped from their bodies. Five more were injured at the Gallop house, which was lifted off the ground and set back down with its stone chimney still intact. A wagon carrying 1,000 board-feet of lumber disap-

Irving Methodist Church. On May 30, 1879, this church became a meeting place and morgue for victims of two of the most devastating tornadoes in the history of the state.

peared without a trace. Barbed wire fencing was twisted like a rope, and most of the livestock, when found, had many broken bones.

Finally, the tornado was past Irving and in the bottom along the Big Blue River, but suddenly, as if it had a malicious afterthought, the funnel turned north up the river and demolished a bridge. Then it was over. The residents of Irving came out of their cellars, felt the rain beat upon their faces, and saw the sun come out along the western horizon. A cold wind sprang up out of the northwest.

"Hardly had the people recovered from the first shock when there appeared at the west a cloud of inky blackness and enormous dimensions."[5] The residents were frightened, and several started shrieking and moaning, their cries joining with those injured by the first tornado. The second storm roared into Irving from the west, flattening what was left of the town. Eighteen houses clustered together were smashed first, then nine others, and then five structures, including two churches and the grain elevator. This time almost fifty buildings were demolished and five people killed before the storm passed, disappearing like the first out onto the empty prairie. Only the devastation and terror remained.

Soon after the storm passed a special relief train carrying nurses and doctors sped out of Atchison to help the injured. In the drenching rain that night the search continued for the dead and dying, and the small stone Methodist church, one of the few buildings that remained, became a morgue for the dead. On Sunday, June 1, 1879, a group of weary friends and relatives formed a procession to the Sylvan Grove cemetery where they buried the victims of the storm. The estimated property damage was nearly $65,000, a large amount of money in those days.[6]

Although a few disheartened settlers left Irving, most of them stayed on to rebuild the town. New businesses replaced the old ones, and Irving soon regained its prominence as a local agricultural center.

In May 1903 after heavy spring rains had drenched the countryside, the Big Blue River went out of its banks, and once more tragedy struck Irving when homes, crops, livestock, and bridges were carried away by the swollen stream. In 1908 the Big Blue threatened to inundate the valley again, but this time the citizens were prepared and worked hard to keep the stream within its banks. Property damage was not so high as in 1903, but two lives were lost.

On a hot night in 1905, the Methodist church bell roused the people to fight a fire at the E. M. Peterson store, but their efforts were futile, and the building and contents were lost. When the church bell rang early on the morning of February 14, 1907, everyone ran to fight the fire that was raging in the J. C. Moore store and in Rutherford's drugstore, but both buildings burned to the ground. Another fire on January 29, 1913, burned the hardware store of Dexter & Guffee, but on August 9, 1916, the town's most destructive fire occurred, and this time almost all the north side of Main Street was destroyed.

Throughout most of the early twentieth century, Irving residents were frequently having to rebuild parts of the town, but in 1910, "all lines of business enterprise is [*sic*] represented. There are good banking facilities, a weekly newspaper—the *Irving Herald*—telegraph & express offices, graded schools, public library, churches of all denominations and 3 rural routes from the post office. The population is 403."[7]

One of Irving's most famous citizens was a noted young aviatrix named Ruth Blaney. After she left Irving, she established two world records for women in aviation, an altitude record of 26,600 feet and the record for piloting her plane nonstop from Vancouver, Canada, to Agua Caliente, Mexico, the longest endurance flight for a woman at that time. In 1930

Today little remains of Irving but this stone marker and a mailbox. Visitors can leave a message in a notebook inside the mailbox for all those coming later who care to read it.

she planned a flight from California to New York, but on the morning of September 18, after she took off in a light fog from San Diego, her plane crashed on a mountainside near Loma Portal. Every citizen in Irving had been following the progress of the town's celebrity, and the news of her death "virtually paralyzed" the townspeople."

The next twenty years were quiet and productive in Irving, and despite a slowly decreasing population, Irving had three general stores, two barber shops, two cafés, two gas stations, a drugstore, feed store, tire shop, butcher shop, and a local doctor.[8] When the proposal for the Tuttle Creek Dam was adopted in 1955, however, the population of Irving began to decrease rapidly, and many businesses closed, including the post office. The *Blue Rapids Times* of May 16, 1957, noted that "Irving's future looks black to many people because it is generally believed that Irving has no future, but life still goes on and we must live for the future."

Some citizens stubbornly stayed on, but their attempts to prolong life in Irving were in vain. The Tuttle Creek Dam finally achieved what tornadoes, floods, fires, droughts, and grasshopper plagues could not: It destroyed a town that had seen more than its share of tragedy.

Today the townsite is part of a wildlife refuge, and visitors can still walk the streets, inspect the old foundations, and find a few relics of the not-too-distant past. One mailbox remains on the site, and there is a notebook inside for visitors to sign and add their comments. In the summer former residents hold a reunion and picnic at the site. Perhaps Irving is not a "dead" town after all.

You can reach Irving by taking an unmarked gravel road that parallels the Missouri Pacific Railroad tracks south and east of Blue Rapids. Turn left at the only junction with another gravel road. A stone marker stating "Irving" indicates the townsite.

ALCOVE SPRINGS
Marshall County

Alcove Springs was never truly a "community"; it was a campground for emigrants destined for California or Oregon, and the lonely site was in all likelihood the most important point along the Oregon Trail in Kansas Territory.

The first mention of the Alcove Springs site by a white man was made in 1827 when James Clyman, a scout for the fur trappers and mountain men, passed through the area as he transported a cargo of furs for William Ashley and the Rocky Mountain Fur Company from the Wind River Mountains to St. Louis. But despite his early reference to the springs, Clyman may not have been the first white explorer to drink from its waters: "No doubt William H. Ashley, Andrew Henry, Jedediah Smith, David Jackson, Jim Bridger, the Sublette Brothers, Thomas Kirkpatrick, Meek, Provost and others crossed there before 1827."[1]

Independence Crossing on the Big Blue River was a well-known point on the Oregon Trail for many years, and the springs were situated just east of the crossing in a small steep canyon. The bed of the canyon was layered with limestone and made a perfect refuge for travelers. John Denton, an early pioneer, gave Alcove Springs its name when he described the overhanging rocks that sheltered the springs, and the designation soon became a common one in the journals of the emigrants heading west.[2]

The springs area was used extensively for a period of about fifty years, and during this time at least 350,000 emigrants camped at the site. Familiar names of explorers and pioneers who stopped there include John A. Sutter and associates in 1839; the Bidwell-Bartleson party of 69 people and Father J. P. de Smet in 1841; and the Dr. Elijah White party of 120 emigrants and John C. Fremont in 1842.[3] Records show that only 107 travelers used

*Today several inscriptions from pioneers can be read in the rocks surrounding Alcove Springs.
This message, "B Death," must be a warning to fellow emigrants that the black death,
or cholera, was prevalent in the area.*

the site in 1842, but this number increased to 19,000 in 1849 and to 30,000
in 1854.

Of all the emigrant parties to camp at the springs site, the most famous
was the ill-fated Donner party, whose members began their trek to California in the spring of 1846 and met disaster in the Sierra Nevada Mountains
when an early winter blizzard caused many of them to lose their lives. Starting on April 14 from Independence, Missouri, they

> had a pleasant and prosperous journey through Missouri and Kansas.
> On reaching the Blue River Ford, known as Independence Ford, . . .
> they were compelled to halt on account of the swollen conditions of
> the river. They went into camp at Alcove Springs and waited for the waters
> to subside. Old Mrs. Keyes, age 75, . . . suddenly became sick and in
> a few days died. She was buried in a rude coffin . . . her grave marked
> with a stone whereon was deeply cut her name, age and date of death,
> May 29, 1846.[4]

Sarah Keyes was not the only emigrant to go no farther than Alcove Springs. A large number of graves were dug near the springs and on the adjacent hills, but no organized burial plot was arranged or permanent markers erected.[5]

The first settlers in the area were a few Kansa and Sioux Indian families who lived near the springs during the 1840s and 1850s until a tragedy occurred that forced them to abandon the site. A band of Osage Indians from near Council Grove attacked the women and children and burned the cabins while most of the men were working in the fields. As the Osage made their escape, they took a young Sioux Indian girl with them. The men dashed in from the fields and gave chase, but the pursuit ended in a nearby clearing where the girl was found murdered. The Indian settlers soon left the area.

In 1849 F. J. Marshall and A. G. Woodward were the first white men to build homes in Marshall County. Although Marshall operated a ferry, a blacksmith shop, and an outfitting store, one of his principal commodities was whiskey, which he sold for 18¢ a gallon.[6]

By the late 1850s few emigrant trains were making the journey westward. The little settlement at Independence Crossing was abandoned, and Alcove Springs was no longer used by the pioneers in such great numbers. The last wagon to use the crossing came through in 1876, nearly fifty years after the first party of explorers.

The Alcove Springs site was largely forgotten until 1941 when the residents in the area began to realize its historical importance. A bill was passed in the state legislature to make the site a national monument, but because of World War II the matter was not taken up by the federal government.[7]

In May 1946 local D.A.R. officials held a 100-year anniversary celebration at Alcove Springs, and the event brought people together who wanted to turn Alcove Springs into a park. After a delay of fifteen years, "the roar of bulldozers and the thud of axes broke the stillness of Alcove Springs valley Sunday afternoon as a corps of about 20 Blue Rapids citizens began renovation of the historic area for visitors."[8] At the same time a committee went before officials of the National Park Service to request that Alcove Springs become a national monument. The National Park Service disapproved the committee's request, but with the help of the local citizens the site became a short-lived community-owned park.

Today the site is on private property where it is a target for vandals and is deteriorating from exposure to the natural elements. Many of the rocks around the alcove have fallen into the water, and most of the original writings and carvings have eroded away. There are only a few inscriptions left, and these are not likely to last much longer. Preservation is the key to the future of this important emigrant stop, or all the reminders the pioneers left behind at Alcove Springs will soon be gone.

Today Alcove Springs is inaccessible. Interested visitors should inquire at the *Blue Rapids Times* in Blue Rapids regarding how to contact the current owner.

2

EAST CENTRAL KANSAS

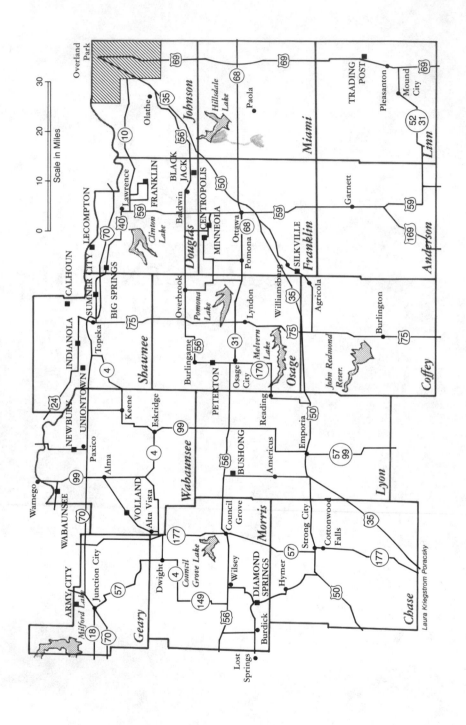

Laura Kriegstrom Poracsky

TRADING POST
Linn County

By 1834 an area near the Marais des Cygnes River was occupied by two
fur traders with the Northwestern Fur Company, Michael Girard and Phillip
Chouteau, who had established a profitable business trading furs with the
local Indian tribes at the Chouteau Trading Post.[1] In 1842 General Win-
field Scott built a log fort near the trading post to house a company of
dragoons, and the fort was in service until after the Civil War.[2] That same
year Girard opened a store he called Trading Post in which he kept a small
stock of goods to trade with the Osage Indians in the area.[3]

In 1845 the traders were surprised to see a steamboat coming down the
Marais des Cygnes River, bringing Girard a stock of merchandise for the
Indians. The steamboat docked at Trading Post, and over 150 people, both
Indians and whites, gathered on the riverbank to greet the steamer and
its captain. In 1848 Girard sold his store to Chouteau, who eventually sold
it to Peter Avery. The last owner was Seth Belch, a Jefferson City, Missouri,
lawyer, who later became speaker of the Missouri House of Representatives.[4]

Trading Post reached its peak of development when a large grist mill was
erected in 1857. A post office was established in September of that year,
and at the suggestion of Mrs. Samuel Nickel, wife of the first postmaster,
it was named Blooming Grove after her old home in Pennsylvania. The
name Blooming Grove was retained until 1880, then it reverted back to
Trading Post because it was the name with which most individuals in the
area were familiar.[5]

The slavery issue became a problem at Trading Post in 1857 when William
Daniels built a saloon that became a stronghold for the Missouri border
ruffians. The tavern and its proslavery clientele were such a threat to the
settlers that James Montgomery and his men raided the saloon and smashed
the barrels of whiskey with a rock, causing the liquor to flow 100 yards
down the road. This action by Montgomery was one of the first
"temperance crusades" in the state, but it only served to provoke the proslavery men and they harassed the settlers even more. Although the free-
state men in town started carrying guns and drilling as a military unit, the
border ruffians continued to torment them until finally a tragic incident
occurred on the banks of the Marais des Cygnes three miles northeast of
Trading Post.[6] Eleven free-state men were lined up and shot by the ruffians; five were killed, five were wounded, and one escaped unharmed.
This episode in Kansas history is known as the Marais des Cygnes Massacre,
and the tragic event was just one of several that turned John Brown against

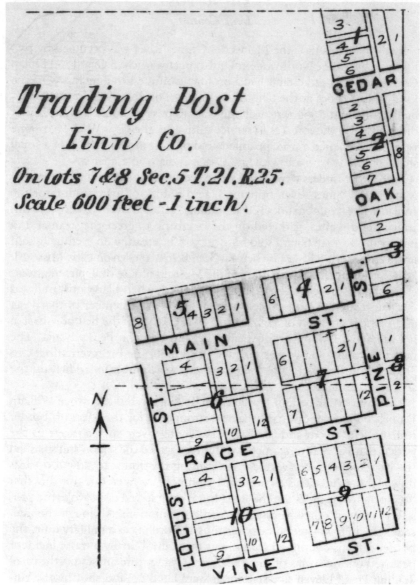

A plat of Trading Post as it looked in 1886. Trading Post was never a large community, but its place in Kansas history is nonetheless secure.

the proslavery faction. Brown, alias "Captain Walker," lived at Trading Post in 1859, and while there he composed his "Parallels Speech," which compared the acts of the proslavery and the free-state men along the border.[7]

During the Civil War, a large group of southern sympathizers from the proslavery town of West Point, Missouri, regularly raided the free-state settlements along the Kansas boundary, and Trading Post was the target of several of these attacks. In 1863 General Alfred Pleasanton and his troops camped at Trading Post just before they engaged Confederate troops six miles farther south in an encounter known as the Battle of Mine Creek, the only major Civil War battle fought on Kansas soil.[8]

Trading Post was prosperous economically until the end of the Civil War in 1865, but after the war Trading Post dwindled rapidly because of the closure of the nearby fort and because trade with the Indians was lost as they moved farther south. During 1867 the Fort Scott & Gulf Railroad was built through Linn County, but it missed Trading Post by a few miles, a fact that caused the town to decline further. In the 1880s the town consisted of three general stores, a drugstore, two blacksmith shops, an agricultural implement dealer, and 100 inhabitants.[9]

Today Trading Post, a quiet little "country town" on U.S. Highway 69 seven miles north of Pleasanton, consists of only a few houses and one or two small businesses. Prosperous during the Civil War, Trading Post was unable to survive the ensuing years of peace.

CENTROPOLIS / MINNEOLA
Franklin County

Before the Kansas-Nebraska Bill was passed in 1854, most of what is now Franklin County was divided into reservations for the various Indian tribes such as the Shawnee, Sac and Fox, Chippewas, and Ottawas. The exception to this reservation land was a three-mile-wide strip along the northern edge of the county, known as the Shawnee purchase, which was opened to settlement on May 10, 1854. Two towns, Centropolis and Minneola, were established within a mile of each other in this stretch. The rivalry between the two was intense, partly because both wished to become the territorial capital. Centropolis had little chance of achieving this distinction because it had proslavery leanings. Minneola could have been the permanent capital of Kansas if it had only attracted popular political interests and the necessary population. Its attempt at prominence, however brief, placed this town in the same class with Lecompton and Pawnee as one of the capitals of Kansas Territory.

By the mid-1850s the slavery issue had become so controversial that many of the settlers came to Kansas with strong political convictions. On June 26, 1854, a group of fifteen men camped on Eight-Mile Creek, near what is present-day Centropolis, and took a vote to see who among them wanted to make Kansas a free state. All voted "free" except for two men—J. M. Bernard and Timothy Keizer; the majority included Jacob Clark, I. C. Hughes, Thomas Doty, John Javens, Franklin Barnes, Johnson Farris, Perry Fuller, Leoander McClellan, John McClellan, and Mansfield Carter. After settling this political matter, each man selected his claim.

After J. M. Bernard opened a store on his claim in March 1855, he was appointed postmaster of the small settlement, which was appropriately named St. Bernard. Although the Kansas Territorial Legislature designated St. Bernard as the county seat in 1855, the town neither grew nor prospered. That summer free-state men in the area raided the town and the post office, as Bernard had become obnoxious over the proslavery issue and had threatened too many people, and shortly after the raid Bernard was persuaded by the free-statemen to leave town. The St. Bernard post office was discontinued on November 26, 1858, and the name was changed to Minneola.

In 1855 the town of Centropolis was off to a successful start in the capable hands of Perry Fuller, who built the first store on the townsite. Fuller believed that his town would become both the county seat and the territorial capital of Kansas, and he named it from a contraction of "central metropolis."

The success of Fuller's store depended on the trade with the local Indians, and the West & James Company of Kansas City kept him supplied with plenty of merchandise. Business must have been good for Fuller that first year because his total sales amounted to $50,000. In 1856 Fuller took William Moore as a partner, and together they bought out the West & James Company and continued the Kansas City–based merchandising business themselves.

After the Centropolis Town Company was organized in 1856, the town grew rapidly, and lots were selling for as high as $500 each. In the fall the first commercial newspaper in Franklin County, the *Kansas Leader*, was published in Centropolis by W. H. Austin. (Previously the Reverend Jotham Meeker had published a missionary newspaper in the county.)[1] Jacob Long opened a tavern and sold liquor to everyone, including Indians. Fuller and Moore did not want this kind of business in their town, so they purchased Long's supply of liquor, smashed the barrels, and let the whiskey flow out onto the ground, thus ending his operation.

Charles B. Lines, the founder of Wabaunsee, wrote a letter dated April 16, 1856, to his hometown newspaper in New Haven, Connecticut, the *Daily Palladium*, in which he described Centropolis:

The place from which this letter is written is what they call here "one horse town." . . . This locality is situated about 18 miles south of Lawrence and is 50 miles from "Kansas City." . . . There are now two or three cabins, a rustic blacksmith shop, and a store. . . . and underlying the whole enterprise is a proposal to make the city the State Capital. The principal parties engaged in the scheme are influential members of the Legislature who, it is supposed, intend to make fortunes out of the movement. . . . It appears also that the members of the "bogus" Territorial Legislature have laid out another site within two miles of this and they are bound to have the capital go there [Minneola]. . . . there is altogether too much of this scheming for great speculation on the part of the leading men of "Kanzas" . . . "the people" should interpose and upset some of their deep laid plans.

I am writing in the store . . . which is situated only a half mile from . . . the tribes from whom they derive their principal trade amounting to not less than $15,000 per annum. The store has been filled with them today. Among the number we noted one fine looking young Chief, decked with all sorts of gewgaws and brass ornaments. There is something sad in moving among these remnants of the powerful tribes of other days and witnessing their despondency as the pale faces are gradually crowding them from place to place . . . and hemming them with narrow boundaries as to crush out the free spirit of their nature.

When Centropolis reached its peak in 1857, there were thirty buildings in town, including four saloons and a prosperous gambling house. But as the free-state forces came into power, the town's proslavery politics proved troublesome. In 1857 the legislature voted against Centropolis's becoming the territorial capital because of its proslavery leanings and because one resident actually owned three slaves.

Minneola had also become a thriving town, and Perry Fuller, who had moved there from Centropolis, was partly responsible for Minneola's new growth. He and his associates purchased fourteen quarter-sections of land just east of Centropolis close to Minneola, and a list of stockholders in the Minneola Town Company included almost every prominent leader in the free-state cause, including a majority of the members of the legislature. In the spring of 1857 the Centropolis *Kansas Leader* was sold to the Min-

This is an artist's 1857 sketch of how the capitol building at Minneola was to appear. Plans for construction of this impressive building never materialized because of lack of funds.

neola Town Company and was given the new name of the *Minneola Statesman* by James H. Lane, the noted free-state leader.[2]

In the fall of 1857 Perry Fuller visited Lawrence, where the legislature was holding an adjourned session, and distributed free shares of stock in the Minneola Town Company, declaring that the legislators might as well locate the territorial capital there. On February 10, 1858, the Kansas legislature passed a bill making Minneola the territorial capital, but this bill was vetoed by Gov. James Denver. An appeal was made by Fuller to the attorney general of the United States, who decided instead that the bill was in violation of U.S. statutes and therefore void. In March another bill was passed that called for a meeting of the constitutional convention at Minneola on the fourth Monday in March.

By March 1858 a seventy-seven-room hotel had been completed alongside a two-story annex that contained a dining room, a kitchen, and a large hall. On the Sunday before the meeting of the constitutional convention, approximately 400 guests took meals at the hotel, and nearly 200 occupied sleeping quarters. Even with the ample accommodations, not everyone found rooms and many had to sleep in the open fields.

After the members entered the assembly hall, Montgomery Conway, James H. Lane's righthand man, addressed the group. He complimented everyone on the nice accommodations and casually mentioned the residents' hopes that Minneola would become the permanent capital of the state. Conway then nominated Lane as chairman of the assembly, and the nomination passed by a unanimous vote of all seventy-four members.

Next, however, the people who did not want Minneola to become the capital moved to adjourn the convention to Lawrence, and an argument ensued. When the assembly reassembled at 1:00 P.M., another motion was made to adjourn to Leavenworth, which only caused more agitation. This session lasted until 8:00 A.M. the next morning without any adjournment. At that time a Minneola man suggested they stop arguing and get down to the important business at hand, and he stated he was more than willing to yield to the motion of adjournment. Unfortunately the motion to adjourn to Leavenworth carried, and as the crowd of delegates moved out of town, the people knew Minneola was not destined to be the capital.

The town continued to prosper for another two years because the legislature adopted a bill that made provisions for a number of railroads to be centered at Minneola.[3] Maps and "bird's eye views" that made the town appear a great railroad center were issued by the town company, but the railroads never came.[4] Any hopes the people had that the legislature would return to Minneola at a later date ended when Topeka became the capital in 1861.

In 1860 Minneola declined rapidly as a severe drought that year caused the farmers to pack up their belongings and move away. The *Statesman* was suspended, and the press was moved to Burlington in Coffey County.[5] After the townsite was abandoned, the land was sold to the county for back taxes. Today the site of Minneola consists of little more than a few ruins and half a dozen farms.

Centropolis has fared better through the years, but only slightly so. The Centropolis *Journal* was first published on March 9, 1864, but was suspended just six months later. By 1880 Centropolis had a population of 175 and two general stores, a hardware store, two blacksmith shops, a wagon and machine shop, a grist mill, a cabinet shop, and a hotel.[6] The post office was discontinued in 1930, and today Centropolis has only a small residential population and a few stores. People drive by without knowing that Centropolis and its now ghostly neighbor, Minneola, were once rivals for the territorial capital of Kansas, and that Minneola actually was the capital for a short time.

You can reach Centropolis by taking U.S. Highway 59 north from Ottawa. Follow the signs and turn west on a paved road; go about three miles. The town of Centropolis is on both sides of the road. Minneola stood approximately one mile east of Centropolis and is today private property and virtually unidentifiable.

Circular Letter,

TO THOSE INTERESTED IN

SILK CULTURE
IN KANSAS.

VIEW OF SILKVILLE.

SILKVILLE, KANSAS, August 1st, 1877.

The number of persons giving attention to the culture of silk in Kansas is rapidly increasing. Silk culture will, in fact, soon be, to many, a valuable and profitable addition to general farming. The object of this circular letter is to answer many questions, explain many facts and correct many errors, in the desire to encourage new beginners and prevent the catastrophe of failure which must come to the most enthusiastic if they work ignorantly.

In my last circular I say, "no success can be obtained without two conditions, viz : Good sound eggs of the finest breeds known, and the best varities of Mulberry trees cultivated for their food."

A sketch of Silkville as it appeared in a circular, dated August 1, 1877, promoting the new colony.

SILKVILLE
Franklin County

The first plans for silk production in Kansas were conceived by a Frenchman named Ernest de Boissiere, an enterprising philanthropist from Bordeaux, France, who had served as an engineer in the French army before resigning to take charge of his parents' estate on the east coast. After Napoleon III came to power in 1852, de Boissiere's ideals and politics were unpopular, and he was advised to leave the country. He came to the United States and first settled in New Orleans, where he established a shipping line, but he was later forced to leave that city because of conflicts with his wealthy southern neighbors.

Ernest de Boissiere had always been interested in the silk industry. While he was looking for a place in the United States that had the right climate for the growing of silkworms, he heard about Kansas from William H. Scofield, the first settler of Williamsburg in Franklin County and a financial agent for Baker University. Through Scofield's influence, de Boissiere chose Franklin County as the site for developing "a system of industrial and social life far in advance of either now prevailing in the world," and he purchased 3,000 acres for his "plantation" and commenced to put his plans for a silk industry on paper.[1]

Ernest de Boissiere was a disciple of Voltaire, and he was imbued with the love of liberty, a philosophy of socialism, and the theory of free love. His plans for Silkville were a curious combination of autocratic and socialistic rule, actually a scheme backed by capitalism yet dedicated to communal ownership. Early in 1870 de Boissiere planted his orchards, which consisted of walnut trees, ornamental groves, and forty acres of mulberry trees.He brought forty families, experts in the silk industry, from France to supervise the work at Silkville.

The first building on de Boissiere's land was a sixty-room house that could accommodate fifty to a hundred persons; it was for a number of years the largest mansion in Kansas. It contained a number of spacious parlors, several dining rooms, numerous offices, forty family rooms, and a library filled with 2,500 volumes of choice literature in many different languages. He built a school at Silkville, the first in Kansas in which the instructors attempted to teach the contemporary world literature of the day, generally known as the "great books."

By December 1870 de Boissiere's farm was nearing completion, comprising the silk factory, a winery, an ice house, an apartment house, and numerous other stone buildings. By 1872 he had added Masonic and

De Boissiere's home in Silkville around the turn of the century. After Silkville was aban-
doned, this structure became the Odd Fellows Orphans Home. It later burned to the ground.

IOOF lodge halls; barns that had a capacity for 300 hogs, 400 head of cattle, and 50 horses; a cheese factory; and a blacksmith shop. Twenty-five miles of barbed wire fence and fifteen miles of stone walls enclosed the tract. In a report to the State Board of Agriculture in 1872, de Boissiere stated that 10,000 mulberry trees were providing luxuriant foliage for the feeding of the silkworms. In a circular published in 1877, he described his farm as having a large peach orchard, 400 four-year-old apple trees, and 1,200 young grape vines. Four of the alianthus trees he planted in the 1870s still stand near the old school grounds.

The French families who arrived to work on the silk farm were required to pay $100 deposit, which was to be refunded at 6 percent interest if and when they left the colony. All persons admitted to the settlement had to pay for their room and board two months in advance and had to provide their own furniture and other articles for their personal use.

By 1873 all operations in Silkville were going well, but problems began to arise. As some of the French laborers became more familiar with the English language and could speak with their American neighbors, they began to leave Silkville for other towns where higher wages were being paid. Since the silk industry was still in its infancy, de Boissiere could not afford

The ruins of de Boissiere's home shortly after the fire, which left only the exterior walls intact.

to compete with the wages of other factories. In the fall of 1873 a severe economic panic shook the nation, and many factories were forced to shut down. This recession, which lasted almost six years, meant that de Boissiere had to market cheese, milk, and butter in addition to silk in order to stay alive. In 1874 he was confronted with problems in the silk market when Italian and Japanese silk became cheaper to buy, a recurrent problem for the Frenchman.

Life in Silkville in the 1870s was different from life in other Kansas communities. The colonists were encouraged to believe as they pleased so long as they accorded to others the same freedom of thought and action. One of de Boissiere's aims was to organize labor on the basis of remuneration in proportion to production, believing that work would be done more efficiently this way. Although there were rumors that the colonists practiced free love, it is unknown whether these rumors were true. Since society was shunned during the colony's early years, this philosophy could have flourished at that time without any outside knowledge.

In 1875 members of Congress became enthusiastic about the Silkville experiment, and Sen. John J. Ingalls asserted that wheat and silk could make Kansas "the most prosperous community on the continent." At the Centennial Exposition in Philadelphia in 1876 a sample of de Boissiere's silk from "the only silk-velvet manufactory in the United States" took first prize, surpassing the finest oriental silkwork.[2]

In 1882, when the silk industry suffered another downward trend, de Boissiere was heard to remark, "When I am in Bordeaux, I'm rich, but when I am in Kansas I eat bread and milk out of a tin can. But I can adapt myself to my income." However, by 1886 de Boissiere had stopped the production of silk altogether and was manufacturing milk by-products. From that time on, cheese from the Silkville Ranch was in great demand, and the production of cheese and butter rose to 1,200 pounds per day.[3] But other communities attempted to follow his example, and by the late 1880s forty-six counties in Kansas were involved in manufacturing silk. These attempts failed as well, however, and all laws created for the silk business were repealed in 1927.

In 1888 de Boissiere's wine- and cheese-making businesses were flourishing in Silkville, but in a few years these too began to falter, and the Frenchman grew restless. By 1892 de Boissiere had recovered his fortune in France and was yearning for his homeland. On May 11 he donated the Silkville Ranch to the Odd Fellows Lodge for an orphans' home and returned to France, where he died two years later at the age of eighty-five. After his death, litigation arose over the validity of his gift to the Odd Fellows, and that and other legal problems concerning the ranch finally caused the Odd Fellows to give up the estate. The ranch eventually became the property of an insurance company and was later sold to several individual owners.

In the 1950s Silkville Ranch was owned by John Netherland and Eldon Koons, and they tried to restore and preserve what was left of the original buildings, the old rock walls, and the mulberry trees that were still standing in the orchard. Unfortunately, their attempts to draw attention to this historical community were unsuccessful, and today the site is only marked by a sign bearing the name of the ranch. The deserted schoolhouse with its alianthus trees and portions of the stable and cocoonery are still there, but they are on private property.[4] As Darrel DeLong wrote in a thesis on Silkville, "The end of an era has come and gone, long gone; for the train doesn't stop and the cattle herds now graze where great silk factories and churches once were. The Silkville community is only a memory to a few and unknown to most."[5]

The site of Silkville is just two miles southwest of Williamsburg on U.S. Highway 50. When you spot the stone schoolhouse on the south side of the road and the sign reading Silkville Ranch, you will be in the area Silkville once occupied.

BLACK JACK
Douglas County

In the early 1850s Black Jack was only a small trail town, but after June 2, 1856, it became well known as the namesake of a battle fought nearby between free-state and proslavery men. The outcome of the Battle of Black Jack gave the free-state supporters a much needed victory and helped change the political system in Kansas.

Black Jack was established as early as 1855 as a supply point for traders and emigrants along the Santa Fe Trail. Little did the residents know that a few months later their community would be in the middle of a bloody political confrontation. When Wilson Shannon was appointed governor of the territory in September 1855, the proslavery supporters had found an advocate. The attacks by the southern sympathizers along the Missouri border increased, and Governor Shannon did nothing to stop them; many of these ruffians were armed with rifles obtained from the U.S. Arsenal at Liberty, Missouri.[1]

In the spring of 1856 a company of border ruffians, under the command of Capt. H. C. Pate, camped at Black Jack and began to terrorize the local residents, who were predominantly free-state proponents.[2] When John Brown arrived in Black Jack in May, he organized a company of free-state men to drive out these marauders.

The company was led by a settler named Howard Carpenter, who took the free-state men to a safe hiding place on Tauy Creek, near the Douglas County line. They camped at this retreat for six days, from May 24 to May 30, 1856, but on May 31 seven proslavery men ambushed twelve of the free-staters, killing or wounding all of them. The next night Carpenter arrived in Black Jack to meet with Brown, and they decided to rendezvous with other free-state men at a church in Prairie City (a small town near present-day Baldwin).

John Brown and his men arrived at Prairie City the next morning and watched the free-state people come in from the surrounding area; some arrived in wagons, some on horseback, and some on foot. "Women cried and men groaned" as the news of the massacre by the border ruffians was revealed to them. Suddenly about 3:00 in the afternoon, a settler reported seeing three men watching the group from some distance away, and several men rode out and captured them. The captives disclosed where their camp was located, and forty men volunteered to ride with Brown to the enemy camp. By 2:00 on the morning of June 2, 1856, they were within a mile of the campsite, and at dawn, they attacked.

This sketch, originally titled "A Family Dying of Starvation at Black Jack, Kansas Territory," appeared in the New York Illustrated News *of January 19, 1861. During this time, settlers in Kansas suffered severely from a devastating drought. Apparently, settlers at Black Jack were not immune to the suffering.*

John Brown and his men charged down the hill to the bottom of the ravine where the enemy had been sleeping, and the gunfire was hot and heavy from both sides. The skirmish continued for five hours until twenty-five more free-staters arrived on the scene, and the proslavery men realized they had lost the battle. The southern sympathizers reported seventeen men wounded out of a force of seventy-five, and two of the men died later at Prairie City. John Brown and the abolitionists had their much needed victory.[3]

The village of Black Jack was incorporated in 1857, and the members of the town company included William Riley, Daniel Fearer, E. D. Pettengill, S. A. Stonebraker, and H. N. Brockway.[4] The first store in town, built by Brockway and Stonebraker, supplied provisions for the travelers on the Santa Fe Trail. During a six-month period in the 1860s, figures show that 4,472 wagons, 1,267 horses, 6,451 mules, 32,281 oxen, and 13,056 tons of freight traversed the trail.[5]

The threat of border warfare continued to be a problem in Black Jack, and on May 8, 1863, Dick Yeager's gang rode into town, robbed the Brockway and Stonebraker store, and stole horses belonging to the Overland Stage Company. On August 15, William Anderson and his men rode into Black Jack and intercepted the Overland mail, stole fourteen horses (eight of them belonging to the Overland Express), and took $2,000 from the passengers. The outlaws also broke into Brockway and Stonebraker's store and carried away $1,800 in merchandise before setting the store on fire. The flames were quickly extinguished by one of the townspeople.[6]

At its peak Black Jack contained a tavern, post office, stage barns, blacksmith shops, hotel, wagon shop, general stores, doctor's office, two churches, schools, and a number of residences. By the end of the Civil War, however, the traffic on the Santa Fe Trail began to dwindle, and since this trade was Black Jack's only source of revenue, the town also began to decline. This downward trend continued into the 1870s, and when the Santa Fe Railroad missed Black Jack by five miles, the town was abandoned.

Today a memorial marker and a Battle of Black Jack Park sign are all that remain to commemorate the armed conflict. Near the townsite and across from the park, deep wagon ruts on the Santa Fe Trail are still visible in the prairie grass. The site of Black Jack is immediately west of Baldwin on U.S. Highway 56. A well-marked battle site and park are just south of the highway. The townsite itself, now unidentifiable, is private property east of the park and south of the highway.

FRANKLIN
Douglas County

The Civil War may have begun at Fort Sumter, South Carolina, in 1861, but the seeds of that conflict were planted in Kansas at least six years earlier. The trouble in and around the town of Franklin, a proslavery stronghold located four miles southeast of Lawrence, was typical of the hostilities in Kansas Territory before the Civil War.

Franklin was founded in October 1853 on the Lewis Wallace claim between the Kansas River and the Wakarusa River. It was one of the oldest settlements and Indian trading posts in the county, and the first stage stop west of Westport (Kansas City).

When Kansas was declared a territory in 1854, many Missourians moved to Kansas, and within a few short months Franklin had been transformed from being a mere stage stop into a town popular with southern sympathizers. Just a few miles to the northwest, the town of Lawrence was established as one of the first free-state strongholds in Kansas, and the proximity of these two towns left little doubt in the minds of the local settlers that there would be trouble between the two factions.

Essentially two battles were fought in Franklin: the first on June 4, 1856, and the second on August 12. During the entire summer, Franklin was continually threatened by attack from the free-state forces at Lawrence, as indicated in a letter written in June 1856 by Col. A. J. Hoole, who lived twelve miles from Franklin:

> These are exciting times here. You may form some idea of them when I tell you that I never lie down without taking the precaution to fasten my door. . . . I have my rifle, revolver, and old home-stocked pistol where I can lay my hand on them in an instant, besides a hatchet & axe. I take this precaution to guard against the midnight attacks of the Abolitionists, who never make an attack in open daylight, and no Pro-slavery man knows when he is safe.[1]

The two battles that occurred at Franklin were preceded by several significant events. In the fall of 1855 Sheriff Samuel Jones, who was holding a free-state man in jail on a minor charge, became extremely annoyed when his prisoner was freed by friends from Lawrence. This event caused Jones to swear vengeance on Lawrence and gave him an excuse to use Franklin as his headquarters for recruiting other sympathizers.

On December 1, 1855, Franklin was swarming with men and horses because a company of Kansas militia had just arrived and 1,500 Missourians were already camped outside of town. Rows of tents, many campfires, two covered wagons with flags flying, and plenty of rifles gave the scene an ominous appearance. The new arrivals had come in answer to the sheriff's call for action and were expected to "help Jones wipe out Lawrence." In the days that followed, the men engaged in target practice, drank whiskey, gambled, and grew increasingly more impatient. As discipline was lax and food was scarce, the plundering of settlers' homes and farms was a frequent form of entertainment for these radicals.

When Gov. Wilson Shannon learned of the true state of affairs in Franklin, he realized the folly of the proposed attack on Lawrence, and on December 8, 1855, he drove through sleet and snow to reach Franklin. Free-state leaders Charles Robinson and James H. Lane arrived from Lawrence, and the thirteen Kansas militia officers met with these men in a small room at the tavern where they calmly discussed the situation. All of the men, except for Sheriff Jones, saw the wisdom of calling off the attack, and a treaty of peace was signed. The militia officers sent their troops back home, and by December 11, the Missourians had left.

This truce did not last long, however, for when the snows were gone, Sheriff Jones resumed his plans. In the spring of 1856, a group of proslavery men arrived in Franklin to join the sheriff's forces, and late in May they sacked Lawrence and burned the Free-State Hotel. Retaliation by free-state men came on the night of June 4, when they attacked Franklin. These abolitionists first prowled around town in an unsuccessful attempt to find "Old Sacramento," a cannon that had fallen into proslavery hands. For several hours there was an exchange of rifle fire between the two groups, and one man was killed and six were wounded. Eventually, however, the free-state men withdrew.[2]

The second battle at Franklin, on August 12, 1856, resulted from the brutal murder of one D. S. Hoyt of Lawrence, who had gone to "Fort Saunders," a fortified proslavery camp south of Lawrence, to confer with the commander, Col. B. F. Treadwell. Hoyt had hoped that this meeting would put an end to the pillaging and plundering around Franklin, but as he left the camp, two men followed him as far as a strip of woods where they killed him and left his body half-buried by the side of the road. That evening, after hearing about Hoyt's murder, twenty-five horsemen and fifty-six infantrymen left Lawrence for Franklin to break up the proslavery headquarters there and again try to retake the cannon, "Old Sacramento."[3] One account of the incident that followed was written by John Lawrie, an abolitionist from Lawrence, in a letter dated April 19, 1857:

In order to carry the stronghold of these Ruffians, artillery was necessary. We had none, but the enemy had one. . . . It was known as Old Sacramento. One night about 75 of us took the road to Franklin. . . . The ruffians were summoned to surrender, but they wouldn't do it, so we replied to their fire in such an effective way that we drove them all to the center of the building. . . . From this position they gave us a pretty hot fire, killing one man named Sackett and wounding two others, Gunther and Brooks. . . . As our fire didn't seem to make much impression on them, a wagon was loaded with hay and run up to the building . . . and set fire to; when our boys began singing out "There she goes!" "There goes the roof!" "Stand off, boys, maybe there's powder in it!" By and by it began to work on the garrison, and they screamed out "Quarter!" "Quarter!" "For God's sake give us quarter!" We told them to march out and stack their arms and we would do so, . . . and then we upset the load of burning hay, and not even the wagon burned, say ing nothing of the buildings. After gathering up their arms and getting Old Sacramento mounted, we started back to Lawrence and arrived there safely.[4]

The troubles in Franklin continued into the fall, but they were more sporadic, and after the proslavery influence in Franklin began to weaken, there was an occasional disturbance, but for the most part, the violence had ended. Elizabeth Williams Smith wrote about living in Franklin after the proslavery forces had left:

We took up our residence in a house that had been used the summer before by the border ruffians as a fort. It was riddled with bullets, and had been taken by the free-state men. . . .

During the summer of 1857 my father built a stone store building and stocked it with general merchandise. Soon he bought an interest in a sawmill located at the east end of the town. There was the promise of good business in the town from the Indian tribes nearby, and the farming country on the Kansas River and the Wakarusa.[5]

In 1857, after Franklin was incorporated, John Wallace established a ferry on the Kansas River north of town, and Dr. R. L. Williams opened a general store upon his arrival that spring.

When the Civil War became imminent, the proslavery power in Kansas had all but disappeared, and Franklin residents who were adamant in their proslavery sentiments kept it to themselves, for the spirit of the community was decidedly antislavery. In fact, many black slaves sought refuge there during the war. One resident, John Ott, has left us vivid recollections of Franklin that would otherwise have been forgotten. He recalled seeing Union troops with glittering bayonets; stagecoaches changing horses at the Franklin tavern; the arrival in town of blacks who praised Lincoln for their freedom; the black school in which "Grandma" Herrington taught; the white school where each pupil furnished his own bench; and the one remaining buffalo that roamed on the prairie near Franklin until it was killed by the local butcher.[6]

The town declined quickly after the Civil War, however. Quantrill's raid on Lawrence in 1863 had created such a demand for houses that many structures in Franklin were moved to Lawrence, and the post office, which was discontinued in 1867, was one of the last stone buildings left in Franklin. The townsite eventually passed to Dr. Williams, who farmed there for many years.

This is an old view of the R. L. Williams residence in Franklin, built in 1857. The house was one of the last remnants of the townsite, which has now practically disappeared.

In 1900 Michael Schutz, a farmer in the area, noted that considerable labor was necessary to fill up the wells and cellar holes on the Franklin townsite. Schutz also found a few coins: pennies the size of half-dollars with the dates 1845 and 1853, an old half-dime with the date obliterated, and five-cent pieces from 1868 and 1871. He discovered bullets that were an inch long and one-half inch in diameter, and lead balls the size of small grapes, some dented and flattened.

All that remains of Franklin is an abandoned farmhouse in a privately owned field about fifty yards from an unmarked gravel road south of state Highway 10, about three miles from Lawrence. Though the exact date of its construction is not known, some people say the house was built around 1857 by S. Crane, the owner of the property at that time. A small cemetery strewn with broken stones and overgrown by brush can be seen near the house.

LECOMPTON
Douglas County

Lecompton can boast of having been both the territorial capital of Kansas and a county seat. Although Lecompton still exists today, with nearly

700 residents and a few businesses, it is hardly the Lecompton of the 1850s, which had a population of almost 5,000, including the surrounding area, and so many businesses that it was nicknamed the "Wall Street" of Kansas Territory.

French fur traders first visited the site while exploring the Kansas River valley in the 1700s, but the region remained sparsely inhabited until nearly a century later. The first settler in the area was William R. Simmons, who had previously fought in the Mexican War and had joined free-state leader James H. Lane's regiment in Indiana. Simmons took a squatter's claim on the Lecompton townsite in 1852 and operated a ferry on the Kansas River. The ferry, affectionately known as the Fairy Queen, consisted of a huge sycamore log twenty feet long and five feet in diameter. Asked about it by dismayed emigrants, Simmons replied, "Don't feel skeery mister, for she's as dry as a Missourian's throat and as safe as the American flag."[1]

In the fall of 1854, Dr. Aristides Roderique and A. G. Boone began exploring the Kansas River valley. After traveling for days, they stopped on a ridge that terminated abruptly at the river and predicted that the place would ultimately be the site of a great metropolis. Boone noticed many bald eagles soaring in the area, and for this reason he named the townsite Bald Eagle. Boone and Roderique returned to Missouri to organize a town company, but their efforts were futile. Newspaper editors would not mention the town either because of its southern affiliations or because they feared competition for trade and residents. Boone and Roderique dropped their plans and did not return to Bald Eagle.

During the winter of 1854/55, Samuel D. LeCompte of Maryland was appointed federal judge of the territory. In his honor, the name of the town was changed from Bald Eagle to LeCompton, and the LeCompton Town Company was organized with Judge LeCompte, president; John Halderman, secretary; and Daniel Woodson, treasurer. In the spring of 1855 the town company reported that D. H. Harting had surveyed the 600-acre townsite and had laid out the principal blocks and streets. As soon as the land office opened, several claims were filed by eager settlers.

On August 8, 1855, the territorial legislature met at Shawnee Mission and designated Lecompton the capital of the territory, granted authority for a bridge and a ferry there, and established the Kansas Medical College. That same year the territorial government began construction of a large stone capitol building in the eastern part of town. When the $50,000 appropriation for the structure had been exhausted after construction of the basement and the first story, however, work had to be discontinued, and the building was used as a fort during the territorial conflicts. The short-

This sketch of Lecompton shows steamboats on the Kansas (Kaw) River circa 1856. In reality, navigation on the Kaw was risky at best: The river was too shallow and had too many sandbars for large-scale navigation.

lived Kansas Medical College, with its board of trustees, never received sufficient funds to begin construction. By 1857 the college was nothing but a memory.

In the fall of 1855 Lecompton became known as a proslavery center and a rendezvous point for outlaws. Many murders and lynchings, blamed by the eastern newspapers on the town's "lawlessness," actually occurred across the river at Rising Sun, and even though it was generally believed that any stranger who entered Lecompton with other than proslavery leanings would be robbed, imprisoned, or killed, Lecompton never had a recorded lynching and only a few murders.

Still, the unrest in the territory over the slavery question made the area's residents uneasy and overly suspicious. One evening a disturbance in his corral caused J. Todhunter to hurriedly reach for his gun, which accidentally discharged, killing him. Despite this uneasiness, a steady stream of settlers, politicians, and land speculators came to Lecompton. Seven four-horse stage and express lines brought emigrants to the fledgling town daily. A large steamboat wharf was built in 1855, followed by a steam sawmill, brickyard, the governor's residence and Constitution Hall, several churches, grocery stores, and scores of homes.[2] Visitors to Lecompton could choose from five hotels: the Virginia, American, National, Alexander, and Rowena. The most luxurious hotel was the Rowena, a three-story struc-

Free-state prisoners arrested and held near Lecompton, from Frank Leslie's Illustrated Newspaper, *October 4, 1856. Lecompton remained a proslavery hotbed throughout much of the territorial period.*

ture finished in walnut and lavishly furnished. Both the town's newspapers—the *Lecompton Union* and the *Lecompton National Democrat*—were radical proslavery publications, but all official printing for the territory (laws, resolutions, and treaties) was done in Lecompton by these newspapers.[3]

In 1855 a free-state convention was held in Topeka, and the 500 delegates who attended adopted a constitution and elected Charles Robinson governor and Andrew Reeder and James H. Lane to the U.S. Senate. Since Kansas was not yet a state, these activities on the part of the free-staters were regarded as an act of treason by the government officials at Lecompton, and in May 1856, a grand jury met at Lecompton to investigate. This group recommended that the two abolitionist newspapers at Lawrence, the *Herald of Freedom* and the *Kansas Free-State*, should be discontinued; the free-state hotel at Lawrence should be destroyed as a nuisance; and Governor Robinson, Andrew Reeder, and other so-called state officers should be indicted for treason. Sheriff Samuel Jones, aided by the territorial militia and the U.S. Cavalry, went to Lawrence. The hotel was burned to the ground, the

newspaper presses were destroyed and thrown into the river, Governor
Robinson's home was burned along with a few other structures, and Robinson and Reeder were subpoenaed to stand trial at Lecompton at a later date.[4]

From 1856 to 1858 between 300 and 500 U.S. cavalrymen and 400 to
600 territorial militiamen were stationed in Lecompton, and their presence
brought a boom to the business in town. Along Halderman Street,
nicknamed "Wall Street," were located the legislative halls, the district and
U.S. courts, the U.S. Land Office, the governor's office, the Rowena Hotel,
the post office, an express office, a book and stationery store, a drugstore,
Leamer's general store, barber shops, a printing office, law offices, real estate
dealers, and three saloons.

Behind Lecompton's success were many prominent men such as Andrew Reeder, the first territorial governor, who was eventually forced to
flee Kansas disguised as a woodcutter; Wilson Shannon, congressman, twice
governor, minister to a foreign court, and an acclaimed lawyer; John W.
Geary, mayor of San Francisco, brigadier-general of the Army of the
Potomac during the Civil War, and territorial governor; and Gen. James
W. Denver, territorial governor, and the man for whom Denver, Colorado,
was named.[5]

By the summer of 1856 the territory's political climate had shifted, and
free-state sympathizers outnumbered the proslavery settlers. Southern sympathizers had to resort to hiding in outlying log cabins and camps, such
as the Colonel Titus cabin one and a half miles south of Lecompton. In
August the free-state settlers decided to destroy Titus's cabin and to burn
Lecompton. Word reached Lecompton, and a force of thirteen men was
sent out to delay the attackers, but when they encountered 200 free-state
men, they took refuge in Titus's cabin. The free-staters attacked the cabin
with the cannon "Old Sacramento," using balls made from newspaper type
that had been thrown into the river at Lawrence. The proslavery men soon
ran out of ammunition and surrendered, and the cabin was burned to the
ground, but not before it had served its purpose. The delay had given the
men in Lecompton enough time to strengthen their defenses, and when
the free-staters arrived they found themselves staring down the barrels of
several hundred guns held by the townspeople. They hurriedly retreated.
Lecompton had been saved, and Titus's cabin was known thereafter as
Fort Titus.

Lecompton was the site of a state constitutional convention late in the
days of "Bleeding Kansas." The convention met on September 7, 1857,
but adjourned to meet again on October 11. When the delegates reassembled
at Constitution Hall, they found several hundred free-state men barring

Constitution Hall, Lecompton. A political meeting place when Lecompton was the territorial capital, this old building was recently purchased by the state of Kansas as a future historical museum.

the entrance. The delegates stayed away until October 19 when more than two hundred U.S. soldiers with brass fieldpieces returned to guard them from the free-state sympathizers. By the end of November the convention had completed its work and adjourned, and the constitution was presented to the citizens of the territory in an election on December 21. Most free-state sympathizers refused to vote, and as a result 6,226 votes were cast for the constitution with a slavery clause and only 569 votes were cast in favor of removing the clause. The constitution was then sent to the U.S. Congress where it failed to gain acceptance. A second election was held in 1858, and this time the constitution with the proslavery clause was rejected 11,300 to 1,788 votes.

In January 1858 the third session of the territorial legislature met at Lecompton, but by this time the legislature was predominantly free-state in politics. Many state offices were moved out of Lecompton because of prejudice against the town's proslavery citizens, and the city began to gradually decline. Each succeeding year until 1861, the territorial legislature would meet first at Lecompton and then adjourn to Lawrence because the free-state forces were determined to boycott Lecompton. After Kansas became a state in 1861, the town declined even further. Lecompton finally lost the county seat. In January 1858, all county offices were moved from Lecompton to Lawrence, which became the new county seat of Douglas County. The political balance of the county had shifted from proslavery to free-state, taking with it most of Lecompton's former affluence.

One of the most enduring institutions in Lecompton was Lane University, which was founded in 1854 as a United Brethren college and named, oddly enough, after the free-state leader James H. Lane. A gift of thirteen acres and the incomplete capitol building were given to the university in 1865 by the state of Kansas, and the university's building, constructed atop the foundation of the old capitol, was completed in 1882. In 1903, however, the school was moved to Holton and renamed Campbell College.[6] The old building in Lecompton has recently been restored and is now a museum.

Today Lecompton is quiet and peaceful. Fire destroyed many of the old buildings downtown; only Constitution Hall is left on a street of small stores, a post office, and an antique shop. It is a silent testimonial to the raucous and violent days before Kansas became a state. To reach Lecompton, take U.S. Highway 40 west from Lawrence. Follow the signs and turn right on a paved road. Lecompton borders the western side of the road before it crosses the Kansas River.

BIG SPRINGS
Douglas County

Big Springs, the oldest settlement in Douglas County, was established in the fall of 1854 by William Harper and John Chamberlain, although the area had always been well known as an excellent watering place along the Oregon Trail.[1] The town was barely a year old when two events occurred that helped Kansans to become victorious over both slavery and the saloon.

One of the first blows against slavery in Kansas was struck at an "official" free-state convention of settlers at Big Springs on September 5, 1855. Determined men gathered from all sections of Kansas and passed resolutions vowing to give their lives if necessary to defend their homes against the border ruffians from Missouri. This meeting was the beginning of an organized attempt to wrest the political power from the southern sympathizers in the territory.

An old stone stable in Big Springs, now known as the Oregon Trail Museum, has more historical significance than any other building in town.

FREE STATE
CONVENTION!

All persons who are favorable to a union of effort, and a permanent organization of all the Free State elements of Kansas Territory, and who wish to secure upon the broadest platform the co-operation of all who agree upon this point, are requested to meet at their several places of holding elections, in their respective districts on the 25th of August, instant, at one o'clock, P. M., and appoint five delegates to each representative to which they were entitled in the Legislative Assembly, who shall meet in general Convention at

Big Springs, Wednesday, Sept. 5th '55,

at 10 o'clock A. M., for the purpose of adopting a Platform upon which all may act harmoniously who prefer Freedom to Slavery.

The nomination of a Delegate to Congress, will also come up before the General Convention.

Let no sectional or party issues distract or prevent the perfect co-operation of Free State men. Union and harmony are absolutely necessary to success. The pro-slavery party are fully and effectually organized. No jars nor minor issues divide them. And to contend against them successfully, we also must be united.— Without prudence and harmony of action we are certain to fail. Let every man then do his duty and we are certain of victory.

All Free State men, without distinction, are earnestly requested to take immediate and effective steps to insure a full and correct representation for every District in the Territory. "United we stand; divided we fall."

By order of the Executive Committee of the Free State Party of the Territory of Kansas, as per resolution of the Mass Convention in session at Lawrence, Aug 15th and 16th, 1855.

J. K. GOODIN, Sec'y.   **C. ROBINSON,** Chairman.

Herald of Freedom, Print.

An advertisement for a free-state convention in Big Springs on September 5, 1855. This convention helped to organize the free-state movement in Kansas and was the beginning of the end of proslavery dominance in the political and economic affairs of the territory.

Some historians claim that the Republican party in Kansas was organized there during the above mentioned free-state convention, while other students of Kansas history maintain that the Republican party was formally organized four years later on May 18, 1859, at the first Republican convention held at Osawatomie. Whichever claim is true, the group of prominent men who gathered at Big Springs in 1855 included many of the same vigorous leaders who founded the Kansas segment of the Republican party and dominated the Kansas political scene during the first few years of statehood.[2]

As travelers emigrated west on the Oregon Trail, Big Springs became an important trading post and was sometimes called the Forks because the trail divided at that point to lead to two different river crossings. A post office was established in Big Springs in 1855, and the first store was opened by two businessmen, Webb and Carter.[3] The Harper House and the Picken Hotel furnished the best accommodations in the area for travelers on the trail.[4]

In 1856 the citizens of Big Springs confronted another important issue—

The Henry Wittich residence near Big Springs, circa 1870.

liquor. Although it was legal for Dr. Carter, the local physician, to prescribe drugs and medicinal alcohol to the townspeople of Big Springs, it hardly seemed proper to the citizens when a Missourian delivered three barrels of whiskey to the doctor's office, and he used this liquor to start his own tavern. After his first night in business, thirty residents sent Dr. Carter a formal notice protesting his saloon, but he ignored their complaints and continued selling whiskey. The next night a mob of forty irate townspeople met outside his saloon and marched into the bar, where they emptied a barrel of whiskey on a pile of wood shavings and set it on fire. After the sober citizens had taken their turns standing on top of the empty whiskey barrel and making prohibition speeches, everyone signed a temperance pledge. This was one of the first recorded temperance meetings in Kansas and the beginning of the crusade that led to more effective prohibition laws in 1881.[5]

Several stories and legends about Big Springs have been passed down through the years, such as the account of the gold that was supposed to have been buried in the area. During the 1850s Kansas Territory extended westward to the Continental Divide, and gold was discovered in what was known then as Cherry Creek, now part of Denver. When a group of miners traveling from the Cherry Creek diggings with wagons loaded with gold were held up by outlaws near Big Springs, a fierce fight ensued and the robbers were driven off, but the miners were afraid that there would be another attempt to rob them so they buried the gold somewhere in the area. Since they were never seen or heard from again, the cache is supposedly still buried in the vicinity of Big Springs.[6]

When the Santa Fe Railroad missed the town in 1869, Big Springs lost much of its prominence and began to decline even though several new businesses were later established. A creamery was built in 1870, and it continued in operation until the hand separator became impractical. In 1887 a cider press was installed and used for several years. The products from these two industries were shipped to Topeka, Lawrence, and Kansas City.[7]

For decades, Big Springs slowly regressed into a small agrarian community. Businesses closed their doors as townspeople traveled to Topeka and Lawrence after U.S. Highway 40 was constructed through Douglas and Shawnee counties. In 1986 the citizens of the community voted to raze the beautiful Catholic church that has graced the west edge of town for fear that vandals would slowly wreck the abandoned structure. The stately rural church now stands neglected and partly disassembled, facing a dismal future. Although the demise of Big Springs has been slow, it does have the appearance of a ghost town today.[8] Big Springs sits on both sides of U.S. Highway 40 between Topeka and Lawrence. It is easily accessible and well marked.

CALHOUN
Shawnee County

Calhoun is the name of not only a ghost town but also a "ghost county," and the relationship between the two was one of dependence, as the loss of the county also meant the loss of the town. Calhoun, named after the surveyor-general of the territory, John Calhoun, was a small proslavery settlement located just east of the present Calhoun Bluffs region and west of the current Shawnee-Jefferson County line. The boundaries of Calhoun County, which included all of what is now Shawnee County north of the Kansas River, were fixed by the territorial legislature in 1855, and Calhoun was designated as the county seat.[1]

On September 24, 1855, the county was formally organized by its commissioners, William Alley, Richard Beeler, and James Kuykendall, and their first official acts were to name the voting places for the election of a delegate to Congress and to present a resolution to build a courthouse "out of brick."[2] The county commissioners met for the second time on September 29, and at that time they fixed the site for the courthouse in "courthouse

The Calhoun County courthouse at Calhoun as it appeared in the 1890s. Built in 1855, this structure was abandoned when Calhoun County was disorganized in 1859. It later served as a hay barn.

square" in the town of Calhoun. They also filed detailed building plans and specifications, indicating that a costly structure was to be built of stone and brick and finished with oak and walnut, but the design proved to be too expensive so the construction of the courthouse was never funded.

The construction of a jail was another important issue. Kuykendall converted an old stone building on his property into a jail, but the first prisoner kicked a hole in the side of the structure and escaped to the river where his friends attempted to get him across on the ferry.[3] This jail break prompted the commissioners to order the erection of an "official jail" at Calhoun as soon as possible.

On May 19, 1856, the legislature ordered that the plans for a brick courthouse "in the town of Calhoun be rescinded," but a small two-story structure constructed of native logs was built at a cost of $2,500.[4] Several important Topeka and Lecompton lawyers opened their first offices in this building, including future Gov. John A. Martin and Judge Samuel LeCompte.

On October 11, 1858, a county seat election was held, and the results favored Holton instead of Calhoun. In 1859 the legislature enacted a law changing the name of the county from Calhoun to Jackson, and the U.S.

government closed the post office at Calhoun.[5] The combination of these events caused businesses in Calhoun to close and the citizens to move elsewhere.

By the time the legislature fixed the boundary line of Shawnee County at its present northern limit in 1868, Calhoun, like many other proslavery communities in Kansas, was a ghost town. Today the name Calhoun Bluffs east of Topeka is all that remains of this once promising town and county.[6] You can no longer see the old Calhoun site because U.S. Highway 24 runs directly over it at Calhoun Bluffs near the junction of state Highway 4 east of Topeka.

INDIANOLA
Shawnee County

Indianola was founded in 1854 a half-mile west of Soldier Creek near what is now the Boys Industrial School.[1] Louis Vieux, a mixed-blood Pottawatomie Indian, sold the land for the townsite to H. D. McMeekin and J. Tutt, the town's first settlers. The Milne House, a large log hotel built in 1854 by a Scotsman named David Milne, was the first business in town.[2]

Indianola's location on the Fort Leavenworth to Fort Riley Military Road helped the town's economic growth; in comparison, the nearby town of Topeka was nonproductive and slow to develop. Although Indianola was a proslavery center and Topeka was decidedly free-state, there were few conflicts as the citizens were far more interested in establishing their businesses than indulging in warfare. However, a skirmish known as the Battle of Indianola supposedly took place in 1856 when several proslavery men were killed after they had barricaded themselves inside a hotel that was destroyed by a group of free-state men.[3] But many people contend that the fight never occurred and the story of the skirmish is nothing but a colorful myth.

By the summer of 1855 four business buildings had been constructed in town, including a log hotel owned by Louis Vieux and a store operated by Lewis Harris.[4] In June 1855, public lots sold for $300 each, but the highest priced lot ($500) went to J. Q. Cowee, who built the Indianola Hotel in the spring of 1857. Other buildings constructed in 1857 were a steam sawmill, a post office where government annuities were paid to the Indians, and a large store owned by William Fairchild.

Indianola attracted some of the rougher elements in the 1850s, and a horse track and two gambling houses were built. Since hard liquor was sold over the bar seven days a week, drunken brawls were not an uncommon occurrence. There were no fewer than six saloons, and all were successful.

The Clinton Hotel at Indianola as it appeared in the 1890s. Most of Indianola was moved to North Topeka after the town was abandoned, but this hotel proved too large and expensive to transport.

In 1862 several outlaws robbed a store of $700, and that same year a young man named Joe Baker killed another man in a brawl at one of the saloons. On another occasion the Confederate general Albert Sidney Johnson caused a great deal of excitement when he and 600 soldiers camped at Indianola on their way to Utah just prior to the Civil War.[5]

Although Indianola had been a proslavery center before the Civil War, Company F of the 15th Kansas Cavalry was organized there shortly after the sacking of Lawrence by Quantrill in 1863, and Orrin A. Curtis, father of Vice-President Charles Curtis, was appointed captain of the company. Company E of the 8th Kansas Infantry, also organized at Indianola, was commanded by Capt. John A. Martin, who saw action at Chickamauga, Missionary Ridge, and the siege of Atlanta.[6]

The Clinton Hotel, built in 1860 by William Clinton, was an impressive building, and it became the most popular hostelry on the military road because it contained a stage station, post office, restaurant, and tavern. The patrons of the stage line, the soldiers, and the government freighters often stopped there to sleep, eat, and "likker up." In January 1868 a public dance was held at the hotel for members of the state legislature who were in session in Topeka, but this dance was Indianola's last big social event as a downward trend in the town's economy was already evident.

The Kansas Pacific Railroad had made plans to build through Indianola instead of following the natural bend of the Kansas River through North Topeka. A contractor from the railroad met with the residents of Indianola in 1865 and arranged for them to provide the ties for the new track. The men went to work cutting timber along Soldier Creek, but when all the ties were cut and delivered, no contractor was there to pay for them. The men were told that Topeka had been chosen as the railroad terminal after all, and they knew their dreams of Indianola's becoming an important railroad center were over. Later the townspeople learned that Sen. James H. Lane, the former free-state leader, had used his influence to have the railroad built through Lawrence and Topeka instead of through Indianola.

When the railroad was completed, the citizens of Indianola moved their homes and businesses to Topeka. The Clinton Hotel was the only building too large to move, so it remained in a vacant field where it stood in ruins for many years.[7] Today the site of Indianola, near the Goodyear Tire Plant on U.S. Highway 24, has completely disappeared.

SUMNER CITY
Shawnee County

One of the most fascinating "paper towns," Sumner City, was to have been located between Topeka and Tecumseh. Preliminary land negotiations took place in the mid-1890s after William L. Eagleson, publisher of the Topeka *Colored Citizen,* proposed a plan to segregate blacks into one community, an all-black town five miles east of Topeka. "He conceived of a community with a population of 1,000–3,000 people with groceries, meat markets, dry goods and notion stores, brickyard, lime kiln, canning factory, lumberyard, and other enterprises. It was to be located on the river bottoms just west of Tecumseh."[1]

In the *Colored Citizen* on July 15, 1897, Eagleson stated that the town would be a haven for blacks, "where the Negro would hold sway and be safe against the wiles of the designing white men," but because of a lack of money and influential backers, Sumner City was never more than a town planned on paper. Instead, many of the blacks congregated in North Topeka, in an area east of the Santa Fe Railroad yards, and in an area called Tennessee Town in the center of Topeka.[2]

UNIONTOWN
Shawnee County

Uniontown was once the largest community in the area, dating back further than any of the other towns. In March 1848 the trading post site for the Pottawatomie Indians was chosen by two government agents, Richard W. Cummins and Alfred J. Vaughn, who worked for "the smith & traders for the Potawatomies." In a March 7 letter Cummins reported, "I have accordingly stuck my stake and christened it union town," and on March 12 he wrote, "The point selected by us is on the south side of the Kansas . . . & very nearly in the center of their [the Pottawatomies's] country."[1]

The location of Uniontown was about a half mile south of the Kansas River on the western edge of what is now Shawnee County. The Pottawatomies north of the river were opposed to there being only one trading site for the Indians because of the dangers they would face in crossing the river when it was high, but Uniontown remained the only official trading post from 1848 to 1853.

In 1849 Uniontown was the only place where the government paid annuities to the Pottawatomie Nation. The Indians would gather for payment, and these gatherings, a time for celebration, would last from ten to fifteen days. The Indians liked to indulge in gambling, drinking, and horse racing in addition to sacred tribal dancing. The government paid each Indian from $6 to $10 as part of their share of a previous land agreement, but unfortunately most of this money was spent before the Indians left town.

In 1849 the town was booming, and the St. Louis *Republican* advised: "Emigrants for California or Oregon, by the way of Independence, Kansas landing, or Westport will find an excellent ford across the Kansas river, at Uniontown . . . the traders with the Indians have a good supply of all articles of provisions, etc. . . . at reasonable rates."[2] Other comments on Uniontown were made by westbound emigrants. On April 22, 1849, William Kelly wrote in his journal: "The trading post is a small hamlet, composed of some half-dozen shops, and a little straggling suburb of wigwams. The shops are kept by white men, licensed to supply the Indians around with the flimsy, fantastic, and trumpery articles they require; liquor being specially interdicted, and very properly so." According to James A. Pritchard, writing on May 7, "There are several white family liveing there & some 4 or 5 stores, blacksmith shop &c. A number of Indians are liveing in the village. . . . There was 2 ferry boats; one kept by a half breed Indian & the other by a white man."[3]

Later in 1849, however, a cholera epidemic in the region spread to Union-town, and many of the settlers panicked and fled. Thomas Stinson, J. R. Whitehead, and T. D. McDonald chose to stay and help the local physi-cian treat those who were sick with the disease, but unfortunately for the settlers, the doctor and his wife also became infected with the illness and died. The Pottawatomie Indians were devastated by the epidemic, and many of them were found lying dead in the streets. Before the remaining white settlers left Uniontown, they buried twenty-two Indians in a com-mon grave in the Uniontown cemetery, and then they burned the town to prevent the cholera from spreading. Uniontown was a ghost town for the remainder of 1849.

In 1850 Uniontown was reestablished as a trading post, and the govern-ment stationed two blacksmiths, a wagonmaker, two gunsmiths, and a physician at the townsite. A branch of the Oregon Trail passed through Uniontown to a ford on the Kansas River, and the emigrants heading west followed this trail directly through the town. Fifty or sixty new buildings were erected, including fourteen stores, and Uniontown became the largest settlement in the region.

Since it was such a convenient place to cross the river, nearly all the trails in Kansas converged at Uniontown including the California/Oregon Trail, the Fort Leavenworth to Fort Riley Military Road, the Mormon route, and a branch of the Santa Fe Trail. A ferry was established in 1850 by Lucias R. Darling "for the use and benefit of the Pottawatomies," and Darling maintained the ferry until January 1854 when John L. Ogee became the new operator.

Some observations of the travelers about the new settlement of Union-town during the spring of 1850 include one description written by Dr. John F. Snyder on May 8–10: "We then came to the Pottawatomie nation, and passed through their trading post, called 'Uniontown,' at the crossing of the Kansas River. This town consists of about fifty log houses, with a population of about 300, nearly all Indians. . . . Crossing the Kansas, we encamped near the hut of a chief, who had the U.S. flag floating proudly over his miserable habitation." On May 15, one Robert Chalmers wrote: "Went 12 miles, passed Union Town. A few Indian huts and two or three stores kept by traders were scattered along the way. Arrived at the ferry and camped for there were so many wagons there that we could not get across till morning. We drove the cattle down to the river to drink and they all got mired."[4] On June 5, 1850, another correspondent noted that "no regular records" had been kept at the Kansas River ferries, but he estimated that 2,700 wagons had crossed the river at Uniontown along with some 4,000 head of cattle in droves of from 150 to 500 head. At four persons per wagon, he calculated that approximately 11,000 emigrants had passed "through this neighborhood alone."[5]

In 1852 two gunmen robbed the government paymaster at the annuity building in Uniontown of $20,000 in gold. The outlaws immediately headed for the Kansas River, but they were intercepted by U.S. Dragoons and killed in the gun battle that followed. The money was not recovered by the Dragoons, nor was it ever located.

In 1854, after Kansas had become a territory and new towns had begun to spring up in the Kansas River valley, Uniontown began to experience a general decline in trade from the overland travelers. As the larger towns of Topeka and Tecumseh gained most of the business, Uniontown was abandoned, and in 1859 the remaining buildings were burned for reasons not adequately explained other than that "evil spirits" dwelt there.[6]

Today some of the ruts of the old Oregon Trail and the mass Indian burial site in the Uniontown cemetery can still be seen. Most of the townsite is filled with the trash of the 1850s such as pipe stems, dish fragments, coins, and assorted metal objects. A portion of the region has become the Green Wildlife Refuge, a public preserve for naturalists.

The site of Uniontown can be reached by taking Interstate 70 west from Topeka to the West Union Road exit. Take this road north about three miles until it curves widely at the site of an old cemetery along the east side of the road. The cultivated fields to the north and east of the road and cemetery were once the site of Uniontown.

PETERTON
Osage County

In the 1870s the rapid development of the coal fields in Osage County was in direct response to the needs of the Atchison, Topeka & Santa Fe Railroad because this transportation giant required a vast supply of coal to keep its locomotives running. The coal in Osage County was close at hand and therefore relatively inexpensive.

The Peterton townsite, purchased by John M. Wetherall in 1870, included an 8,000-acre tract between Dragoon and Salt Creeks. After geologists had explored the area and confirmed the presence of a large bed of bituminous coal near the surface, railroad officials lost no time making an offer for the land, and Wetherall sold most of this tract to T. J. Peter, the manager of the Santa Fe line in Topeka and the president of the newly formed Osage Carbon Company. In the mid-1870s several mining companies began to

View of an engine explosion at Peterton in 1896.

sink shafts in the region, and a branch line of the Santa Fe was constructed through the heart of the Osage County mining district, and directly through the small town of Peterton, to make shipment of the coal to Topeka easier.[1]

Andreas, in his *History of Kansas,* painted a pleasant picture of Peterton during the town's formative years: "[Peterton] is located about three miles north of Osage City. It is exclusively a mining town and has few business houses. . . . [The population] consists almost entirely of miners. The houses are comfortable and are all frame structures and owned generally by their occupants."[2] Other reporters were not so enthusiastic. The *Topeka State Journal,* October 11, 1887, printed a rather derogatory description of the town: "Peterton is an uninviting little mining town down in Osage County. The houses are not kept well painted, the fences are tumble down and everything looks unpleasant and uncomfortable."

In 1884 the first annual report of the State Inspector of Mines noted that out of 91 shafts in Osage County, 5 of them were around Peterton.[3] One of these mines was owned by the Coughlan brothers, and they employed 21 miners "including boys," who worked an average of 250 days annually. Other large companies in the area included the Peterton Coal Company and the Osage Carbon Company, which employed 180 workers and produced nearly 1 million bushels of coal in 1887 alone.[4] By 1890 the towns of Peterton and Osage City were growing and enjoying the fringe benefits of the coal mining industry, which had brought hundreds of miners and their families to the communities.

There were eighty-one shaft, slope, and drift mines and fifty-four strip banks in operation in Osage County in the late 1800s. The major companies at that time included the Scandinavian Coal Company, George Bass & Company, Osage Carbon Company, Coughlan Brothers, Webster & Russell, Peter March & Company, George Hartzwell Company, Jones Brothers, Peterton Coal & Mining, and the John Craig Mining Company. Over 300 miners were employed, including a number of boys thirteen years old or younger, as the employment of young boys in the mining fields was relatively common in the nineteenth century.[5]

The positive effect of the mining boom on Peterton's business district and population was evident as the population increased from 100 in 1878 to 600 by 1891, and the town expanded from 12 blocks to 145 blocks. Despite the workers' attempts to construct straight thoroughfares, the streets in Peterton still resembled those of a mining town in the midst of a boom—the houses were built just anywhere based on the whims of their owners, and the streets were rutted and zigzaggy, becoming quagmires of mud during heavy rains. Businesses included two grocery stores, two hotels, two livery stables, a meat market, two general stores, a drugstore, a confectionary, a justice of the peace, a physician, two carpenters, a boot and shoe shop, and a local band known as the Peterton Cornet Band.

By the late 1890s the business boom in the region began to show signs of slowing down. The demand for coal, especially from the Santa Fe Railroad, had increased at such a rapid rate that the Osage County mines could no longer keep up, and mining companies in the region around Pittsburg in Crawford County began to dominate the coal industry in Kansas as they offered more coal to the railroad at a lower cost per bushel. In time this shift changed the focus of the industry and eventually the coal mines in Osage County were forced to cease production.

The population in Peterton reflected this change in the county's coal industry. By 1900 the population of the town had fallen to 400, and by 1904 it was only half of its 1891 high of 600. Since local miners had left the area for jobs in the coal region in southeast Kansas, most of the mines around Peterton had to close down, and by 1910 only about 200 people were left in the community. Many of the businesses closed their doors, the post office was discontinued, and Peterton was now only a railroad shipping point for the farmers. During the 1930s most of the coal

Prohibition did not end all drinking in Kansas. Posing for the camera are a number of beer drinkers enjoying a party at "Grandma Blooms" shanty in Peterton, circa 1910.

mines in Osage County were closed, and Peterton became a ghost town.

Today the townsite contains a few ruins and some old residences from the coal mining days, but for the most part, the town has disappeared. Peterton's citizens witnessed the rise and fall of one of the first and most successful mining booms in the history of the state.[6]

To visit Peterton, take a two-lane road that parallels the Santa Fe Railroad tracks north from Osage City. When the railroad tracks cross the road, you are in the vicinity of Peterton.

BUSHONG
Lyon County

Compared with other early Kansas settlements, especially in the eastern third of the state, Bushong is a relatively new town. In fact, until the mid-1880s, the Bushong townsite was an empty field owned by Joseph Weeks, but when the Missouri Pacific wanted to build a station in the area, Weeks donated twenty acres to the railroad for that purpose. He then platted another twenty acres and sold it to a developer who laid out a town

The Bushong Garage on Main Street. This building still stands and is well preserved.

near the station. Although the town was first named Weeks, the railroad construction gang renamed it Bushong in honor of a former big-league baseball player for the St. Louis Browns, Al "Doc" Bushong. (This was not the only instance of such a name. Another town along the railroad in Lyon County, Comiskey, was named for a baseball player from Chicago.)

Bushong was basically an agricultural town with a railroad, and by 1927 it had over 150 residents. The town suffered a major setback, however, when three large buildings on Main Street—a restaurant, a garage, and a community hall—burned down and were never rebuilt. The many open spaces on Main Street today indicate where other fires occurred.

In its prime, the business district was composed of a hardware store owned by George Harder; a grocery store operated by Claude Decker; a gas station owned by Virgil Weeks; hardware and groceries delivered by H. E. Hubbard; an elevator operated by U. R. Pykiet; a garage owned by Paul Gilbert; and a blacksmith shop run by Ernie Pykiet. Today these places have closed. Signs on Main Street advertise Coca-Cola and Butternut Bread, but the stores that once sold these products are no longer open. Nor are the high school and consolidated grade school built to serve the district.

Even though there are a few people still living in the immediate area, Bushong bears quite a ghost town appearance. But because of its late arrival in Kansas history, Bushong can be visited before the remaining traces of the town are completely gone. It can be reached by taking U.S. Highway 56 west from Allen. Follow the signs and turn south at a marked road; drive on it for one mile. Bushong is on the east side of the highway.

This building served many uses in Bushong, including a gas station and tavern. Today it stands wide open and abandoned. (Photo courtesy of Don Miller.)

VOLLAND
Wabaunsee County

Volland was originally called Grafton, but its name was changed in 1888 as Volland was a prominent family name in the community. The first general store in town was in a small frame building opened by John Cromer, who ran the business successfully for several years. In 1904, he sold his store to J. W. Kratzer, who operated it for many more years, along with another general store in the same building. Kratzer's store flourished as Volland became a major cattle shipping point on the Rock Island Railroad. The store, which was open seven days a week, did as much business on Sunday as on the other days combined. In 1913 a large two-story brick store was built, and it took over much of Kratzer's clientele.

Cattle shipping remained a big business in Volland until the mid-1920s, when shippers began taking their herds to larger railroad towns, such as Alta Vista and Alma.[1] The depression of the 1930s also adversely affected the town, and many citizens eventually left during that decade.

Today, Kratzer's frame store and the two-story brick store, which stands

Interior of the Kratzer General Store at Volland. Contrary to popular belief, the store owner did not sell mules.

just across the road, are the last remnants of the community. They have been renovated to resemble typical stores of the early twentieth century, and items with brand names from by-gone days line the shelves—Watchdog Lye, Fairy Crackers, Jap Rose Toilet Soap, Mica Axle Grease, Mayfair Tea, Zeno Chewing Gum, and Houn Dawg Chewing Tobacco. The brick store is also filled with old antiques of every shape and size from the not so distant past. Periodically open to tourists, nearly 3,000 visitors have visited the stores, which are owned by Lowell Thierer, who lives on a nearby farm.

The two stores seem so alone and so out of place on the Flint Hills prairie that they naturally attract the curious eyes of passers-by. But Volland is definitely worth a visit because it may not be long before all vestiges of rural town architecture, such as those represented at Volland, will be gone.[2]

Volland can be visited by taking an unmarked gravel road southwest of Alma paralleling the Rock Island tracks. Volland, well marked, is immediately south on another gravel road. The buildings, however, are on private property.

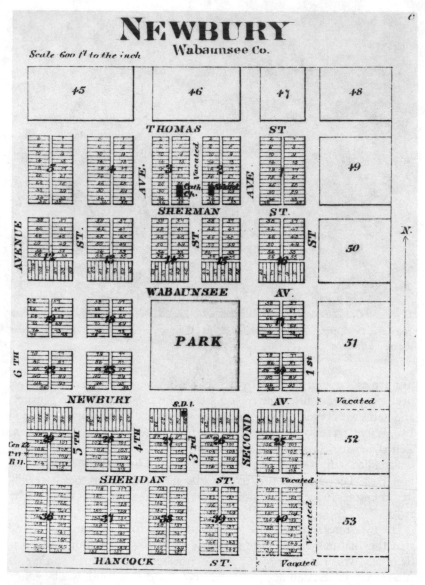

Newbury had several streets, according to this 1886 plat of the community. Today, most activities in town center around the large Catholic church, which is visible for miles in any direction.

NEWBURY
Wabaunsee County

The founding of Newbury dates back to the fall of 1869 when four German settlers—John Mock and his father, Joseph Glotzbach, and Martin
Muckenthaler—were the first white men to purchase land in the area. By
the spring of 1870 these men had laid out the town of Newbury and had
erected several dwellings and commercial buildings in the town.

In 1871 Newbury vied for the privilege of being the county seat, but Alma
eventually won the election. Although some of the settlers were disappointed with the outcome of the vote and moved away, most of them
chose to stay. That fall the firm of Goldstandt & Cohen built a general
merchandise store, which was followed by a drugstore, lumberyard, post
office, hotel, harness shop, and a dozen homes.[1]

Newbury was a prosperous agricultural community for several years, but
new settlers chose to build homes in other towns in the area—the closest,
Paxico, being only a mile away. Paxico began as a mill site in 1879, but
when a store and a post office were constructed there, Newbury and Paxico became business rivals.

This competition became especially apparent when the Rock Island
Railroad began laying track in the area. Both towns "wined and dined"
the railroad officials, but in the end Newbury lost, and the Rock Island
built the railroad through Paxico.[2] Losing the county seat was not a major
factor in the decline of Newbury's economy, but losing the railroad in 1886
was. Most of the businessmen in town either sold out or moved to Paxico
when it became the railroad shipping point for the local farmers, and
Newbury nearly became a ghost town.

Among the settlers who called Newbury and Paxico home during the
1880s were a number of "exodusters," or black emigrants who were escaping
the collapsed economy of the post–Civil War South. In celebration of their
newfound home and freedom, they staged an "Emancipation Day" every
August I, and excursion trains from Topeka and Kansas City brought other
blacks to a camping area near Paxico and Newbury known as Zeller's Grove.
However, since some people objected to this gathering, violence
was sometimes only narrowly averted. On one particular Emancipation
Day in the 1890s, a group of white men tried to crash a dance, and when
several of the blacks did not take kindly to the intruders, a brawl ensued.
One black man was killed, and this tragedy ended the riot, but it left bitter
feelings in the hearts of the blacks for many years. However, the celebration
of Emancipation Day continued to be a popular event through the 1940s.[3]

Most of Newbury's businesses were gone by the 1890s, but the citizens who remained were active in the religious and social affairs of the community. The first church in town had been built in 1874 at a cost of $614, but within ten years the community had outgrown the structure and a new, larger stone church had been built to replace it. In 1921 this church caught fire and burned to the ground, but the citizens did not give up easily. The next year construction began on the new Sacred Heart Catholic Church, and this beautiful building remains a memorial to its builders.[4] Today the church, which still has an active congregation, is within sight of Interstate 70 at the Paxico exit and is worth seeing. It is a majestic monument to the religious fervor of the community.

WABAUNSEE
Wabaunsee County

In 1856 Charles B. Lines of New Haven, Connecticut, formed a colony to emigrate to Kansas, and nearly a hundred people pledged to go with him. On March 22, when the group met to organize the trip, they were inspired by the well-known abolitionist Henry Ward Beecher, whose rousing sermon heightened the crusading fever in all of them. When one man suggested that in order to fight slavery they needed to defend themselves, money for twenty-five Sharpe's rifles was immediately pledged. Beecher himself pledged enough money for another twenty-five. The group prepared carefully for the trip to Kansas, and the rifles, accompanied by twenty-five Bibles and hymnals, were all packed in boxes innocuously labeled "Beecher Bibles." Beecher wrote: "Let these arms hang above your doors as the old Revolutionary muskets do in many New England dwellings. May your children in another generation look upon them and say, 'Our father's courage saved this fair land from blood and slavery.' "

After their departure from New Haven, the *New York Tribune*, April 4, 1856, remarked: "A nobler looking body of men was never seen than the New Haven colony. They are mostly large, athletic men with strong hands and hearts. Among the colony are two ex-members of the legislature, one clergyman, one physician, one or two theological students, and quite a number of the members of the colony have their diploma from old Yale."[1] Although the group was harassed by a few proslavery sympathizers during the trip west, they were never actually attacked. They arrived by steamboat at Kansas City on April 10, 1856; bought farm implements, oxen, and other supplies; and pushed forward to search for a satisfactory location. On April 20, they camped on the prairie on the east side of Antelope Creek and decided to settle there.

Henry Ward Beecher provided financial and spiritual assistance to the colonists who first settled Wabaunsee. He is best known for supplying rifles to the colonists in crates marked "Beecher Bibles," in order to sneak them past the eyes of suspicious proslavery men.

The site was not deserted when the colonists arrived. One of the first settlers in the region was a French-Canadian named Peter Sharai, a speculator and promoter who had preempted a claim nearby. In 1855, a year before the New Haven settlers arrived, he had prevailed upon a Mr. Goodrich to take an interest in the area and to establish a store on the site. Goodrich had purchased merchandise in Kansas City and left the goods with John Nesbit while he returned to Kansas City to get his family and another load of merchandise. On the return trip Goodrich died, and Nesbit took charge of the business. Nesbit was also appointed postmaster at "Waubonsa" on December 29, 1855, but a few months later, the cabin that served as the store and post office burned down.[2]

During the spring of 1856 the colonists laid out their town and named it for a local Pottawatomie Indian chief. Included were parks, a tract of land for a university, and even a few lots for a Kansas state capitol building. The settlers were confident that Wabaunsee was destined to become the "New Haven of the West." On May 2, Charles Lines wrote, "Our men have generally staked out their claims. The surveyors are at work finding the boundaries and the appraisors fixing their . . . value." Church services were held every Sunday, "at the Company tent, in the store, in log cabins, and dugouts, according to circumstances."[3]

In May 1856 the men from Wabaunsee were called upon to reinforce the free-staters at Lawrence who had been expecting a raid on their town. Capt. William Mitchell and Dr. E. Root reached Lawrence safely, but on their way back they were captured by southern sympathizers, and Captain Mitchell was threatened with hanging. After being held for a few days at Lecompton, both men were released unharmed. Upon their return to Wabaunsee, they organized the Prairie Guards, and with Captain Mitchell leading, the group marched to the aid of Lawrence. The so-called surprise attack from the proslavery men was easily repulsed, but this incident gave Wabaunsee the reputation of being a "damned Abolition nest."

Life in Wabaunsee that first summer was spartan. "Tea is a luxury," Charles Lines wrote, "and chicory a delicious beverage." The men brought home game occasionally—mostly buffalo, deer, turkey, and prairie chicken. After some of the settlers had lived on hasty pudding, molasses, and bacon for a month, they butchered one of the plow oxen in order to have the fresh meat they needed to survive.[4] Still, the first Fourth of July was celebrated with feasting as Lines had just returned from a trip to Kansas City for provisions. The "bountiful feast which the ladies spread on the prairie grass" consisted of roast and corned beef, cold tongue, rice and Indian puddings, pear and apple pies, three kinds of cake, and lemonade. This picnic inspired a toast (drunk with lemonade) to "the ladies of Wabaunsee: May we truly appreciate their value as Heaven's best gift to man— doubly precious in a government like ours. And may an abundant supply soon take the place of the present scarcity" (there were only five women in the colony). The good effect of the women on the community was the subject of Wabaunsee's first lyceum debate topic: "Resolved: That a wife will do more to promote the happiness of man than a fortune."[5]

By late July many of the colonists had grown tired of Henry Ward Beecher and his stern ways. Some favored naming a street after him, but Moses Welch objected on the grounds that he had become a symbol of bold repulsiveness and bad judgment. John Gould fancied that if they felt this way, they ought "to send back to Mr. Beecher, the 25 rifles and 25 Bibles he was instrumental in furnishing us with." That motion was rejected, but the street was named Plymouth instead of Beecher.[6]

During the winter of 1856 the free-state–proslavery conflict forced many of the men to be away from home for several months. When they returned to Wabaunsee, sick from exposure and poor food, they found provisions short and expensive. Some of the colonists became discouraged and left the settlement; a few left because they felt that the affairs of the colony had been handled in a dictatorial manner and that aid from New Haven had not been fairly distributed.

Near the end of the year, an underground railroad for routing slaves north was established through the settlement. The attic of the William Mitchell house, east of Wabaunsee, served as a hiding place for the slaves until Mitchell could move them on to Joshua Smith. Smith then escorted them north to the border.[7]

In the spring of 1857 more settlers, including women and children, arrived. The need for a permanent church became apparent and about thirty of the colonists organized the First Church of Christ in Wabaunsee, congregational in form but not in name. Many new homes were built, gardens and fields planted, a school organized, and a town hall and a temporary church built. During the summer, new businesses were constructed, including a four-story hotel (costing $20,000) and a cheese factory. Also during the summer, however, flu and fever, more commonly known as the shakes, had a devastating effect on the children of the community, and the death rate among them was high. Diphtheria also took a number of lives.

In 1858 Charles Lines traveled to New Haven to raise funds for the construction of a stone church. About $500 was collected for building the church and another $250 for the erection of a schoolhouse. In 1859 the colonists began construction of the church, and over the next three years nearly everyone in Wabaunsee donated their time so that on May 24, 1862, the church was finished and dedicated as the Beecher Bible and Rifle

The First Congregational Church, or "Beecher Bible and Rifle Church," at Wabaunsee. This photo was probably taken around 1870.

Church. It was a one-story stone building with a rectangular floor plan. The entrance was at one end and the chancel opposite; as was customary, a divider was placed down the middle of the church to separate the men from the women.

The Civil War greatly affected the town as more than a third of the voting population, twenty-seven men, enlisted. Capt. F. C. D. Lines, the son of Charles Lines, of the 2d Kansas Cavalry was the first to enlist from Wabaunsee; he was killed on September 1, 1863, near Fort Smith, Arkansas. When the town of Lawrence was destroyed by William Quantrill in 1863, Wabaunsee citizens were quick to bring relief as the two towns had always been staunch supporters of one another.

After the Civil War the townspeople hoped for a railroad, but the first one built in the area went north of the Kansas River, and Wabaunsee grew slowly. In 1879 Charles Lines noted that three-fourths of the residents were related to the original colonists by marriage or direct lineage. He remarked, "While none have become wealthy, we have no paupers, but all are com-

The Beecher Bible and Rifle Church at Wabaunsee as it looks today. Most of the remainder of the town has disappeared.

fortably situated—have good farms with fine orchards."[8] There was also much religious activity in Wabaunsee. On July 9, 1897, the *Wamego Times* listed the Beecher Bible and Rifle Church membership at 137, and in addition there were three other churches: the Methodist church and two black churches, the Baptist and the Methodist.

By the turn of the century, many settlers were leaving Wabaunsee and going to the larger towns nearby. The branch line of the Manhattan to Burlingame Railroad that had been built through the town pulled up its tracks in 1898, but the Rock Island soon built through the town. In 1905 a large lodge building, Woodmen Hall, burned down, but another lodge was constructed within a few years. In 1910 when the "Golden Belt" highway was built from Wabaunsee to Manhattan, the old blacksmith shop became a garage.

For a few years during the 1920s and 1930s the Beecher Bible and Rifle Church closed its doors. Then in 1948 renovation began, and by 1958 the church had been restored to its once-proud position in the community. The name was changed to the Wabaunsee Congregational Church, and in 1971 it was placed on the National Register of Historic Landmarks. Sunday services are still held at the church.

An interior view of the arcade building in Army City, circa 1918. Army City was built chiefly for entertaining enlisted men.

Today Wabaunsee consists of about twenty houses and assorted buildings, including the Beecher church. The old stone building still stands as a historic monument to that original band of colonists who left their comfortable New England homes for the unknown and

> Crossed the prairies as of old,
>   The pilgrim crossed the sea,
>   To make the West as they the East,
>   The homestead of the free.[9]

To visit Wabaunsee, take state Highway 99 south from Wamego. Turn west at the junction with state Highway 18. This road will take the traveler directly through the community.

ARMY CITY
Geary County

The coming of the First World War brought with it a massive increase in the number of troops in training at Fort Riley. In order to entertain

On August 4, 1920, the Army City Theatre went up in flames. Built to house hundreds of enlisted men during World War I, it was never rebuilt.

and provide various services to these soldiers, the community of Army City was established. It was located north of Fort Riley and adjacent to Camp Funston. The land was purchased by the government in 1917, and lots were auctioned off to enterprising businessmen who wanted to establish stores, shops, and theaters near Camp Funston.

A. D. Jellison of the Jellison Trust Company was largely responsible for the general layout and financing of the town. He gave the streets military titles and financed major projects such as the construction of sewage systems and water lines. Jellison was also owner and president of the Military State Bank.

In late 1917 the population of Army City was around 1,500 and was composed largely of the town's businessmen and their families along with some officers and enlisted men who were housed there from time to time.[1] The community offered entertainment for the men at Fort Riley and Camp Funston because the town was closer to these installations than to either Junction City or Manhattan. Army City had a host of stores and shops, including both a Y.M.C.A. and a Y.W.C.A., a church, and two movie theaters—the Orpheum and the Hippodrome.

Army City's closest competitor for the business from the two army in-

Auction Sale

250 BUSINESS AND RESIDENCE LOTS

| Adjoining Ft. Riley Reservation | **ARMY CITY** | Commencing at 10 o'clock each day |

WEDNESDAY and THURSDAY, AUGUST 1 and 2

SALE TO BE HELD ON THE GROUND. Kansas' Greatest, Biggest, Busiest New Town. Located less than 100 feet from America's largest Cantonment—60,000 population in 60 days, within a radius of two miles. Great opportunity for all business lines. Pay Roll will be over $2,000,000 a month. The U. S. Government is spending sixteen million dollars in improvements. Army City will have sewer, water, electric lights, telephone, great white way. 40 miles of new paving leading to Army City. Theaters, Banks, Hotels, Restaurants, Business Houses, now under construction.

The Greatest Sale of High Class Business and Residence Lots Ever Held in the West. EXCURSIONS ON ALL RAILROADS. Buy tickets to Junction City, Ft. Riley or Ogdensburg. Your chance to mop up big profits. Something doing in Army City every minute. Get in the prosperity procession Wednesday, August 1. A very convenient place for friends or relatives to stay while visiting soldiers. 10 miles from Manhattan, 10 miles from Junction City, on the Manhattan and Junction City Interurban, the Golden Belt Road, the U. P. Railroad.

| TERMS: One-Half Cash, Balance March 1, 1918 | Train Leaves at 8:48 A.M. Fare is $1.44 |

Army City Townsite Improvement Co., Owners
Office, Central National Bank Building, Junction City, Kansas

Carolina Land Development Co.
Sales Managers and Auctioneers. Western Office, Salina, Kan.

After the war, Army City's usefulness ended. From 1918 to 1922, the town was auctioned off or torn down. This is an advertisement to auction 250 business and residential lots in Army City.

stallations was called the zone—a second Army City located within Camp Funston. The zone was not built with the intention of eliminating Army City. In fact, there was more business in the area than both towns could handle.

On June 4, 1918, Army City held its first election. A mayor, police judge, and three councilmen were voted into office, and a post office was established.[2] This show of permanence was little more than an outward facade, for after the Armistice was signed in November, there was no further need for the town. During the next four years all of the buildings were either torn down, burned, or moved away. In September 1922 six of the town's eight citizens met at the local tailor's shop, and they voted 6 to 0 to unincorporate.

Army City had been 100 percent dependent on the war, and after 1918 the town had no reason to exist. It became a victim of a peaceful America, and today little remains to mark the site.[3] The Army City townsite adjoins old Camp Funston on the Fort Riley Military Reservation. Inquire at Fort Riley regarding access to the site.

DIAMOND SPRINGS
Morris County

Diamond Springs was one of the most important points along the Santa Fe Trail in Kansas, and the history of the town reads like the plot of a western novel or movie with one exception—the events actually happened.

When the Santa Fe Trail was first surveyed in 1825, Diamond Springs was called the Diamond of the Plain, and records of Santa Fe traders who passed by Diamond Springs date back as early as 1821 when William Becknell, called the father of the trail, combined several Indian paths and created a line of commerce between the United States and the residents of Santa Fe, then governed by Mexico. The surveyors and explorers were fortunate to find the springs site because good water was often hard to locate, especially in that region of Kansas.

Maj. George Sibley held a council with the Osage Indians on August 10, 1825, and then traveled southwestward until he reached Diamond Springs at the headwaters of Otter Creek. Sibley recorded in his journal that the "Diamond of the Plain" was a remarkably fine, large fountain spring near a good camping ground. In 1839 Sibley wrote even more enthusiastically: "The spring gushes out from the head of a hollow in the prairie, and runs boldly among the stones into Otter Creek, a short distance. It is very large, perfectly accessible, and furnishes the greatest abundance of most excellent, cold water—enough to supply an army."[1]

Diamond Springs became a favorite stopping place for the overland trains and caravans carrying goods to and from Santa Fe, and it was frequently mentioned in emigrants' journals of the 1840s as a popular spot where smaller caravans could rendezvous to form larger trains for protection from marauding Indians. The region west of Diamond Springs was considered unsafe for the emigrants as, not only was water in short supply, but also bands of Cheyenne, Comanche, and Kiowa often attacked the wagon trains.

As the traffic along the Santa Fe Trail increased, Diamond Springs became an established stage station, and several large two-story stone buildings and corrals were constructed there in 1849 by Waldo Hall & Company, the holder of a contract from the U.S. government to carry the mail from the Missouri River to Santa Fe. These stone buildings and corrals could hold several hundred head of livestock and were the largest of their kind between Council Grove and New Mexico. One of these buildings served as both a hotel and a stage station, another was a storehouse for supplies, and next to it was a blacksmith shop where horses were shod and wagons and stages repaired.

Several encounters between the emigrants and the Indians occurred near Diamond Springs, and in the fall of 1852 a troop of U.S. Dragoons, encamped just east of the springs, found themselves surrounded by Indians, who nearly destroyed the camp by starting a prairie fire in the tall dry grass. Col. Percival G. Lowe described the incident:

Returning from a trip to the forts along the border in the fall of 1852, nothing of special interest occurred until we reached Diamond Springs. The weather had been frosty at night and days sunny . . . grass dry as powder. All day we had seen little bands of Indians a mile or two off the road, traveling in our direction and watching us. This was the Kaw country and no other Indians were there. Of course, the Kaws knew our troop and they had no love for it, but we were slow to believe they would attack us.

We camped on the higher ground east of Diamond Springs on the south side of the road. . . . We had finished dinner, about two hours before sunset, when . . . fire broke out in a circle all around us not more than a mile from camp. A stiff gale was blowing from the south, and when we noticed it, the fire in the tall grass was roaring furiously and the flames were leaping twenty feet high. . . . Every man used a gunny sack or saddle blanket and worked with desperate energy. The utter destruction of the camp was imminent, and we faced the fire like men who had everything at stake. Success was ours, but the battle left scars on nearly all. I have never seen fifteen minutes of such desperate work followed by such exhaustion.[2]

Such an incident was all too typical of the events that occurred near Diamond Springs during the 1850s. In fact, this portion of the Santa Fe Trail was once dubbed the Journey of the Dead because dangers from Indian attacks to starvation and lack of water ended the life of many a foolhardy trader or emigrant. For several decades the trail was strewn on either side

An old general store at Diamond Springs as it looked circa 1890. When the railroad built tracks through the area, a small community and siding were established near the old springs site.

with the bleached bones of oxen, horses, mules, buffalo, antelope, and deer; sometimes even the unburied skeletons of men were found. These scattered bones were seen from Council Grove westward across the plains until the coming of the railroad brought a group of men known as the "bone pickers," who made a living by gathering the bones and selling them to factories that ground them into meal.

At one spot near Diamond Springs, a deep gulch was filled for many years with tons of bones that dated back to the peak period of commerce on the Santa Fe Trail when a freighting team that included 1,500 oxen was returning late in the season from a successful trip to New Mexico. When the team reached the springs area, a winter storm with blinding wind and snow swept down upon the unsuspecting party just as they were settling down for the night. Frightened by the storm, the oxen stampeded and fell to their death in the gulch, filling it to the top with their carcasses.

Diamond Springs was also the scene of a tragic incident during the Civil War period. In the spring of 1863 a noted desperado named Dick Yeager and his gang were in the springs area, and they murdered several settlers and destroyed property along the Santa Fe Trail as far west as Diamond Springs. The band would split into groups of two or three men so that their movements would not arouse suspicion, and then at a prearranged point, they would all come together to carry out their plans. On May 5, 1863, their plans included raiding the stage station and store at Diamond Springs. Augustus Howell, the store proprietor, was killed, and his wife was badly injured trying to defend him. After robbing the store and damaging the property, the gang scattered to the east, leaving behind a trail of destruction.

By mid-summer 1863 Diamond Springs was nearly deserted as the Santa Fe Trail traffic had been declining for some time. The town no longer was a stage and supply station, but it was still a favorite camping spot for settlers heading to their claims in central and southwest Kansas. A few years later the abandoned town became part of the Diamond Springs Ranch, a large spread owned by several investors primarily interested in ranching.[3]

When Samuel A. Kingman passed Diamond Springs in 1865, he recorded the following in his diary: "We passed Diamond Springs. The remains of 3 buildings of stone 2 stories high tell their story of violence. . . . A small room used as a dramshop is all left fit for use save a large stone corral surrounding 5 or 6 acres with a small supply of hay."[4]

A few of the ruins at Diamond Springs can still be seen in this picturesque area of the Flint Hills, and a granite monument in the local cemetery is a final tribute to the era of the Santa Fe Trail. Diamond Springs can be visited by taking U.S. Highway 56 west from Council Grove. Turn south at the junction with state Highway 149 and stay on this road for several miles. The Diamond Springs site is at the crossing of the Santa Fe Railroad tracks.

3

SOUTHEAST KANSAS

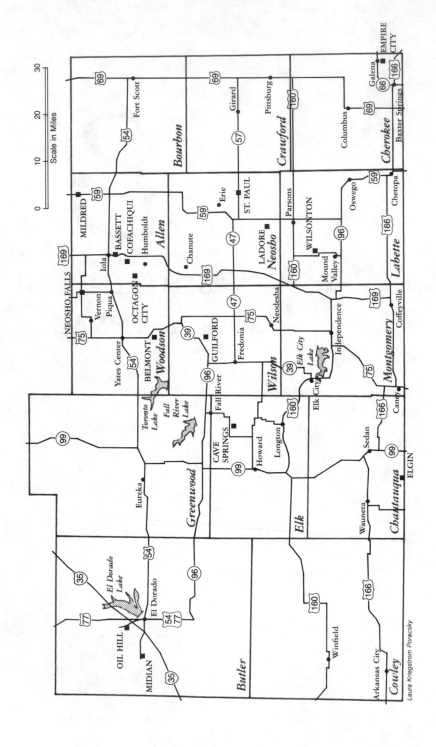

Laura Kriegstrom Poracsky

EMPIRE CITY
Cherokee County

In the 1870s the news of the discovery of lead ore on Short Creek in Cherokee County brought a number of prospectors back from Nevada and California, inasmuch as the mines in the western states were declining and miners were looking for another big strike. Although gold was never discovered in the Short Creek diggings, lead and zinc were valuable enough to pique the interest of any nineteenth-century entrepreneur.

In 1877 the influx of emigrants to the Short Creek area was unbelievable, and almost overnight several large settlements were established. After lead was discovered on the Nichols Tract, a town company was formed by Gov. George Crawford and Pat Murphy for the purpose of promoting a new town called Empire City on the south side of Short Creek. On the north side of Short Creek the town of Galena was organized, and from the beginning there was intense rivalry between the two communities.[1]

On May 21, 1877, Pat Murphy and Governor Crawford hired Elijah Lloyd to survey the townsite. After Lloyd had officially located the town on a high hill overlooking the diggings, the happy trio, along with Matt Clary, Solon Cheney, and M. Van Bennett, established their headquarters under an oak tree and began marking the lots and the major streets. On May 23 the town was formally dedicated, and 200 lots were sold. Empire City was on its way.

On May 25, 1877, a large multipurpose building was completed and occupied by a saloon, restaurant, town company office, hardware store, the offices of Murphy and Chency, and the office of J. J. Davis; when night came everyone used it as a hotel. The local newspaper, the *Empire City Mining Echo,* edited by T. B. Murphy, was in operation by June 1.

Empire City was incorporated as a third-class city on June 18, 1877, and within three months over 3,000 inhabitants occupied the townsite.[2] News of the boom town spread to Topeka, St. Louis, and Kansas City, and a reporter from the *Topeka Daily Commonwealth* was sent to Cherokee County to find out about this overnight wonder—Empire City. He wrote:

The most wonderful sight I ever beheld was the original town of Empire. . . . Such a motley collection of houses, men and women, I never saw before. . . . The town looked as though it had been heaved up by volcanic convulsions. . . . Houses had been erected with no regard to architectural beauty, regularity of line or locality. The streets are as crooked as illicit distilleries, and from morning till night they are filled with people

Main Street, Empire City, as it appeared around 1877. These makeshift buildings with false fronts were erected rapidly to handle the rush of miners who came to the area.

and teams. Saloons and gambling houses are the most frequent objects. Gambling quarters are in such great demand that several members of the profession are compelled to conduct their operations in the open streets.[3]

Empire City's redlight district was one of the wildest in the West, and the *Kansas City Star* had this to say about the wicked side of this boom town: "The principal thoroughfare was known as Red Hot Street. It became so true to the name that all legitimate business withdrew and left the street to saloons, gamblers, and dance halls. For several months the orgies that held sway on Red Hot Street were perhaps never exceeded in any other frontier mining camp."[4]

At Empire City's first city election held on June 30, 1877, 224 legal votes were cast, and Solon Cheney was elected mayor. The *Mining Echo* remarked that "if [Empire City] continues to improve as rapidly in the future, it will certainly be the 'Boss Town' of the Southwest." This prophesy, however, never came to pass.[5]

The Empire Mining Company had been officially organized on July 6,

A group of miners pose in front of a wagon at Empire City during the wild summer days of 1877.

1876, and at that time the company purchased forty acres of land for mining purposes. Between May 5 and June 30, 1877, its mines produced 109,196 pounds of lead and zinc, and in July over sixty shafts were sunk on that one claim. The largest amount of mineral ore removed from one shaft in one day was 5,500 pounds. The Nichols Tract, also owned by the Empire Mining Company, produced 225,000 pounds through July. During most of 1877 Empire City surpassed Galena in the production of lead ore.[6]

By late summer of 1877 the mining companies in the Empire City and Galena fields had become so competitive that the rivalry between the two towns almost turned to violence. A mile-long stockade fence was erected by the men of Empire City in an attempt to keep the miners from leaving and going to the Galena fields. The only opening in the fence was on Red Hot Street, and at midnight on August 28 some Empire City men began to close even this gap. The mayor of Galena and a strong body of men confronted the Empire City workers and ordered them to tear down the fence. A shot was fired from the Galena side of the street, slightly wounding an Empire City man, but when the gunfire was not returned, the Galena men started to cut the stockade into pieces and set it on fire. Armed men from both towns gathered at different points along the fence, and a showdown seemed inevitable. Luckily the men finally calmed down and called a truce, and no conflict occurred.[7]

Near the end of the nineteenth century the ore was depleted at Empire City, and the mining interests dwindled. The last chapter in the history of the community was written on July 9, 1907, at a joint meeting in Galena. Due to Empire City's financial troubles, the businessmen had decided that the town should be annexed to Galena, and the citizens of Empire City sadly agreed to the proposal.

Today there are a few vestiges left of the original community as some of the old Empire City buildings are still maintained by Galena residents. Galena, the victor in the feud, is a quiet prosperous community in a once important mining section of Kansas. Empire City, the loser in the rivalry, no longer exists. Empire City is now within the city limits of Galena along Short Creek.

WILSONTON
Labette County

Elenor (Ella) B. Ensor, a pioneer reformer in the women's suffrage movement, was married to Augustus Wilson of New Madison, Ohio, on December 1, 1863. After the couple suffered the loss of their only son, John Emory Wilson, in 1865, the Wilson family moved to Parsons where Augustus became president of the Parsons Savings Bank. When Augustus died in July 1885, he left Ella a wealthy widow.

Both before and after her husband's death, Ella Wilson was occupied with activities outside the home. In 1879 she was active in the temperance crusade and was made a lifetime member of the Kansas Temperance Union; in 1881 she was a delegate to a prohibition convention in Chicago; and in 1897 the magazine *American Woman* identified her as one of the more powerful women in the suffrage movement in Kansas. Mrs. Wilson was known regionally and nationally as a reformer. The *American Nonconformist* stated, "There is probably no more characteristic a woman in Kansas than Mrs. Augustus Wilson."[1]

Prior to the Wilsons' arrival in Parsons, the town had had only a small reading room for a library, but when Ella became president of the Parsons Library Association, this situation changed. She solicited contributions from around the state to help finance a new library, and she alone contributed $18,000 of the $40,000 needed to construct the building that, when completed, covered half a city block. In a few years the library ex-

perienced a financial setback when an eastern bank foreclosed on the mort-
gage, but when Mrs. Wilson offered to help by contributing an additional
$12,000 to meet the mortgage payment, the city refused her offer and sold
the building for $12,500.

In 1887 Ella Wilson was actively involved in building a new community,
Wilsonton, and many people believed that the town was actually established
as a memorial to her husband. A marker at the site attests: "Erected to
the memory of Augustus Wilson who departed this life in 1885. Husband
of Elenor E. Wilson and father of their only child John Emory Wilson.
A living faith in God inspires a hope beyond."

Ella Wilson was described by those who knew her as a small woman who
nearly always wore black, and who often walked down the road with her
long skirts trailing in the dust. Most people in the community thought
she was eccentric, but a few admired her and said she had a brilliant mind.

In 1888 Ella Wilson built a large two-story house at the edge of Wilsonton. The bottom floor was used free of charge by the community as a hall
for public gatherings, including the Women's Republican party and a men's
labor party. The printing press that printed the *Wilsonton Journal*, edited
by Mrs. Wilson, was housed on the top floor of the house, along with
her living quarters.

By 1890 Wilsonton had two stores, a railroad depot, a church, six houses,
and a cemetery. Most of the townspeople were not so wealthy as Ella
Wilson, and her house atop a hill overlooking the town was a constant
reminder of her prestige in the community. By 1896, however, Ella Wilson
was deeply in debt. On October 18 a sheriff's deed transferred the bulk
of her estate to the county, including most of her land except for the
townsite of Wilsonton, or about forty acres, which was saved because her
brother, John T. Ensor, held the deed in his name. On June 11, 1903, he
sold the townsite back to Mrs. Wilson for "one dollar and love and
affection."

Although deprived of most of her holdings, Ella Wilson did not abandon hope until January 12, 1912, when J. W. Plummer filed a petition in
Labette County Probate Court to have Samuel Carson appointed guardian of both Mrs. Wilson and her estate "in order that she be properly
cared for and that her property may be protected." Dr. J. A. Vaughn of
Mound Valley sent a letter to the court stating that he judged Mrs. Wilson
to be unfit to manage her own affairs. Accompanying the letter was a list
of fifteen witnesses who attested to this fact. On January 27 a notice was
sent to Mrs. Wilson setting forth the charges of "feeble mindedness" against
her, and on February 3, after a brief trial, a jury returned with the verdict

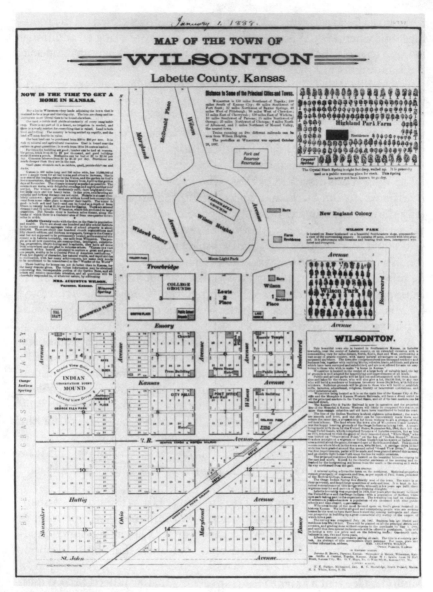

A promotional plat of Wilsonton (circa 1888) shows such attractions as an Indian Mound, a college, a widows' colony, Wilson Park, and a tabernacle. Visitors, however, would have been disappointed because most of the sites on the map were more fanciful than realistic.

of insanity. A guardian's sale was held on March 5, and an undated, unsigned letter described the sale: "The sale of the Wilson home brings sadness to our minds as we reflect on what might have been. . . . There in her home lay scattered in waste and ruins the fruits of a lifelong effort. In a little house not far away from her home lay Mrs. Wilson feeble in both mind and body, while the selfishness of mankind was striving and grabbing to gain possession of the last vestige of her lifelong toil."[2]

The *Parsons Sun* reported that Ella Wilson had been taken to a hospital in Bartlesville, Oklahoma, and that she was being cared for by a niece. A woman named Ensor signed a court document acknowledging the arrival of Mrs. Wilson at the hospital, and the probate court records show that she lived there until May 1913. Samuel Carson petitioned the court to be released as her guardian on September 30, 1913, stating that Mrs. Wilson had died a few weeks earlier, although a search of the records revealed no death certificate for her in either Kansas or Oklahoma.

Ella Wilson's attempt to establish an enlightened, progressive town had ended in failure. At the time of the guardian's sale, an article about her in the *Parsons Sun* was obviously disrespectful. It quickly passed over the facts that Mrs. Wilson had entertained three Kansas governors and Julia Ward Howe, and that she was nationally known in the women's suffrage movement, and dwelled instead on the failure of the Parsons Library and Mrs. Wilson's physical and mental degeneration.

Ella Wilson was a woman who was ahead of her time at nearly every point of her life in Kansas. She was the lifeblood of Wilsonton and when she passed away, so did the town.[3]

To visit the site of Wilsonton, drive north and east from Mound Valley. A rural cemetery in the immediate area marks what is left of the townsite.

OSAGE MISSION/ST. PAUL
Neosho County

During its existence, St. Paul (originally called Osage Mission) has been an Indian mission school, a Catholic school, an early trading site, a county seat, a railroad center, and finally a small country town. It is still the last—there are still a few stores and houses in the town—but St. Paul lost the drive it needed for success that so characterized the town's early years.

Over 160 years ago, before the community existed, there was a small missionary school for the Osage Indians on the site. In 1822 Reverend Charles De La Croix visited the Indians at the school and baptized two French-

An early view of what was perhaps the first Catholic church in Osage Mission. A simple frame building, the oldest portion dates back to 1848.

Indian children, James and Francis Chouteau, the first children baptized in southeast Kansas.[1]

Twenty-four years later, in 1846, Father John Schoenmakers visited the Osage Indians and made plans to organize another school to "Christianize" the Osage children. When he returned in 1847 he was joined by Reverend John Bax and three Jesuit brothers. In May Father Schoenmakers built two structures—his residence and a manual labor school for the Osage Indian boys—and thirteen boys enrolled. Five months later, on October 10, a girls' school was established by four sisters of Loretto, and Father Schoenmakers's plans were complete. His choice of the name "Catholic Osage Mission" was retained for over twenty years. In 1848 a Catholic church was built. A simple log structure that measured only thirty feet square, it served the settlers for many years.

In 1851 Father Paul Ponziglione arrived at Osage Mission to be confronted with a serious problem. The nearby Osage villages had been ravaged by black measles and typhoid fever, which had decimated the Indian population. The measles were traced directly to the Osage Mission schools where the children had become infected and then carried the disease back to the villages. Father Ponziglione tried desperately to halt the epidemic by isolating the sick and disinfecting the schools and the villages, but the death toll was high. Still, he won the respect of the Indians, and they continued to send the children to the schools.

As more white settlers arrived in the area, they began to displace the Osage Indians at the mission. The first white settler in Neosho County was Samuel J. Gilmore, who located a claim on land near the mission. His log home was used as a combined hotel, store, and post office, which he established under the name Catholic Mission. He was soon followed by a few more white settlers who started farming nearby.[2]

Before the Civil War the mission schools were at their peak of activity, but after the war broke out, enrollment dropped drastically because Osage Mission was perilously close to the hostilities. Troops from both the Confederate and the Union armies camped in the area at various times, but the soldiers seldom caused any trouble at the mission. After the war the mission schools never ministered to the Osage Indians in the same way again, and by the end of 1867, the Indians had left the area. In order to keep the schools open, Father Ponziglione focused all his attention on the white settlers and their children. The boys' school was reorganized and renamed St. Francis Institute, and the girls' school became St. Ann's Academy, but one detail remained the same in spite of the reorganization—the schools still lost money.[3]

By 1867 a community had developed around the mission, and in addition to the Gilmore store and post office, several more buildings were constructed, including a large two-story hotel called the Neosho House, which was acclaimed as the finest hotel in southern Kansas.[4]

Late in 1867 Father Schoenmakers donated land a half mile west of the old mission for a town, which was also to be called Osage Mission. At the same time Erie was founded five miles northwest of the mission, and from the beginning the two towns were bitter rivals.[5]

In November 1867 an election was held with the towns of Osage Mission, Geographical Center, Centerville, and Erie all vying to become the county seat. Geographical Center had the most votes, but in 1868 the commissioners moved the county records to Erie as more suitable buildings were available to store them there. Another election was held in 1868, and Osage Mission won with 582 votes to Erie's 543. Since this election was contested by Erie, it was not until January 1870 that the records were finally moved to Osage Mission, and the town was officially declared the county seat.

The growth of Osage Mission was vigorous. In August 1868 over twenty-

St. Francis Catholic Church, Osage Mission. Made of native stone, this church still stands as one of the prettiest churches in southeast Kansas.

four buildings were being built at the same time, including eight dry goods stores, two mills, three drugstores, one hardware store, two boot and shoe

The James J. Owens store in Osage Mission was one of the largest stores in town. Here crowds gather in front of the store on a summer afternoon in 1896.

stores, four blacksmith shops, and facilities for three stage lines. By 1870 the town had a population of 500, and Osage Mission had begun to over-shadow the other communities in this section of the state. The town was the center of business activity in the region just prior to the coming of the railroads, and many of the stores on Main Street were the distributors for country stores in the smaller towns. A solid line of businesses extended for two and a half blocks on both sides of Main Street, and in February 1871 the Missouri, Kansas & Texas Railroad built into Osage Mission, which helped to further boost the economy of the community.

Not so assured, however, was Osage Mission's status as the county seat of Neosho County. Erie residents were still striving to win the county seat back to their town, and in 1872 another election was held. Osage Mission was again the winner, but the results of this election were contested in the courts for two years. The court finally decided in favor of Erie after the votes were recounted and Erie received a majority.[6]

The decade of the 1880s marked Osage Mission's "peak period" when the population of the town reached 1,508 in 1885. But problems arose. The town of Chanute became the largest city in the county and began to dominate the trade in the area, and two banks in Osage Mission failed in 1885, one closing due to fraud. The most annoying problem, however, was the financial difficulties of the two mission schools. By 1890 St. Francis Institute was $27,000 in debt, and it was forced to close its doors. St. Ann's

An elaborate gasoline station for its day, the Grillot Brothers Texaco Service Station was open for business in St. Paul, circa 1940.

Academy was also in trouble, and it closed in 1892. The Jesuit fathers withdrew from the mission, and the church and school were placed in the charge of two laymen. In the mid-1890s both schools reopened, but St. Ann's met with disaster in 1895 when it and a neighboring chapel burned to the ground. St. Francis Institute also burned down.

In the late 1890s Osage Mission continued to decline, although a few major improvements were made such as the laying of stone sidewalks and the planting of trees. A committee known as the Board of Trade was organized, and one of the board's first moves was to change the name of the town. Osage Mission did not seem like a progressive name for a community, so the name was changed to St. Paul.[7]

But the name change did not help the economy. On November 5, 1911, a $125,000 Passionist monastery was dedicated at St. Paul, the fifth in the United States. Its library contained 4,000 volumes, some more than 400 years old. Unfortunately the monastery did not bring back the prosperity the town had once known.

Plans were made to rebuild St. Ann's Academy in 1915, but with the coming of World War I, all construction on the site stopped and never started again. In the 1920s and 1930s new highways and better automobile transportation adversely affected the town because most of the residents began driving to Chanute or Erie for their merchandise and services, leaving St. Paul's businesses neglected and ignored.

Today St. Paul is a small residential community with a beautiful stone Catholic church still standing on the east side of town. The church and the community are closely linked together, but the church was there before the town, and it will probably outlast St. Paul's few remaining businesses. To reach St. Paul, take U.S. Highway 59 south from Erie to the junction with state Highway 57 and turn east. St. Paul borders both sides of the road.

LADORE
Neosho County

Lynchings occurred in Kansas, but not nearly so often as the movies like to portray; however, the town of Ladore was the site of a mass lynching that surpassed any depicted in the pulp western novels or in motion pictures.

On September 30, 1869, when Ladore was incorporated by the Missouri, Kansas & Texas Railroad, only a few settlers were in the area, including Addison Roach, P. McGaugh, and Joseph Haskett. In the spring of 1870, L. A. Bowes was foreman for the contractor who was building the railroad, and his headquarters was at Ladore, which bore the unfortunate reputation of being "as rough as they make 'em!"

Bowes reminisced about his life in Ladore during those boom years, and left us his impressions of the town and the violence that occurred there in May 1870:

It was the toughest place I ever struck. Whiskey was sold in nearly every house in town. Vice and immorality flourished like a green bay tree. One day about noon seven hard-looking characters came into town. They commenced to fill up on "tangleleg." That evening about dusk they began operations by knocking men down and robbing them. As they were heavily armed, they soon had full possession of the town. . . .

An old man by the name of Roach kept a boardinghouse about a quarter of a mile south of town, close to the railroad. Twenty-five of our workmen were boarding with him. . . . About seven o'clock that night the seven desperadoes went down to the Roach house, placed two men at the foot of the stairway with revolvers to hold the twenty-five men upstairs, while the other five took possession of the lower part of the house and captured the inmates.

Roach, his two daughters and a hired girl went downstairs. They beat Roach over the head with their revolvers until they thought he was dead. . . . They captured the three girls, carried them outside and kept them all night. . . .

Along towards morning the citizens began to organize for the capture of those devils. . . . We caught two of them before daylight in a drunken sleep in one of the saloons. We captured one in the timber with one of the girls shortly after daylight. The leader of the gang and two others [were] captured on the way to Osage Mission. . . .

We locked the men up in a log barber shop, put a guard over them, took them out one by one, led them down past the Roach house, had them identified by the girls, [and] swung them up on a large projecting limb of a hackberry tree. By eleven o'clock five men hung lifeless on that one limb.[1]

The five men were "convicted" of attempted robbery, murder, and rape, and "three hundred of the best citizens participated" in the trial and hangings. Hanged were William Ryun, Patrick Starr, Patsey Riley, Richard Pitkin, and Alexander Matthews.[2]

In 1872 the Missouri, Kansas & Texas Railroad decided to make Ladore a junction on the main line and made plans to build shops there, but the residents of Ladore refused to sell their land at a reasonable price, forcing the railroad to negotiate with another town farther down the line. From that time on Ladore was just a sidetrack on the railroad. This lack of foresight by the townspeople proved to be a costly mistake, for in less than two years, Ladore was a ghost town.[3]

Unfortunately, what little remains of Ladore is virtually inaccessible because of its isolated location. Inquire with local residents regarding the exact location.

OCTAGON CITY
Allen County

Octagon City, an unusual social experiment on the Great Plains, was founded in New York City in 1855 by the Vegetarian Settlement Company directed by Henry S. Clubb, Charles H. DeWolf, and Dr. John McLauren. Eastern families on a vegetarian diet were persuaded by the company to sell their property and buy shares in the association so a colony could be established for them in the West.[1] Prospective settlers, from about six eastern states, were drawn to the philosophy of the colony by the rosy picture

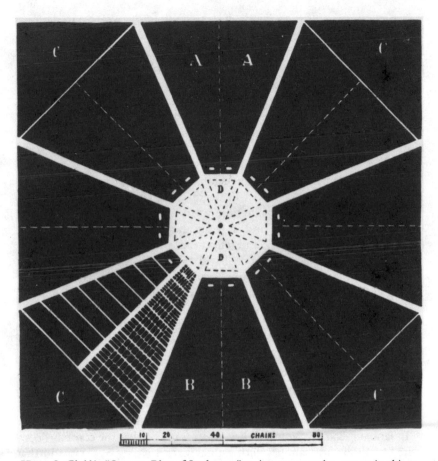

Henry S. Clubb's "Octagon Plan of Settlement" as it was supposed to appear in this experimental southeast Kansas colony. Disaster after disaster beset the colonists, and Clubb's dream never materialized.

of prosperity painted by the company and by the promise that they would live in a community where no meat would be consumed.

The vegetarian company began organizing the first party of settlers who were chosen to head west to the new colony.[2] At their first public meeting on May 16, 1855, forty-seven people signed an agreement to emigrate, and twenty-six more indicated that they would go along with relatives and friends. All applications for membership were approved by the board of directors of the company, and each member was asked to pay $10 to aid in erecting a sawmill and a grist mill and to purchase a stock of provisions, seed grain, tents, and utensils.

Henry Clubb thought that the unpopulated Kansas Territory would be a suitable place to start a colony, so in the fall of 1855 Dr. McLauren was sent west to search for a good location. In the meantime families selected by the vegetarian company for the settlement were told to abstain from the consumption of meat, tea, coffee, tobacco, and other such stimulants.[3]

The community way to be laid out according to an octagonal plan, which Clubb proclaimed was the only sensible way to "commence a city." There would be four octagonal villages, which would form Octagon City, covering sixteen square miles with an octagonal green of 584 acres in the center. Clubb wrote of his endeavor: "To begin with, every settler would thus live in a village, and at the same time be in the best possible situation on his farm—between pasture land in front and arable land in the rear . . . of his dwelling and barn . . . and reflect that in isolation men become indifferent to the refinements of civilized society. Why sirs, they may sink into barbarism. But living in these Octagon Villages as a part of a great Octagon City, would cause emulation to excel in the arts of domestic and social life."[4] No land in the Octagon City development would be sold except to those who voluntarily signed a pledge to abstain from liquor, tobacco, and the flesh of animals, and to those who took the pledge, the land was offered at $1.25 an acre.

Clubb and Dr. McLauren found land in Kansas Territory that was available for homesteading claims, and Clubb and his colonists obtained title to 32,000 acres. The selected site lay six miles southwest of present-day Humboldt on the Neosho River, near a creek now called Vegetarian Creek.

In January 1856 the *New York Tribune* announced that the company consisted of about fifty families with capital stock totaling $75,000 and that the shareholders were one-third practical farmers and two-thirds mechanics and professional men.[5] In all, 108 people left their eastern residences in 1856 to venture to Octagon City and the "wild and woolly" Kansas Territory, having been told by the vegetarian company that the "immense and gorgeous" Central Octagon Building would be ready to accommodate them when they arrived and that sawmills and grist mills were "about to commence."[6] Actually the Central Octagon Building was only a modest cabin, and no other structure was built before the arrival of the settlers.[7]

In the spring of 1856 Clubb arrived with the first group of colonists, to live in tents, not the accommodations promised. One colonist, Mrs. Miriam Colt, kept a diary and told of the expedition to Kansas; the daily life in the settlement; the sickness and death from dysentery; the fear of the Indians; and the storms, droughts, and all the other adversities that eventually forced most of the settlers back east. Mrs. Colt had this to say when she reached the site of Octagon City:

> Can anyone imagine our disappointment this morning on learning from this and that member that no mills have been built; that the directors, after receiving our money to build mills, have not fulfilled the trust imposed in them; and that in consequence some families have left the settlement. Now we all have come, have brought our fathers, our mothers, and our little ones, and find no shelter sufficient to shield them from the furious prairie winds, the terrific storms of the climate.[8]

Mrs. Colt stated that by May 17, 1856, most of the members of the original company had started back to Kansas City, but a few remained and others continued to arrive. After the corn was planted that spring, the colonists felt that there was a chance the settlement might succeed. Then the "ague" struck the little community, and there was no medicine in the town for the chills and fever. Hot weather in July caused further problems as the springs and streams dried up, and when no rain fell for weeks, the corn withered and died. Dozens of settlers died that summer from various illnesses, including Henry Clubb, and only four colonists stayed in the settlement that fall—Charles Baland, Z. J. Wizner, J. Watson, and S. J. Stewart.[9]

The Octagon City venture was not just a land-selling scheme concocted by Clubb and his associates to dupe the colonists; they simply used poor judgment and were bad managers. The vegetarian concept was new in those early days in Kansas and was similar to other novel ideas that failed.[10]

All that remains in the area today is the stream called Vegetarian Creek. Only a few cabins were ever built on the site, and the specific location where the colonists camped is unknown.

COFACHIQUI
Allen County

Cofachiqui, one of the earliest settlements in Allen County, was named for an Indian princess. In the spring of 1855, a group of proslavery men from Fort Scott formed a town company and laid out the town just east of the Neosho River. In July 1855, the territorial legislature passed an act incorporating the Cofachiqui Town Association.[1] The incorporators were William Barbee, J. C. Anderson, Samuel Williams, and Charles Passmore.[2] The legislature granted the association the authority to locate and hold a tract of land not to exceed 900 acres around the proposed townsite and passed an act making Cofachiqui the permanent county seat of Allen County.

The first store in Cofachiqui was built by James Gilbreath, and by the end of the summer, three more stores were doing business in town. A post office was established in the fall of 1855, and Haden W. Linn was the first postmaster.[3] Also in 1855 the first sessions of the district court in Allen County were held in Cofachiqui. By 1856 the businesses in Cofachiqui were thriving as trade with the Osage Indians in the area was profitable, and that summer the first sawmill in the county was erected at Cofachiqui by Joseph Ludley.[4]

Cofachiqui was one of the largest proslavery strongholds in southeast Kansas, and one settler, S. H. West, gave this account of his experiences in the town:

> On arriving at Coffychee, I found about a dozen men sitting about the log cabin hotel. I hitched my horse, talked with the men, telling them I was looking at the country. One of them asked me where I stayed the night before. . . . They at once concluded that I was a spy from the enemy's side. I afterward learned that one of the men I was talking with was Capt. Gordon, of South Carolina, who had brought a company of armed men from that state to Kansas to help make it a slave state.[5]

The Reverend Cyrus R. Rice, fresh from Tennessee, was assigned to organize Methodist societies in Kansas Territory in 1856, and he gave this further description:

> We put up at the best hotel in the place. . . . It consisted of two log cabins with an entryway between and two clapboard "lean-tos." . . . We found the proprietor, James Barbee, and his good wife accommodating and ready to do everything possible to make things pleasant for the guests.
>   Cofachiqui . . . was the largest and most impressive city in the great Neosho valley. It consisted of the hotel, two hewned log store rooms with rooms overhead, one log dwelling, a small cabin saloon, and a number of beautiful vacant lots.[6]

On August 19, 1856, the court ordered the construction of a county courthouse in the public square of Cofachiqui on a lot donated for that purpose. However, on January 7, 1857, for no apparent reason, all orders pertaining to the courthouse were rescinded.[7] By the end of 1857, other towns were beginning to develop in Allen County, and Cofachiqui was declining. On January 11, 1858, a mail route was established from Leavenworth to Humboldt via Carlyle and Cofachiqui, which helped to revitalize the town for about a year. By the end of 1858, however, many of the county seat offices had been closed, and within two years most of the town had been moved to Iola.

There were several reasons for Cofachiqui's economic difficulties. Not only was the town built in a rugged hilly region, but also well water was scarce and the people were obliged to get their drinking water from the Neosho River, an impure and unreliable source at best. In addition a number of proslavery men had settled in town, which caused a great deal of political unrest among the citizens. Furthermore, two nearby towns, Iola and Humboldt, were rapidly increasing in size, and they were taking business away from Cofachiqui. When the two most prominent businessmen in town, James Faulkner and Aaron Case, left for Humboldt, that signified the end of Cofachiqui.

In the election of March 26, 1860, Cofachiqui received only two votes for the county seat, which caused the site to be vacated by the territorial legislature. After the Civil War all that remained of the town was a barn, which was torn down after it was the scene of a hanging in 1870. In later years, the townsite was owned by the LeHigh Portland Cement Company of Iola, which operated a quarry there. Today nothing remains of Cofachiqui except the old quarry site.[8]

MILDRED
Allen County

In a period of thirty years the town of Mildred rose from a cornfield, became an industrial center, and then reverted to being a cornfield. Why? The cement plant that still stands north of the community is a constant reminder of the fickleness of an economy that caused the men in the area to trade their farmers' overalls for white shirts and then to go back to overalls, all in one generation.

In the spring of 1907 Sam T. McDermott of Kansas City approached two farmers, John Winterbottom and Hiram Lieurance, who were planting corn on their farms just east of the Missouri, Kansas & Texas Railroad tracks, and asked them if they would sell all or part of their land. Within a few days McDermott had secured options to purchase 260 acres of land from these farmers for the Great Western Portland Cement Company.

McDermott was soon followed by other men who began inspecting the

Main Street of Mildred as it appeared in 1909. Today most of the buildings are gone.

ledges along Coal Creek, surveying and measuring the water flow, and what they discovered was good enough to begin work on a $2 million cement plant and to lay out plans for a new city just south of the plant. In a few months a large labor force began constructing a dam across Coal Creek to provide water for the plant, and a surveyor was laying out the town lots. By the end of 1907 two or three stores were in operation, a school was under construction, and a few residences had been completed.

J. W. Wagner, president of the Great Western Cement Company, named the town Mildred after his daughter. C. McLaughlin, chief engineer, directed the construction of both the factory and the town, and by the spring of 1908, the dam had been completed, a powerhouse was nearly finished, and the main factory was rapidly taking form. The first loads of cement were shipped in April 1909. After only two years, the old cornfields were now the site of a full-fledged industry employing 300 men.

The town of Mildred boomed along with the cement factory. Turner Smith opened the first hardware store in Mildred, and a general merchandise store was built by Russell Cubbison & Company. Dr. R. R. Nevitt moved to Mildred in 1909, and he built a large two-story building, using the upstairs as a clinic and an emergency hospital and maintaining his residence and a drugstore on the lower floor. Mildred's population reached its peak in 1912 at nearly 2,000. Businesses that year included a newspaper,

Mildred cement workers pose for the photographer outside the plant office around 1914.

two hotels, two barber shops, a town band, and a church. The plant employed 325 men, and its payroll amounted to thousands of dollars a week.

During World War I all the cement companies in the area encountered stiff competition from companies in other states, low prices, and a general slump in the building industry. This economic recession forced the plant at Mildred to close down for a year, and although the company reopened the plant in the 1920s, it never operated at full capacity again. With the coming of the depression in the 1930s, the plant closed down permanently, and in 1935 much of the equipment was moved to another company-owned plant at Fredonia in Wilson County.

After many of the houses in Mildred had been sold and moved elsewhere, most of the land became a cornfield again. The local school remained open for a few years after the plant closed, and some of the stores stayed in business to accommodate the farmers.

Today Mildred resembles a typical ghost town. The streets are still there, and some of the stores are still open, but many of the lots are vacant. The ghostly ruins of the cement plant rise like a behemoth above the thick underbrush and trees, reminiscent of some last remnant of a prehistoric civilization. The buildings are a monument to the material from which they are made—these cement structures have remained intact while the town of Mildred, built of frame and stone, has almost disappeared.[1]

Mildred is located on U.S. Highway 59. Take 59 north from Moran. The townsite and the cement plant are both accessible on the west side of the highway.

BASSETT
Allen County

In the early 1900s, when the zinc, lead, and coal mining companies in southeast Kansas were attracting a lot of attention from the press, the cement factories were second-page news. For a brief time, however, cement plants were operating at capacity, and several communities became small industrial centers, including the town of Bassett.

In 1900 the Iola Portland Cement Company, established by James A. Davis, was the largest cement plant in the United States, producing 5,000 barrels of cement a day, and it consisted of a large complex of buildings. From 1900 to 1903 Iola Portland was the largest single employer in Allen County, and a housing project named for S. H. Bassett, an official at the plant, was built two miles south of Iola. Kansas Portland Cement established another plant four miles northeast of Bassett, and a company town named Concreto was built there. These two communities were connected to each other and to Iola by the Iola Electric Railway, an interurban system that handled both passengers and freight.

In 1907, over 1,000 men were employed at the Iola Portland Cement plant, and most of them were living in Bassett, which had a boom town appearance. The houses were constructed close together on narrow streets, resembling the "shotgun style" that was so prevalent in cheap housing. In fact, most of these houses were so identical that the only notable difference between them was the street number on the front.[1]

The cement company officials strived to treat everyone equally, but not all things were equal to all employees. Although labor and wage disputes affected the plant occasionally, most of the conflicts were over the attempts of management to hire foreigners and blacks for less money, and one altercation occurred when the native white workers forced thirty-three newly employed Italian workers to leave town. In Bassett the black employees lived in a segregated section of town, and occasional outbreaks of racial strife shattered the tranquility of the community. Such incidents were not

A street scene in Bassett, circa 1914. A long row of shotgun houses on each side of the street was accepted housing for the cement plant workers who lived in Bassett and worked in the Iola Portland Cement Plant.

unique as they occurred in many communities where industries hired black and foreign labor in order to cut employment costs.[2]

Iola Portland's peak year, and Bassett's, was 1907, but that year also saw the beginning of a money panic that undermined the financial security of the community. The cement industry overproduced, the market was flooded with cement, prices dropped, and construction slowed down. Although Bassett survived this crisis, other towns were not so fortunate. In 1911 Kansas Portland closed down, and Bassett's neighbor, Concreto, became a ghost town.

Iola Portland managed to stay in business for several more years, and in 1915 the city officials in Bassett even issued $10,000 in bonds for improvements to the town.[3] But cement production experienced another slump just before World War I, causing some consolidations in the industry, and when Iola Portland sold out to LeHigh Portland Cement in 1917, the change in ownership did not benefit Bassett financially.

In the 1920s Bassett essentially became a suburb of Iola, and any differences between the two communities became less and less noticeable. By the 1930s, Bassett's population was only 194, and the slow encroachment of Iola caused an "identity crisis."[4]

Today Bassett is still included on a few maps, and a resident population is still there, but its "golden days" are over. Only a few shotgun houses and some of the original streets and walks remain as "concrete" remnants of the boom years of the cement industry in Allen County. Bassett is a southern "annexation" of Iola. U.S. Highway 169 bypasses Bassett's western border immediately south of Iola. Follow the signs.

BELMONT
Woodson County

The town of Belmont was founded in 1857 in a wooded area on Sandy Creek, and a fort known as Fort Belmont was built nearby to protect the settlers from the Indians and the Missouri border ruffians. A military road from Fort Leavenworth came through the site from the north, and the army used it to bring supplies to the Indians who were camped along the Big Sandy and its tributaries. A part of the old trail can still be seen southeast of the Belmont Corner crossroads.

Belmont was a thriving town from 1857 to 1865. Stagecoaches arrived daily, bringing more settlers, as the town was a main stop on the route between Humboldt and Eureka. At its peak Belmont had a population of 600 and a number of businesses including a general store, post office, hotel, blacksmith shop, stage station, tavern, grocery store, and an Indian agency. In 1858 Belmont was a contender for the county seat of Woodson County. An election was held there on September 16 at the house of "Lowe and French," but the community lost to Neosho Falls, which was designated the county seat.

After the first guns of the Civil War were fired in 1861, additional forts were established in eastern Kansas, but most never saw any military action and neither did Fort Belmont. The latter consisted of three or four small cabins, referred to as the officers' quarters, and a few yards north of these cabins stood the actual fort, mostly earthwork with logs placed on top. The parade ground was located a mile east of the officers' quarters. For a short time Fort Belmont was actually manned when Companies C and G of the 16th Regiment, under the commands of Capt. Joseph Gunby, 1st Lt. James Watkins, and 2d Lt. Robert Daniel, called Fort Belmont "home" for a few years.

These companies left the fort in October 1864, and the Indian agency, which was no longer needed, was closed. In 1867 a severe smallpox epidemic in the area caused many of the settlers and Indians to go elsewhere, leaving Belmont nearly deserted.[1] The Belmont post office stayed open for ten more years but was finally discontinued in 1877.[2]

Today a portion of the old trail from Fort Leavenworth and a section of the earth embankment on the site of the old fort can still be seen, but these remnants are not easy to find and are slowly disappearing. Belmont is now private property and not easily accessible. Inquiries should be made with local contacts regarding a visit to the site.

NEOSHO FALLS
Woodson County

Neosho Falls is the oldest town in Woodson County, and it was named after the river that flows nearby. On April 6, 1857, Col. N. S. Goss and I. W. Dow arrived in the area from Iowa, and just before reaching the Neosho River, they found the cabin of Judge John Woolman. Another settler named John Chapman was living on Spring Creek just north of the Neosho River. These two men were the only known settlers in the county because it was still the New York Indian Reserve and not open to preemption.

Late in 1857 the company of Ruggles & Stevens built a cabin on the south bank of the Neosho River and sold merchandise to the Indians. In 1858 when the county was opened for preemption, the firm erected a hotel called the Falls House and a frame store building they rented to Clark & Company. Although these two buildings were among the first in town, they were preceded by some crude log cabins constructed by a few settlers along the banks of the river.

On August 16, 1858, Neosho Falls was formally declared the county seat, and money for a courthouse and a jail was presented to the town by Col. N. S. Goss.[1] Judge Leander Stillwell of Yates Center remembered the courthouse and gave a vivid description of it:

Court was being held in a ramshackle two-story frame building, which was situated, as I remember, on the east side of the principal street running north and south through the village. The court room was in the second story of the building, and one gained access to it by means of a flight of rickety stairs built on the outside. The stairway was . . . built on the ladder plan, with open steps. I remember that at intervals some of the steps were gone. . . . The court room proper was small and stuffy, with the ceiling villainously low. No matting or carpet of any kind was

The Township Hall in Neosho Falls. Built in 1922, this building was a useful meeting place until it was damaged by the 1951 flood. Today it stands abandoned.

upon the floor, but in lieu thereof it had a topdressing about half an inch thick of fresh, green timber sawdust.[2]

When the Missouri, Kansas & Texas Railroad built its line south from Junction City through Neosho Falls in order to handle the shipments of Texas cattle, it erected a round house and a land office there. The coming of the railroad added numerous families to the community and gave it a feeling of industrial permanence.[3]

Misfortune, however, awaited the citizens of Neosho Falls. In other sections of the county, the people were resentful of the Falls's status as a county seat. Agitation grew until 1867 when an election was held on the issue, which Neosho Falls won by a vote of 129 to 118 over its rival, Yates Center. Again and again the county seat controversy was renewed until finally, on September 12, 1876, the question was decided permanently when the citizens of Woodson County cast 488 votes for Yates Center against 426 votes for Neosho Falls.

Due to the construction of a railroad line from Junction City directly to St. Louis and Chicago, the Neosho Falls branch of the railroad became a local line only, and the round house and land office were moved away.

In spite of these setbacks, Neosho Falls had a population of 1,200 in 1878.

In the fall of 1879 President Rutherford B. Hayes visited Neosho Falls and spoke to thousands of people who came from all over southeast Kansas, southern Missouri, and northern Oklahoma to hear him. Hundreds of people had to camp in the fields outside of town because the hotels and rooming houses could not handle such large crowds, and several descriptions of the visit were written.[4]

On the day the Pres. and his retinue arrived, they were met at the M. K. & T. depot with a six-horse coach, brass bands, and a large delegation of leading citizens. I never will forget the noise and the music as the stately procession wended its way across the bridge, under the beautiful arch and into the shady grounds, where thousands and thousands of Kansas people had gathered for the great occasion.[5]

A week before the fair opened people were arriving in covered wagons and before the President was due to arrive, 1,000 were encamped nearby. . . . At 9 o'clock A.M. September 25, the presidential party, accompanied by General Sherman with a military escort arrived here. The President's first remark was "Where is the city?" Upon entering the grounds Hayes was honored by a salute of 21 guns given by the troops from Fort Riley. Seeing the vast throng of people the President exclaimed, "Where did they come from?" The attendance was estimated at 40,000.[6]

During the 1900s Neosho Falls suffered one disaster after another. When steam and electricity replaced water power, mills were closed down. A hydroelectric plant was constructed, but before long it too was abandoned. In 1926 a disastrous flood on the Neosho River caused thousands of dollars in damages and cost one person his life. In 1927 natural gas was discovered near Neosho Falls, but the wells were shallow and were depleted within a short time. In the 1930s Neosho Falls lost its only newspaper, the *Neosho Falls Post,* the oldest paper in the county, and in August 1933, Neosho Falls's only bank closed its doors. Soon after building a branch line from Neosho Falls to Yates Center, the Santa Fe Railroad abandoned the line and the town was left without any rail service.

Neosho Falls's last chance for prosperity came in 1937 when several men drilled for oil in Dr. A. J. Lieurance's backyard. At 1,145 feet the drillers struck oil, and the well produced 150 barrels in the first few days. This strike sparked a great deal of interest on the part of oil companies in the Neosho Falls area, and many more oil wells were drilled south of town.

This photograph of stained glass windows was taken at a Neosho Falls church (later City Hall) on Main Street in 1976. Three years later the window was removed by townspeople in order to preserve it.

Within fifteen years, however, the oil had stopped flowing, and the wells had been abandoned.

During the 1940s and 1950s several destructive fires and floods left the town in ruins. Many buildings on Main Street are deserted now except for an old café on the east side and a post office several blocks away on the west side. The once modern high school of the 1930s is abandoned, and the community hall looks neglected and forlorn with an old broken piano standing mutely inside. A church with its pretty purple stained glass windows awaits the same fate that has affected most of the rest of town as it, too, is deserted.[7]

Neosho Falls can be visited by taking U.S. Highway 75 south from Burlington. Directions are well-marked; watch for signs to Neosho Falls. Turn east on a marked road and go ten miles. The town is on both sides of the road.

GUILFORD
Wilson County

The history of Guilford goes back to May 1861 when J. H. Gunby built the first cabin on the townsite on the west side of the Verdigris River. He had intended to stay in the area but instead sought shelter elsewhere when the Indians burned his cabin. In the fall of 1865, after a treaty had been made with the Indians, Andrew Akin and his sons erected a sawmill at the Guilford townsite. A post office was established in 1868 with Akin as postmaster. After Guilford was formally platted in 1870 by the Guilford Town Company, the Akin family constructed a flour mill there. In addition, the town had a newspaper, law office, doctor's office, printing plant, shoe shop, blacksmith shop, the Guilford House hotel, and a snake antidote resort, all built in 1870.[1]

In the early 1870s the settlers at Guilford were periodically plagued by disease. The editor of the *Guilford Citizen* noted that many of the lowland farms had to be abandoned because of the ague and malaria that took a heavy toll in sickness and death every year. Each spring the paper carried advertisements offering quinine and other ague remedies for sale. The sickness was seasonal and was apparently taken for granted, considering that each year the arrival of the "plague" was ushered in by one of the local editors' printing the annual joke proclaiming that "the ague is here and willing to shake." The disease was so prevalent that those who could afford it bought or rented upland farms and moved during the hot, wet months, staying away from the bottoms except to plant and harvest their

The Lugeanbeal general store and post office in Guilford, circa 1890.

crops. This "small annoyance" did little to hamper Guilford's boom, as in 1870 the editor of the *Citizen* counted no fewer than ten emigrant wagons a day rolling toward homes in the southern part of the county.

In 1872 bandits and robbers also found Guilford a good place to "ply their trade." "Our county," wrote the editor of the *Citizen*, "during the last ten days has been infested with a gang of horse thieves who have displayed a boldness in their operations which is rarely to be met with, even among these long-haired, hemp-deserving scoundrels."[2] In October Constable A. G. Lowman was killed by Alonzo Snodgrass, but no newspaper account states whether the perpetrator ever served time for this murder.[3]

In 1874 an alarming explosion occurred:

On Wednesday, May 27th, the usual quiet and repose of the village of Guilford was startled by a report scarcely excelled by a heavy cannon, and followed by a violent shaking of the earth, . . . on visiting the mill pond of Akin & Bros., where a party of well diggers were drilling for water, the cause of the shock became evident. . . .

The gentlemen engaged in drilling a well on the premises of the above, having reached the depth of 120 feet, all at once noticed the drill descend about six inches, evidently meeting with no obstructions, and at once a deep rumbling sound, like heavy thunder, came forth from the well, and drove the person who was tending the drill . . . to the surface. . . . Having reached the top, the drill was immediately withdrawn, but no water becoming visible, the drill was again lowered, and a few strokes given, but the noise became so terrific that all operations were suspended.

A slight odor was emitted from the well, and the conclusion that something inflammable was escaping, induced the gentlemen to test its burning qualities. A match was at once lighted on the edge of the well, and had hardly commenced to burn when the report and shock that has been described took place, and the adventurous well digger, with whiskers, eyebrows, and hair missing, lay at some distance from the well, evidently meditating upon the peculiarity of combustibles. A solid column of flame shot up from the well at least 40 feet, and continued to burn, attended with that same rumbling sound that at first indicated the presence of something escaping from the well. . . .

At last it . . . burned brightly until extinguished by the heavy rain on Sunday night. . . . No water of any quantity has appeared. The noise has ceased, the usual quiet again "reigns around."[4]

Apparently it never occurred to anyone that what they had found—natural gas—might be more valuable than the water they were looking for.

The rapid development of other larger towns in the area, such as Fredonia, caused Guilford to decline, and in 1876 the site was partially vacated by the legislature. As a further blow, in May 1886 the Missouri Pacific and Santa Fe railroads intersected at the site of the town of Benedict, which had already been surveyed, and the post office at Guilford and most of the buildings were moved to Benedict, four miles northwest of Guilford, in 1888 and 1889.

On the site of Guilford, eight miles northeast of Fredonia, there are today only a few ruins left to mark the town. You can reach Guilford by taking state Highway 47 west from Altoona. Turn north on the first road and drive until you reach a second junction with an east-west road. Take this road west about one mile. Turn north again and follow the road until it leads to the site of Guilford—a few ruins and structures on both sides of the road.

The Cave Springs Hotel, circa 1890. This huge building had the luxury of water piped into each room for guests who came to bathe in the medicinal waters of the springs nearby. The hotel was eventually torn down when the town was abandoned.

CAVE SPRINGS
Elk County

On April 2, 1949, Gov. Frank Carlson affixed his signature to a legislative act vacating "the original townsite of Cave Springs in Elk County, Kansas, and the streets and alleys of such townsite." In so doing, he closed the book on the last chapter of a once prosperous town that was founded by a man ready to exploit any settler who was gullible enough to be swindled.

After discovering the springs in the 1860s, Dr. John Long, who was known more for his promotional ability than for his expertise as a physician, decided to establish a health resort near the site. He acquired the title to the eighty acres of land that included the springs,[1] and in 1875 the town of Cave Springs was built by Long[2]—a name derived from an overhanging rock that formed a cave over the springs.

Dr. Long's plat of the town consisted of sixty-four square blocks divided into lots, which were sold to settlers eagerly waiting to buy them. Long kept the blocks that included the cave and the springs so that he could erect a hotel on one of them.

Dr. Long made ridiculous claims about the restorative powers of the spring water, and as soon as he advertised the resort and hotel in eastern newspapers, unsuspecting people with various ailments began to arrive by the hundreds. When Long built the resort, he had the water piped directly from the springs into the hotel for the convenience of those patients who were too ill to leave their rooms. During the late 1870s the hotel was filled to capacity most of the time.

At its peak Cave Springs had grocery and general stores, a drugstore, barber shop, newspaper office, livery stable (with a pool room in the loft), millinery shop, and post office. Definite figures are not available regarding the amount of business transacted at Cave Springs during those years, but apparently the stores and the hotel were financially successful.

In the 1880s people began to question the healing properties of the water and to doubt the good faith of Dr. Long. When he realized his patients were no longer trusting and foolish, he traded his resort for 300 acres in Mississippi, which he soon discovered to be swampland. Before he could dispose of his holdings at Cave Springs, however, one of the local ranchers became ill while driving a herd of livestock to market. When Dr. Long was called in to treat him, he swindled the rancher by trading him the Mississippi swampland for his cattle. Long quickly disposed of the cattle, and the people of Cave Springs never saw him again.[3]

By 1900 only three of the original businesses in Cave Springs were still in operation. When the post office was discontinued, the building was torn down and the lumber was used on a nearby farm. Today a few old structures can still be seen, but Dr. Long's resort, built to take advantage of his gullible patients, has vanished completely.[4] The Cave Springs site is located on an unmarked gravel road south of Fall River. The site is now on private property.

ELGIN
Chautauqua County

Romulus (Rome) Lysurges Hanks, one of the town's founders and Abraham Lincoln's cousin, rests peacefully in the Elgin cemetery, and above the entrance to the cemetery, there is a large sign commemorating him. Rome Hanks was born in Kentucky in 1822, and when he was a young man he married and moved from Kentucky to Knoxville, Iowa, where he ran a livery stable. The Civil War years were tragic for the Hanks family. Two brothers, Remus and Ream, were both Union soldiers who died during the war; another, Lucious, served in the Confederate army; and yet another, Granville, was with the Lexington Rifles. Rome served as a captain in the 117th Iowa and after he was wounded at Shiloh in 1862, he was captured and taken to Andersonville prison.

Four years after the war, Rome moved with his family to Elgin, which at that time was an unincorporated collection of cabins, shacks, and soddies. Here they erected a cabin that Myra Hanks, one of Rome's four daughters, found to be a great disappointment. Her remarks concerning Elgin were that the town "isn't much." In time, however, Rome was instrumental in establishing Elgin as a major cattle shipping point.[1]

Rome Hanks lived in Elgin for seven years and operated the trading post and the post office. (This ivy-covered stone building is standing today, home of the Episcopal church.) He kept a journal that is still in excellent condition with the first entry dated April 27, 1872, and the last entry December 8, 1876, just twenty-two days before his death.[2]

Elgin was actually built three times. The first site called Hudson, destroyed by fire in 1887, was just east of the present location. The town, renamed Elgin, was rebuilt two miles west, but since the settlers wanted to be near the Big Caney River, it was moved again to its present site almost on the border between Kansas and Oklahoma. It was so close to the line that drunken cowboys could ride along the Oklahoma side, out of the law's reach, and shoot out the lights in the town.[3]

One of the darkest days in the town's history occurred on August 23, 1873, when three black men, all brothers, were lynched for horse stealing. According to the *Junction City Union*, August 30, 1873, the hanging of these men did not satisfy the posse, so they also hanged their mother. The next day the bodies were cut down and nailed to a downtown store front for all the citizens to see.

Elgin's growth was slow before the Santa Fe Railroad arrived in 1886. When the town was founded there was supposed to be plenty of rich farmland in the area, but the government intervened and apportioned most of the good land to the Osage and Kansa Indians. Fortunately for the community, the coming of the railroad literally transformed the town.

Thousands of lean, hungry cattle were driven every spring from the plains of Texas to Oklahoma Territory to be fattened before they were shipped to eastern markets in the fall. Because most of these cattle were infested with ticks and had "Texas fever," corrals were built and huge dipping vats were installed for the cattle to pass through. After they were dipped, they were herded along the "Quarantine Trail" into Oklahoma Territory, and in the fall the cattle were driven to the railroad at Elgin for shipment to market.

The Browns Shoe Store and Elgin State Bank, Elgin, around the turn of the century. Elgin was once the largest shipping point in the world, but today it is a quiet semi-ghost town.

The first load of cattle was shipped on June 23, 1890, and by 1902, 6,500 carloads had been shipped from Elgin to the markets in the East. The town was dubbed by those in the cattle shipping business as the biggest shipping point in the world, and in fact for a few years, it was.[4]

Elgin had a population of only 300 in 1889, but in ten years it had 1,100 people. Unfortunately, along with the prosperity brought by the cattle trade, there came the cowboys, outlaws, and gamblers, and in order to satisfy their thirst, thirteen saloons were opened in Elgin. In spite of the prohibition laws in Kansas, Elgin had been transformed into a "hell-for-leather cowtown."

For nearly ten years, drunken revelry was the custom in Elgin, and shoot-outs and killings were commonplace. Many a night after the first cowboy yell was heard, the citizens would head for home, darken their windows, and stay inside until all was calm again. Judge C. A. Gilman, who was a deputy sheriff during Elgin's boom years, recounted that "nine-tenths of the trouble was caused by cow men trying to keep the settlers out. They'd get up massacres just to scare people—and just for the fun of it."[5]

Since the outlaws used the hills and caves around the countryside for hideouts, they could wander in and out of Elgin whenever they chose, and no man dared to lift a gun against them. Bob Dalton, Bill Doolin, Jesse Newcomb, Jesse Jackson, Ben Cravens, "Dynamite" Dick, and "Buckskin" Joe were all frequent visitors in town. These outlaws were a problem to Sheriff Gilman, but he had more trouble with the bootleggers who sold their homemade whiskey to the Indians.

One of the most successful cattlemen in Elgin, G. M. Carpenter, pastured hundreds of longhorns just outside of town. Others who profited from the cattle business were shippers Ed Harris, Dick Russell, the Hazzard brothers, Roll White, Bob Ledbetter, Tom Moore, John and Jenk Block, Joe Herrard, and Neville Fleming.[6]

The railroad moved farther south in Oklahoma, and the days of cattle drives to Elgin came to an end in the early 1900s. In 1902 oil was discovered in the area, and Elgin had an oil boom that lasted until 1924 when the smaller and more shallow wells dried up and were replaced by the deeper, more productive ones in Oklahoma. After the wells went dry, the oil men left town, just as the cattle shippers and cowboys had done years before.[7]

In the 1930s Elgin was hard hit by the depression; many businesses closed, and most of the residents left. Financial failures in Elgin continued through the 1940s, and on June 24, 1952, the *Topeka Daily Capital* printed this description of the town: "Now the saloons, outlaws, blanketed Indians, and herds of cattle have vanished. . . . The railroad station has vanished, and fewer than 200 people remain. . . . The old timers now only sit in front of the brand-new liquor store and talk about the old day."

The *Wichita Eagle*, January 22, 1956, listed the remaining businesses in Elgin: "There is no hotel, one liquor store [which had been robbed recently], a small drug-grocery store [the largest grocery had been destroyed by fire the night following the liquor store robbery], and two filling stations."

Today Elgin has a wide street paved with brick through the main section of town. There are rows of deserted business buildings on this street, and an old 1880s stable with signs inside the doorway that read:

Horse & Mules bought and sold.
Feeding charges—tie in, to hay and water 25¢, per day 50¢
Grain feed 40¢, per day $1.00
Feed charges must be paid when stock is taken out
Pen feeding on full feed—Mules 50¢ per day, horses 70¢ per day
Arrangements can be made for teams, horses, mules, cattle
Everything else must be strictly cash.

Next to the town museum stands the Elgin Café where the food is good and reasonably priced, and its walls are covered with old newspaper articles and scores of photographs that date back to the days of the cattle drives. Perhaps the numerous comments on Elgin's demise are the reason for a sign on Main Street that depicts the hard stubbornness of the towns-people. It reads: "Elgin—A Town Too Tough To Die."

You can reach Elgin by taking a two-lane paved road west from the town of Chautauqua. Clearly marked signs provide directions to the site.

MIDIAN
Butler County

In the early days of oil exploration in Kansas, near the end of the nine-teenth century, some experimental wells were drilled, but no oil of any consequence was found. In the twentieth century, however, gushers transformed the Flint Hills around El Dorado and Wichita into a lake of oil as millions of barrels came flowing from the earth. This region, especially surrounding the small town of El Dorado, became known as the El Dorado oil field boom; it attracted thousands of transient workers and created several large communities in the heart of the oil fields. Two important oil company towns, Midian and Oil Hill, were established in the region, and Midian became one of the largest "boom and bust" oil towns in the United States.

The first oil drilling began at the El Dorado fields in December 1914, and by February 1915 the drillers had struck a small ledge of oil capable of from one to three barrels a day. On June 8 they hit black shale, a good sign of oil, at a depth of 2,500 feet, but two months later money prob-lems and well cave-ins ended the drilling, and El Dorado town investors lost $12,000 in the venture. It was not until the famed Stapleton No. 1 gushed in October that the oil boom really began.

Midian, which was named after the Midian Temple in Wichita, was built in early 1916 and was maintained by Cities Service Petroleum Com-pany and Gulf Oil Company. The town's boundaries were hard to define because there were also houses and buildings built by other oil com-panies such as Sinclair and Standard in the area. The field itself was di-vided into twenty-eight different leases ranging from 80 to 640 acres, and over 1,135 wells were drilled on these leases, which covered approx-imately seven square miles. Frank Shirk, a former Midian oil field work-er, stated that "it was quite a sight to view the drilling rigs and to hear the engines at the pumping wells. Nearly all the wells came in from 100 barrels to as high as 20,000 barrels a day."[1] The first oil well in the El Dorado pool to produce above 500 barrels a day was in the Midian field, which had twenty-three oil leases in 1918 and was said to be worth nearly $100 million.

One resident of Midian stated: "People came in hoards and there wasn't enough places for them to sleep or eat. . . . There were strings of shacks, covered wagons, and tents all the way across the north end of the Paulson lease. This was known as 'Skinner's Row.' It looked as if the horses lived better than their owners and in some cases they did."[2] An oil worker, Harry Black, told of learning "about Midian through friends. Jack Ronesburg wrote us on how he was making $100 a month and I thought that if you could make a hundred dollars a month you would soon be a millionaire, so I quit the grocery business at Emporia, Kansas, and moved down. I made around $2.00 or $2.50 a day."[3] Some men did make over $100 a month—good wages in the 1920s.

There were several disasters at Midian during the boom days. The first occurred on August 9, 1918, when a bad wind storm damaged over 300 rigs. On August 15, after the rig at Revert No. 1 had been rebuilt, a wooden oil tank burst, sending a stream of oil to the nearby boilers and causing a fire. The flames spread to only one other rig, but Revert No. 1 was damaged again and had to cease operating for several days.

An estimated 6,000 people were either coming or going in Midian from 1917 to 1920. Many businesses had been established by 1920, the houses built by Cities Service were placed on a good upslope to control problems with sanitation, foul odors from outdoor toilets, and disease, and the town was provided with wide streets, good water, and fire protection. A doctor, a nurse, and emergency hospital services were available for the workers, and a "welfare hall" was built by the company and used for dances and motion pictures. Baseball was one of the favorite pastimes of the workers, and a friendly rivalry existed between Oil Hill and Midian in the annual summer play-offs. During the 1920 season, Casey Stengel played ball at Midian.

Midian boomed until 1925, when the oil began to run out. The town then went into a gradual decline. Its school district was discontinued on January 29, 1940, and the students were transferred to schools in Oil Hill and El Dorado. The post office closed its doors on July 22, 1950. By the mid-1950s most of Midian had been abandoned. Many of the buildings were torn down or moved away; only two houses, a church, and a tool shed are left today to indicate where Midian once stood. William A. Green's book, *Midian, Kansas: History of an Oil Boom Town,* is an excellent source of additional information.[4]

The site of Midian is located west of El Dorado near the junction of state Highways 254 and 196. It is now private property.

OIL HILL
Butler County

The most important town established in the El Dorado oil fields was Midian, but another notable one that also became a ghost town was Oil Hill.

On October 6, 1915, the Wichita Natural Gas Company staked a test well in Butler County on land belonging to John Stapleton, and within a week the drill bit picked up sand at 549 to 557 feet that yielded a heavy showing of oil. Although the well was put under guard immediately, the news that there was oil in the area was hard to keep secret. Soon "great crowds thronged to the well, driving across the prairies in horse-drawn vehicles or bumping along in the few automobiles possessed by El Dorado citizenry."[1]

The Stapleton strike opened the rich El Dorado oil field, which was a dominant factor in the economy of Butler County for decades, and a flurry of leases and land sales followed the discovery of oil at the site of Stapleton No. 1. Early in 1916 one well was turning out 175 barrels of oil a day at a depth of 2,465 feet, and by mid-November there were eight more rigs in the field. From 1916 to 1918, nearly 2,000 wells were drilled. In 1917 Kansas advanced to third place in oil production in the United States, but peak production actually came in 1918 when the field output averaged more than 80,000 barrels a day.

Oil Hill became a Cities Service town, and the company built offices, warehouses, a garage, a livery stable, a first aid and fire station, pipe yards, lumberyards, and a planing mill. By 1918 the company had constructed homes for its 2,700 employees and residents, and in 1920 the first prefabricated oil rigs, constructed of both steel and wood, were manufactured at Oil Hill.

In 1934 Oil Hill was also the headquarters for the Empire Gas & Fuel Company, which constructed an additional 137 company-owned houses. At that time the town had a store, post office, garage, drugstore, and two filling stations. In April the town mapped out a community playground next to the company swimming pool for croquet, tennis, kittenball, and horseshoes, and there were two Girl Scout troops. The Empire Golf Club had laid out its course, and the Cities Service Colts was the company's entry into the Ben Johnson baseball league. So long as the oil kept flowing, there was growth and prosperity in Oil Hill.

But in the late 1950s, the oil boom began to subside, and the town was left with no other industry to base its economy on. In 1969, after the Em-

A view of Stapleton Well No. 1, the oil derrick that started the great El Dorado oil boom in September 1915. Today a marker commemorates this historic well.

pire Gas & Fuel Company and Cities Service had transferred all their offices and employees to Oklahoma City, the Oil Hill Café, the last business in town, closed its doors. Oil Hill was a ghost town.[2]

The site of Oil Hill is northwest of El Dorado near the Oil Hill Road overpass on the Kansas Turnpike. Most of the site is now privately owned.

4

NORTH CENTRAL KANSAS

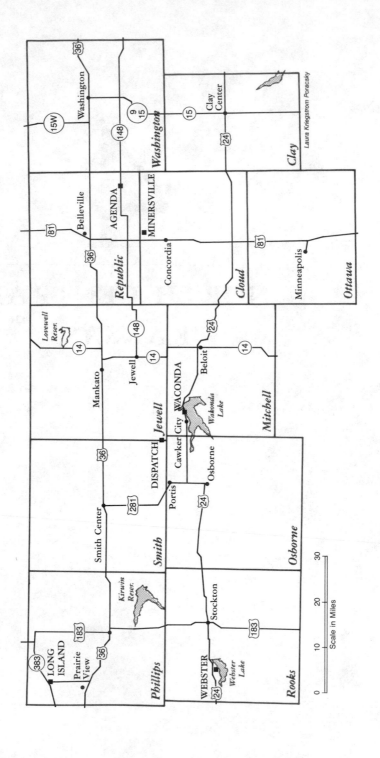

Laura Kriegstrom Poracsky

The J. D. Henderson coal mine at Minersville. This horse-powered piece of machinery appears to be breaking up large chunks of coal.

MINERSVILLE
Cloud County

In 1869 coal was discovered on the Minersville site by Heim Nelson. During the early 1870s three more mines were opened in the same area, and Minersville soon became one of the most successful coal mining towns in Kansas.

Minersville was spread out and temporary in appearance as many of the residences were just dugouts or shacks. Some dugouts were more elegant than others with fancy curtains at the windows, and a few were divided into sections for extra sleeping rooms used by some of the single men who worked in the mines. By the 1880s, when Minersville was at its peak, there were only five buildings in town made of wood. The rest either were constructed of rock or were dugouts.

Coal mining was hard, dirty work for both the men and the women. Water had to be hauled for cooking and washing, and lunches had to be packed and carried to the men at the mines. Some meals were prepared at the Alexander Henderson house where a number of workers boarded in the winter. As the mine shafts were always dark and dusty, each miner had a small lamp filled with oil, called a pit lamp, which resembled a metal teapot with a wick sticking out of the spout, and these wicks had to be cleaned hourly in order to get a little respite from the darkness. The mines operated in the fall, winter, and spring but were closed in the summer months since there was no demand for coal in hot weather. Many of the miners would leave in the late spring and never return.

In the early 1880s the coal mines were highly productive. The *Belleville Telescope* noted that the output of the mines was 100 tons a day, and the miners were receiving $2 per ton for their labor. In 1883 nineteen mines were operating at full capacity, and the 20,000 tons of coal produced that winter was worth $55,000 at the mines. The coal was found at a depth of twenty-five to fifty feet; the shallow places were worked by slopes and the deeper ones by means of shafts. All were operated by horsepower. Between 1883 and the 1920s, twenty-eight mines were in operation, and as many as 500 men were employed at one time.[1] At least one fatal accident occurred—in 1894 Albert Parker was killed during a cave-in in one of the shafts.

On December 7, 1882, a reporter for the *Telescope* gave this description of Minersville:

> A stranger entering Minersville about 10 or 11 o'clock a.m. would take it for a deserted village, but when the dinner bell rings, the miners come, like gnomes, from the caverns of the earth—dusky, it is true, but in a few moments afterwards they appear as well clad gentlemen of culture and education.
>
> On a close calculation, there is at present over 500 employees in and depending on coal mining in this town. . . . In the busy season there has been as large a number as 150 wagons waiting for coal in Minersville in one day. . . .
>
> Minersville has a concert band of vocal and instrumental musicians and the miners spend their evenings after the labor of the day in furnishing excellent music.
>
> The "Minersville Store," at this place, is well stocked for a town this size, doing a large retail business; the proprietor is certainly making money, judging from the daily crowded conditions of his store.

Both counterfeiting and gambling were popular pastimes in Minersville. One miner, who made lead dollars that looked like silver, lived in a wooden shack just south of town and kept his molds along with his cache of counterfeit dollars behind a stone wall in the cellar. The miners would be displeased when they received their pay in this lead money, but so were the mine owners whenever they counted each day's take and found that part of it was counterfeit. The town's gambling dens resembled the miners' old shacks. Inside would be an ordinary stove, table, and bed, but underneath the stove there would be a well-hidden trap door and stairs down to a room where cards were played and drinks were sold.

In the early 1900s low coal prices combined with stiff competition from other Kansas mining companies forced most of the Minersville operations to close down permanently. Since the majority of the Minersville residents made a living in the mines, there was nothing to keep them in town so they moved on. Several mines operated into the 1920s, but after that time all work ceased in the area.

Today the Minersville site is located eight miles north of Concordia, east of U.S. Highway 81 on the Cloud-Republic County line. Some of the mines, houses, and a few foundations are still visible from the road, but the wooden shacks and dugouts are gone. The Minersville cemetery is still there, a memorial to a once busy but shabby little mining town.[2]

AGENDA
Republic County

On April 19, 1880, a small country post office was established in Republic County. It was first called Neva, but since another town in Kansas already bore that name, a new name had to be selected. The story goes that at one of the town meetings someone remarked, "What is next in the line of business?" Another person said that the town had to have a new name and since that was next in the line of business, they should name it Agenda. It evidently had the right sound, for Agenda was chosen, and the name has endured for over 100 years.[1]

After the Chicago, Kansas & Nebraska Railroad, which was later absorbed by the Rock Island Railroad, laid its tracks through Republic County and Agenda in the 1880s, the community began to prosper, and the railroad remained the focal point of the town's development and economy. The town was formally laid out in 1887, and that fall Joseph Cox and George Smith built the first general stores in town. An elevator was constructed in 1889 to store the farmers' grain until it could be shipped by rail to the eastern markets. At the turn of the century, Agenda's businesses consisted of the Drovers Home hotel, a farm implement store, a furniture and hardware store, the Agenda State Bank, and a blacksmith shop. By 1912 the Fairmont Creamery and a newspaper called the *Agenda Times* had been established, and the population had reached 300 by 1917.[2]

There have been several tragedies and near tragedies in the town's history. A passenger train derailed south of Agenda in June 1924, and ten years later, a freight train derailed just as the engine passed the Agenda depot. This wreck caused the death of three hobos who were riding in one of the boxcars. Since none of them carried any identification, their bodies were buried in a corner of the Agenda cemetery, and to this day they remain nameless.[3] On May 14, 1909, Agenda came perilously close to being destroyed by a tornado. The funnel demolished much of the town of Hollis to the southwest and then damaged several farms and the Manning schoolhouse in the vicinity of Agenda, but luckily it missed the town. Another storm, this time a blizzard, struck the Agenda community on April 9, 1920, and completely isolated the town for three days.[4] These were just two of Agenda's close calls with destructive spring storms in the years of its existence on the Kansas prairie.

In 1917 the first oil field in Republic County was located near Agenda. On February 1, five carloads of casing and a drilling outfit were unloaded on the site, and a derrick was erected by the Jayhawk Producing Company. Success, however, eluded the crew; after drilling 2,500 feet without any positive signs of oil, the disappointed crew dismantled the derrick and left town. What had been a promising oil boom ended as quickly as it had begun.

The farmers at Agenda experienced hard times during the depression years of the 1930s, and record books in the register of deeds office at Belleville show that many went bankrupt or sold out to the banks. The Rock Island Railroad was unaffected by the depression, however, and continued to offer its passenger and freight services as usual until conditions changed in the 1950s. On October 17, 1957, passenger train service was suspended, and in 1961 the depot at Agenda was torn down. When the Rock Island declared bankruptcy years later, the slow decline of Agenda accelerated.

Today the main street in Agenda is cluttered with abandoned buildings and houses. Caught between the loss of the Rock Island Railroad and the present farm crisis, Agenda is living proof that towns can become ghostly even amid the hustle and bustle of the twentieth century. To visit Agenda, take U.S. Highway 81 north of Concordia to the junction with state Highway 148. Turn east on 148 and go twelve miles. Agenda borders the highway and is well-marked.

WACONDA
Mitchell County

The location of Waconda, eighteen miles west of Beloit on the Solomon River, was near the site of an old Indian spring known as Waconda Spring, from which the town got its name. According to legend, Waconda was the daughter of a great chief, and she was in love with the son of the chief of a hostile tribe. Despite attempts by their parents to break off the affair, the lovers refused to part, and this led to a fight between the two tribes on the plain that surrounds the spring. After Waconda's lover was severely wounded and weak from loss of blood, he fell headlong into the pool. Waconda, frantic with grief, turned on her father and charged him with murder. The irate father bent his bow and a moment later sent an arrow crashing into her skull, and her body followed that of her lover into the spring. The Indians then named the spring Waconda and believed that the spirit of the maiden dwelled there.[1] Since the spring was supposed to possess mystical powers, the Indians came there to celebrate their victories and to bury their dead.

Waconda Spring was a peculiar formation or mound about 500 yards from the bed of the Solomon River, and in the center of the mound was a pool 30 feet or more across. The spring was fed from shale overlying Dakota sandstone 300 to 800 feet below the surface. Collectors found many Indian beads and other ceremonial artifacts on the surface, indicating that certain rituals had indeed been performed there. When an engineering company from Philadelphia made an unsuccessful attempt to pump the spring dry around the turn of the century, in hopes of making some sort of medicine from the water, it temporarily lowered the water level sufficiently to recover several complete skeletons and many more artifacts.

When settlers began staking claims near the spring, three stockades were manned by government soldiers to protect them from the Indians. In 1869 Dr. D. C. Everson and his wife were attacked by Indians thirteen miles east of Waconda after they had joined with four other wagons at a night camp. Early the next morning the Indians rushed them, but the settlers were well armed and repulsed the Indians by using the wagons as a barricade. In another Indian raid east of Waconda three women were captured, but they were returned unharmed the next day.

In 1870, when the Indians were pushed farther west after the arrival of more settlers, the "Great Spirit Spring of Waconda" became little more than a watering place for emigrants. The military stockades were abandoned

An early stereoscopic view of a crowd surrounding the Great Spirit Spring of Waconda. The spring constantly attracted curiosity seekers and Indian-artifact hunters, many of whom claimed that the springs were bottomless.

because the Indians were no longer a threat, and small towns began to dot the landscape.[2]

In 1871 the town of Waconda was established by James W. Terry one mile south of the spring. Terry soon attracted more homesteaders to the site, and on September 8, 1871, the *Waterville Telegram* reported that "there is a large amount of building in process there and the houses are of the most substantial character, nearly all of them being of magnesium limestone." The article also noted that James Terry, P. B. Calkins, and Billy Jensen were building three buildings and there were plans for five more; B. F. Mudgett was putting in a steam grist mill and a sawmill; Charles E. Patterson had a general store on Main Street; and R. W. Lundy had a fine drugstore. There were also land agents in the town as well as contractors in stone masonry. At the end of 1871, Waconda had a population of only about 25, but there were 200 residents by the end of 1872.[3]

Among the new arrivals in 1872 was the town's first physician, George Chapman, who came to Waconda from Canada. Besides being a doctor, Chapman was also a shoemaker and an amateur geologist who gathered rock specimens from across the countryside and displayed them on the second floor of his home.[4] Before his death, Dr. Chapman donated a cabinet full of his geological finds and his medical books to the Cawker City Public Library. Along with his many other enterprises, he experimented with silk production, and once he asked the legislature for an appropriation of $10,000 to be used for the cultivation of silk, but the money was not granted because of the unfortunate failure of the Silkville experiment in Franklin County at approximately the same time.

Despite the town's growth, the year 1872 also brought a problem to Waconda that eventually led to its demise. Another town, Cawker City, was founded two miles north in that year, and its promoters offered big financial inducements to settlers and businessmen to move there. One important businessman who came to the area at that time, A. Parker, planned at first to open a large general store in Cawker City, but the Waconda Town Company made him a better offer and he decided to move his store there. Cawker City's promoters countered Waconda's offer with a better one, so he returned to Cawker. This "see-saw" bargaining continued for several weeks until Cawker City finally made an offer that Parker could not refuse, and he left Waconda for good. After Parker had moved his business to Cawker City, other settlers followed shortly thereafter. One of those was Col. W. C. Whitney, who opened a hotel in the Scrafford & Emo Building at Cawker City. After a few months Whitney moved back to Waconda, but by 1873 he had realized that Cawker City was destined to be the more prosperous town in the area, so he erected the Whitney House hotel there. In the summers of 1873 and 1874 swarms of grasshoppers destroyed the crops, and many of the farmers moved to other parts of Kansas. Without their business, most of Waconda's merchants were forced to move to Cawker City.

In 1878 the railroad built south of Cawker City instead of through Waconda. This loss ended any hopes for replacing the previous loss of population and businesses, but by that time there were few residents left in Waconda to complain.[5] The townsite, comprising 120 acres, was purchased by P. T. McNair, and in 1883 Andreas, in his *History of Kansas,* noted that "now nothing remains but a dwelling or two. The hotel is a large farmhouse, the brewery an unoccupied building while nearly all the stores are torn down, burned down or moved to help build up its rival, Cawker City. A large 2-story stone schoolhouse which was built in the spring of 1873, is the most conspicuous landmark left—like a headstone erected to the memory of a departed life."[6]

In 1890 another town named Waconda Spring was laid out near the site, and the planners hoped that this town would become a successful health resort. Streets were laid out and named, lots were sold, and trees were planted, but the town never materialized.[7]

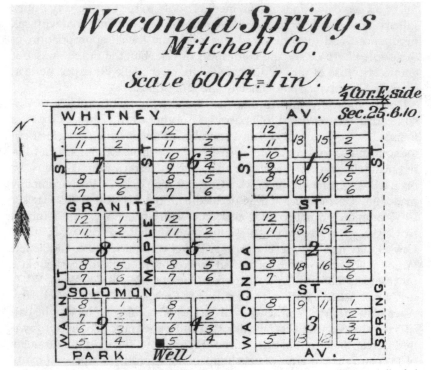

A plat of Waconda Spring, circa 1890. The town, however, never really materialized; it was too close to Cawker City.

In 1952 the site was threatened by Waconda Lake, built by the U.S. Army Corps of Engineers for purposes of flood control. When the lake was finished, the site of Waconda was inundated. An editorial in the *Topeka Capital* of November 13, 1952, expressed the feelings of many citizens:

> If the descendants of the original Plains Indian tribes are still loyal to their ancestral shrines as were their forefathers, we may hear war-whoops emanating up and down the Solomon Valley. Waconda Springs was one of the reasons the tribesmen fought to the death against white encroachment upon their lands. If there ever was a time when the Indians deserved help from their paleface brothers, this seems to be the opportunity to partially make amends for the ill treatment meted out to a noble people.

Unfortunately no one could stop the government engineers, and the lake was built. Progress once again triumphed over the heritage of "a noble people."

DISPATCH
Smith/Jewell Counties

In the years following the Civil War, buffalo hunting was a popular but dangerous sport in central and western Kansas. The danger was greatest when the hunters were competing directly with bands of Indians, who hardly considered buffalo hunting a "sport" since they relied heavily on the buffalo for survival.

Such was the hard lesson learned by Jim Higgins, John Owens, and Matt Freeman, who embarked on a hunt sometime in the late 1860s. After following the North Solomon River, they established a campsite on a high bluff just west of the future town of Dispatch. When Higgins went out to gather brush for a fire, he discovered that a band of Pawnee Indians was about to attack the hunters, and he hid in the tall grass, hoping the Indians would not discover him. The Pawnees did not surprise the other two men because Owens saw them coming and fired his rifle, killing one of the Indians.

Since they were outnumbered, the two men knew the only smart thing to do was retreat. Owens ran to the east edge of the bluff and jumped off, sliding and rolling until he reached Oak Creek where he hid under some brush in the water. The Pawnees never discovered his hiding place, and by traveling at night and hiding by day, he finally made it back to town.

Back at the campsite Freeman successfully made his escape, but the Indians took possession of the camp, which they plundered and burned. Then they searched in the grass until they found Higgins, whom they shot while he was trying to get away. A few days later another group of hunters arrived in the area and found his scalped and mutilated body. The bluff where the campsite was located is known today as Higgins Bluff, and the story is that Higgins was buried somewhere nearby.

The site of Dispatch was near Higgins Bluff on the Smith-Jewell County line. The original town, called Rotterdam, was located a mile south of the site of Dispatch. Rotterdam consisted of little more than a store and a post office, and after a windstorm wrecked both structures, the town was moved to a new location.

The first settlers in the area were a colony of Dutch immigrants, who settled in Smith County in 1869, lured by cheap land and stories of the romantic West. They established the little town of Rotterdam, which they named after their home city in Holland, but when they moved the community after the storm, they changed the name of the town to Dispatch because the post office was, after all, a place to "dispatch news!"[1]

The community developed slowly. In 1871 a Christian Reformed church was built, a general store and hardware shop opened, and a sod school with home-made cottonwood benches was erected. Farming was difficult because markets for the settlers' grain and livestock were too far away. Getting corn ground into meal was a two-day ordeal, since it took a day to get to the mill at Glen Elder twenty miles away and another day to return. Moving wheat to a railroad shipping point was a trying experience, as Waterville, the closest depot, was a hundred miles to the east.[2] Lumber was difficult to obtain as it had to be purchased from Hastings, Nebraska, a six-day trip by ox team.

A railroad would have made a big difference in the economy of the community, but unfortunately, Dispatch never attracted one. The town remained little more than a local settlement of Dutch emigrants sharing a common past. As farms grew larger, there were fewer residents, and many of these left the security of their circle of Dutch friends to live in larger towns.

Today a church and a few homes mark the site of Dispatch. The town is almost gone, but many of the descendants of the first Dutch settlers are still in the area, working the way previous generations did to carry on the old traditions. To visit Dispatch, take state Highway 181 north from the Smith-Osborne County line. Turn east on the first unmarked gravel road; stay on this road as it goes east and then turns south. This route takes the traveler by a rural cemetery and the few structures that remain of Dispatch.

WEBSTER
Rooks County

Webster's existence dates back to 1885 when two towns were established in the same township. A land patent was first issued in June for the town of Webster, platted on 48 acres by Oliver Beck. Three months later the town of Belmont was platted just south of Webster on 120 acres of land, and a friendly rivalry developed between the two communities over the business and trade of the settlers in Rooks County.[1]

In 1886 the Missouri Pacific Railroad was building westward, and the settlers were hopeful that either Webster or Belmont would become the first railhead west of Stockton. Unfortunately the township failed to vote sufficient bonds for the railroad, and the Missouri Pacific workers stopped laying track at Stockton.

During the next few years both Webster and Belmont grew slowly in

The J. W. Anderson General Store at Webster on a busy Saturday around the turn of the century. Today most of Webster has disappeared to make way for the construction of Webster Dam.

terms of population and business, and eventually Belmont was annexed to Webster. During the late 1880s the population of Webster was nearly 500, and businesses in town included the Fulkerson House, the Webster House hotel, the Bank of Webster, three grocery stores, three livery stables and feed barns, two blacksmith shops, two doctors, two churches, a real estate office, hardware store, lumberyard, drugstore, and furniture store. The town also had four newspapers during these years: the *Webster Eagle, Webster Enterprise, Merchants Journal,* and *Webster Blade.*

If violent crime was any indication of the prosperity of a community, then 1888 was Webster's boom year. In one incident H. I. Price was knifed by F. W. Hiddelson in front of the Webster post office. At the trial the jury returned a verdict of justifiable homicide, and Hiddelson avoided a "necktie party" at the town's expense.[2]

Webster began a slow decline in the 1890s for two reasons—a severe drought in the area and no prospects for a railroad. In 1907, the town's economy was temporarily revived when the Gulf, Plainville & Northern Railroad organized and made plans to reach the community by fall. After construction began and the roadbed was graded through Webster, many of the citizens were eager to invest in railroad bonds, and the businessmen

Main Street, Webster, around the turn of the century.

in town were more than happy to sell supplies to the workmen on credit. Unfortunately, a severe depression in late 1907 caught the speculators by surprise, and they lost money on their investments. The workmen never finished the roadbed or the tracks, and two businesses in town failed due to overextension of credit to the workers.[3] Webster's last chance for a railroad had not succeeded.

In 1918 truck transportation began to increase, and after a highway was built through Webster, trade improved. In 1920 E. F. Jones built a grain elevator to store wheat, and he also operated a fleet of trucks to haul the wheat to the railroad at Stockton. Unfortunately, for the next three years wheat prices were poor, and the trucking company and elevator went bankrupt.

In 1930 oil was discovered two miles south of Webster, and the townspeople had fantasies of wealth in the form of oil refineries and pipe lines. Although the geologists were certain that more wells would be drilled, nothing came of the oil discoveries, and once again Webster started to go downhill. By 1930 there were only 200 people on the townsite; in 1953 Webster consisted of only two churches, two stores, and 113 people.[4]

In 1953 a few of Webster's more outspoken citizens tried to make the dream of a dam on the Solomon River a reality, and it was due to the endeavors of Mrs. Curtis Fry—her petitions and her hearings before state conservation officials and the U.S. Army Corps of Engineers—that Webster Dam was eventually constructed. When the bill was approved on December 2, 1953, the Corps quickly began implementing plans for the reservoir.

It was necessary to condemn the old townsite, and the U.S. Army Corps of Engineers agreed to build a new school a mile south of the dam near the new townsite. After some controversy over the location, a schoolhouse was erected, and a store and a few houses were constructed nearby. The Webster cemetery had to be moved, which proved to be a major undertaking. Over 200 bodies were moved to the Stockton cemetery.[5]

Even though several prominent Webster families were willing to gamble on losing their town in favor of the reservoir, other townspeople moved to Stockton or other nearby communities instead of the "new" Webster. As a result, the new schoolhouse stood empty, waiting for students who never came.

Today a small community still exists near the dam, but it does not compare to the old town of Webster in its heyday. The residents took a gamble when they vacated the old townsite, and most of them lost; but the hardy few that stayed behind have kept the spirit of Webster alive.[6] You can reach Webster by driving to the east side of the Webster dam area. Although a few new structures still stand, you cannot see the old town at this new location.

LONG ISLAND
Phillips County

It is difficult to visualize that Long Island really is built on an island, but the town's founders were correct when they named the community as maps and aerial views show the town situated on a finger of land, nearly eight miles long, bounded on the north by Elk Creek and on the south by Prairie Dog Creek.[1]

Settlement in this region of north central Kansas came early. One of the first settlers in the area was Amos Cole, who built a homestead about five miles west of the site of Long Island in the late 1860s. Cole was an adventurous easterner who loved to hunt buffalo, and he soon found that his favorite pastime was not only an exciting sport but also a way to make a comfortable living. However, before long he realized that the local Indian tribes depended on the buffalo for their existence, and they resented the presence of white men on their hunting grounds. Cole knew that if he were to survive as a buffalo hunter, he was going to have to trick the Sioux by imitating them, so he learned the Sioux language, dressed himself like a Sioux hunter, and trained himself to imitate their posture and gait whenever walking or running. He never fooled the Indians, but he was always quick enough to escape with his life. After the buffalo herds began

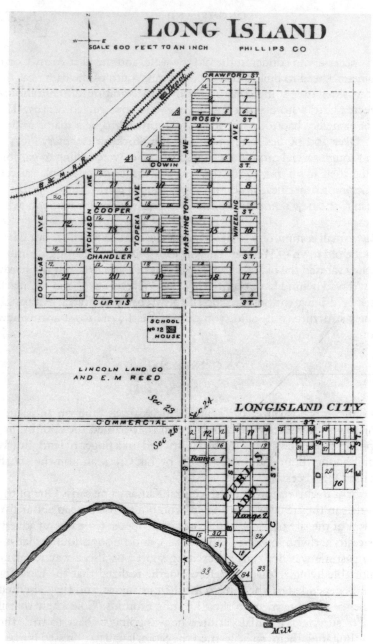

Plat of Long Island, 1886. This sketch is unusual because it shows both the old townsite to the south and the new townsite, which was moved north to the Burlington & Missouri River Railroad tracks about this time. Only a short distance separated the two communities.

to move farther west, Cole turned to agricultural pursuits and settled down near the site of Long Island.[2]

During 1870 and 1871 the area around the Long Island site was populated by a group of Dutch settlers, who began to lay out the town.[3] After finding an adequate water supply, W.T. Weed, his son E. M. Weed, and J. N. Curl filed claims and built log houses, and Weed started a grocery store in his home, the town's first business.[4] In 1876 John Bertwell and A. H. Mischke built a saw and grist mill, and it was followed by a hotel, an implement building, a blacksmith shop, and a general store.[5] Before the end of the year the community had been formally platted.

During the town's early years its residents discovered that disasters were commonplace on the western plains. In 1876 a prairie fire nearly destroyed the community, and by contrast, in 1877 the area was deluged with water. A town located on an island has certain inherent disadvantages, and floods often occurred after the heavy spring rains.

In 1885 when the Burlington & Missouri River Railroad was laying track through Phillips County, it missed Long Island, but the citizens solved that problem by moving the townsite to the railroad. Several old businesses from the original Long Island townsite were reestablished, and a number of new ones were opened including the P. J. Curl Merchandise Store, Lindley Drug Store, Romick Brothers General Store, Figley Furniture Store and Photo Gallery, J. O. Atkins Café, a doctor's office, a recreation parlor, two blacksmith shops, a meat market, a hardware store, two real estate offices, a lumberyard, a clothing store, two hotels, two millinery shops, a brick kiln, the Long Island Bank, and the People's Bank.[6] Long Island had four short-lived newspapers—the *Long Island New Leaf, Long Island Argus, Long Island Leader,* and *Phillips County Inter-Ocean*—and all were helpful in promoting the new town.[7]

A town in the middle of the western Kansas plains that could boast of having its own steamboat might be considered opulent, and Long Island had one in 1888. It was a little steamer called the *Minnie B,* and it plied the waters of a nearby lake in Fairy Land Park on Prairie Dog Creek just south of town. Due to the eventual lowering of the water level, however, the *Minnie B* was a short-lived source of community pride.

There were several destructive fires at Long Island during the 1880s and 1890s. The first one occurred on February 1, 1889, and continued out of control for hours, burning the southwest side of Main Street. Ten months later another fire destroyed the Curl Building, and in 1909 a devastating fire destroyed most of the downtown area. Much of Long Island was rebuilt with brick structures in order to ensure against any more such disastrous fires.[8]

A locomotive rolls into Long Island, circa 1915. The town still exists today, although the population and the business district have decreased markedly.

Long Island remained an active community with a population of around 300 for several decades, but the advent of good roads and automobiles and the decline of the railroad brought about a recession in the town. Businesses closed, and their owners left for Phillipsburg or other nearby towns. By 1952 only one of the original buildings was still standing on the townsite. Today Long Island still exists, and there are a few businesses, but the glorious days of Fairy Land Park and the *Minnie B* are gone. You can visit Long Island by taking U.S. Highway 183 north from Phillipsburg. At Woodruff, 183 becomes U.S. Highway 383. Take this road seven miles to Long Island, which borders the road.

5

CENTRAL
KANSAS

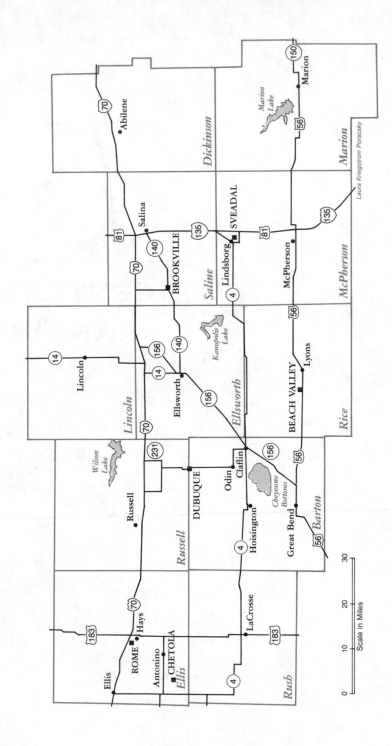

Laura Kriegstrom Poracsky

BROOKVILLE
Saline County

When the Union Pacific was moving west through central and western Kansas, the Indians became angry because the railroad trespassed on their hunting grounds, and this intrusion on their land often led to warfare. Trains ran only in the daytime, under military escort, and it took a great deal of courage on the part of railroad crews to start out from a terminal to cross unfriendly Indian country when they knew there was a possibility of an assault on the train before they completed the run.

One Indian raid occurred at a small settlement called Brookville in 1867. When a large body of Indians attacked the town, the settlers rushed to the roundhouse where a barricade was hastily thrown up. The Indians surrounded the building, piled railroad ties against it, and tried to set the structure on fire. Railroad crew members jumped on an engine already under steam, crashed it through the doors of the roundhouse, around the turntable, and with whistle and bell sounding, headed for Salina to get help. This action caught the Indians completely off guard, and they fled. When the engine reached Salina, a dead Indian was found lying on one of the wheels.[1]

In 1869 the town of Brookville was officially surveyed and laid out by the Union Pacific Railroad. Since the company had granted the right-of-way for the townsite, it could also impose a special regulation on the townspeople: Liquor sales were to be prohibited within the city limits. This rule may possibly have caused some inconvenience, but it did not put an end to the local liquor traffic.

In 1870 Brookville became a third-class city, and William Brownhill was elected the first mayor. The town prospered and all was quiet until December 1874 when a tragedy occurred that horrified the entire community. In a saloon a gunfight resulted in the murder of two brothers by a man named Barney Bohan. Excitement over the double murder ran high, and loud threats were made by the citizens about lynching the guilty party, but Bohan was hurried off to jail in Salina. The lynch mob rode to Salina and broke into the jail, but luckily they were stopped by the marshal before they could lay a hand on Bohan.[2]

Brookville had a population of nearly 2,000 people during the 1870s. The town was an important cattle shipping point on the Union Pacific, and Texas cowboys drove their cattle north to Brookville and loaded them on freight cars. During one season, over 200 freight cars of stock were shipped from Brookville, along with large quantities of grain. At its peak,

The Kansas Pacific roundhouse and buildings at Brookville circa 1872. For a time this town was a regional hub for the Union Pacific Railroad, but in time the roundhouse was abandoned, leaving Brookville little more than a shipping point.

the town's businesses consisted of a furniture store, hardware store, flour and feed stores, a cigar and tobacco shop, grain elevator, restaurant, flour mill, two hotels, a livery and feed stable, two lumberyards, a Knights of Pythias building, and four general merchandise stores.[3] There was employment in the local railroad shops and the flour and grist mills, and Brookville residents looked forward to a prosperous future.[4]

The town was not without a few disasters, and one of them, the Great Blizzard of 1886, cut off Brookville and many other towns from any outside contact. A cut on the Union Pacific track near Brookville, twenty feet deep and a quarter of a mile long, was completely filled with snow, and trains were delayed for several days. On December 4, 1890, a disastrous fire destroyed an entire business block in Brookville, including a bank, hotel, and three residences.[5] Just a few months before, after another fire, Mrs. Samantha Baker and her son Harry had been found burned to death in a stable on her farm three miles west of town.[6]

Brookville's economy suffered a severe blow when around the turn of the century the town lost the prestige of being a major shipping point on the railroad. Much of the cattle business moved to the larger communities of Salina and Ellis, and when the Union Pacific moved its point of operations to Salina, Brookville became little more than a flagstop. During the depression of the 1930s the migration of the residents to larger

Brookville today is best known for the Brookville Hotel, where fried chicken dinners with all the trimmings bring crowds daily. The hotel, built in 1870, is one of the oldest hotels in continuous operation in the state.

cities to look for jobs finally transformed Brookville into a quiet country town.

Brookville has a population of only 200 today, but the Brookville Hotel, one of the oldest hotels in continuous service in Kansas, attracts people from all over the state because of the fried chicken dinners served there. The hotel was built in 1870 and was first known as the Cowtown Café and later as the Central Hotel. In the old hotel registers there are several prominent names from the past: "Buffalo Bill" Cody, J. C. Penney, and Henry Chrysler of Ellis, Kansas, whose son Walter founded Chrysler Motors. Business at the hotel had declined considerably, but during World War II the military personnel at Smoky Hill Air Force Base discovered that the fried chicken dinners were delicious, and hundreds of men began to patronize the hotel. Today the Brookville Hotel still serves dinners to travelers at modest prices and in the same old tradition, unaltered during the last ninety years.[7]

Perhaps the same statement could be made for the town of Brookville. Progress has not changed this country town; it too is unaltered by time.

This small building was the office of Justice of the Peace L. N. Holmberg in Sveadal. Court was held in the cellar, and the tower served as a lookout for hostile Indians, as well as for overseeing Sveadal's farm laborers.

Brookville can be visited by taking state Highway 140 west from Salina. Most of the town is immediately north of the highway.

SVEADAL
McPherson County

In 1868 Maj. L. N. Holmberg, who claimed to have royal blood and who always used the title "Major" to impress people, homesteaded in the region that was to become McPherson County. He had emigrated from Sweden, where he had been a lieutenant in the Swedish army, and he had been awarded the title of major in the Union army during the Civil War. Soon after homesteading, Major Holmberg decided to build a town on his property, so he constructed a one-story general store and hung out a sign that proclaimed the town's name, Sveadal, a derivative of the name Sweden. In 1869 Holmberg received two government appointments: postmaster and justice of the peace. The latter was a dubious title since he always carried a gun and often used it to scare his farm laborers, just to "get 'em goin'."

Peaceful citizens across the Smoky Hill River from Sveadal were appalled at the way Holmberg treated his workers, and some of them claimed that he was "possessed by the devil." Due to his offensive nature and his mishandling of his business affairs, he soon lost both government appointments.

When McPherson County was organized on March 6, 1870, in Major Holmberg's store, the crudely constructed building became the first county courthouse, and after the first county election, on May 2, 1870, the governor declared the town the temporary county seat. During that summer a military company was organized to protect local settlers from the Indians, and Major Holmberg assumed command of this unit. Unfortunately, Sveadal showed no signs of growth so in 1871 the post office was discontinued, and the county seat was moved to Lindsborg.

Now the Sveadal townsite is almost within the city limits of Lindsborg, another town settled by Swedish immigrants. About 100 yards from the spot where the old general store still stands are the ruins of an eight-sided brick building that once had a wooden tower from which Major Holmberg kept an armed lookout for Indians. After Holmberg died, some people believed that his spirit roamed that odd-looking building after dark, but one former neighbor recalled that raccoons used to fall into the cellar of the building and become trapped. Those wild animals were probably the "spirits" responsible for the mysterious night noises that so frightened people.

Today the Sveadal store and former McPherson County courthouse is used as a tool shed on a farm just outside Lindsborg. It has withstood floods, fires, and man's destructive nature. The only other reminder of the town is the old Sveadal sign, which was rescued by G. N. Malm and is now on display at the Old Mill Museum in Lindsborg.[1]

BEACH VALLEY
Rice County

Just west of Lyons where the Santa Fe Trail crossed Cow Creek, Joseph Brown surveyed the area in 1825 and described it as being "good for wood, water, grass, and buffalo." In 1857, L. B. Wolf of Company K, 1st U.S. Cavalry, belonged to a detachment that was sent to escort government surveyors and to guard emigrants, mail carriers, and stations along the Santa Fe Trail. The detachment was headquartered at Asahel and Abijah ("Doc") Beach's ranch on Cow Creek, and Wolf noted that "the Doctor has quite a trading station here, his stock consisting of 'dead shot' whiskey, sugar, flour and bacon and it is also a mail station and post office."[1] This ranch later was incorporated as a town, but although a true town never developed, its location was the scene of many exciting encounters between the Indians and settlers, emigrants, and traders.

After a post office was established on February 10, 1859, the Cow Creek ranch became known as Beach Valley,[2] and later that year a gold seeker, named Charles Post, recorded that he had "made the acquaintance of Dr. Beach, who keeps a ranch on the east side of the creek. He is a young man who together with his father and four hired men are trading with the Indians, the Kowahs, and slaughtering buffalo, the meat of which they prepare by salting, smoking and drying and hauling to Kansas City, where they find a ready sale at 25¢ a pound."[3]

William Mathewson, the original "Buffalo Bill," was one of the "four hired men" referred to by Post. In an interview in 1893, Mathewson was quoted as saying while he was at Beach Valley "there were plenty of buffalo roaming the plains, but the Indians were thick and hostile, and the settlers unused to Indian warfare."[4]

Beach Valley was incorporated as a town on February 23, 1860, when Gov. Samuel Medary approved the incorporation of the town company. A. J. Beach, I. A. Baker, and Samuel Shaff were listed as the founders, but after Asahel Beach was found unconscious later that spring, near Diamond Springs in eastern Kansas, any further attempts to develop the Beach Valley townsite ceased.[5]

There had been trouble with the Indians ever since the ranch was established, and William Mathewson stated that in the summer of 1861, he had a personal encounter with Satanta, chief of the Kiowas. Word was sent to Mathewson that the chief intended to kill him for shooting one of the braves he caught stealing his horse. A short time later Satanta, accompanied by several Indians, entered the trading post with drawn bows and told him they had come to kill him. After knocking Satanta down with his revolver, Mathewson quickly covered the others with his weapon and ordered them out of the store. When they had gone, he proceeded to give the chief such a severe beating that the Indians had to return to carry him back to their camp. After this confrontation, the Indians called Mathewson "Sinyah Yilbah," or the "Long-bearded Dangerous Man."

But the troubles with the Indians continued unabated until 1865. A preliminary peace treaty was signed by the chiefs of the Comanches, Kiowas, Arapahoes, and plains Apaches on August 15, 1865, at the mouth of the Little Arkansas near Wichita. By mid-October permanent peace agreements had been made with most of the plains Indians, and much of the warfare came to a halt around Beach Valley.

On June 22, 1866, the post office was permanently discontinued at Beach Valley, and William Mathewson left. No activities at Beach Valley from June 1866 to June 1872—when a Methodist Episcopal church was established nearby—were documented, so there is no record of those years at the place described as "three houses and a good corral" and "three or four little lumber shanties built in a row on the east side of Cow Creek."[6]

Today only a well remains on the Beach Valley site. It has been described as "about 40 feet deep and walled almost from top to bottom with sandstone slabs which could not have been procured closer than 15 miles away."[7] Even though the well was constructed in 1857 when the Beaches started their ranch, it has frequently been referred to as "Buffalo Bill's well." The *Lyons Daily News* of April 12, 1961, reported that "Buffalo Bill's well now has its curb, has been cleaned out and will soon receive a wooden superstructure which has been built for it. Then the old well . . . will become part of a small park."[8] Today Beach Valley is private property. Local contacts should be made for permission to visit the site.

DUBUQUE
Russell/Barton Counties

Robert O'Brien of Dubuque, Iowa, received quite a shock when in 1962 he traveled 586 miles southwest of his hometown and came upon the remains of Dubuque, Kansas. For a moment he thought he was going in circles. According to a newspaper account of his visit,

> [In] the rolling hills clothed with yellowing maize that surround it is the tall spire of a church and two other faded wood buildings, one a small public school, and the other a home for three nuns.
>
> But for O'Brien's curiosity, the little Kansas village might have passed unmourned.
>
> He was passing through Central Kansas while on vacation recently, stopped his car to take a picture of the church, set amidst a grove of honeysuckle trees.
>
> Then he saw the sign: "St. Catherine's Catholic Church, Dubuque, Kansas."[1]

Shortly after the Civil War, Polish emigrants arrived in the area from Wisconsin, Illinois, and Indiana. They were followed by German-Russian

The elaborate Dubuque Catholic church could be seen for miles across the prairie. Although the town slowly disappeared, the church remained active.

colonists from Minnesota, Wisconsin—and Dubuque, Iowa. The town was officially founded in 1887. A check of twentieth-century local telephone directories revealed that some of the original surnames from the late 1800s still appeared, such as Woydziak, Redelzkes, Polzin, Murray, Driscoll, Schauff, Harrington, Neys, Kehough, Huberty, Scharpf, and Weber. Dubuque was always a community of mixed nationalities.

The colonists devoted their time to homesteading and planting crops, and the Turkey-red wheat they planted in Kansas proved to be more adaptable to the climate and soil than the soft wheat of the Mississippi Valley, which thrives in damper soil and climate.

When the settlers were faced with bad weather and economic problems, they erected a church in the hope that it would help bring peace and faith to their struggling community. The first Dubuque church was built in the early 1870s about a mile south of the present St. Catherine's structure, which was built in 1901 and is on the National Register of Historic Places.

Even at its peak in the early 1920s, Dubuque had only a few stores and a post office. With the advent of more mechanized farm machinery, some of the owners of smaller farms sold out and moved away, and the farms that were left became larger in size. Dubuque lost its status as a center, and the more prominent towns in the area took over the local trade.

Today Dubuque consists of only the church and a cemetery. Even the school, where the pupils were taught by two Dominican sisters, has closed. Dubuque has become a relic of an era characterized by native limestone ("post-rock") architecture, and its church is the last remnant of a simpler time. To visit Dubuque, take an unmarked county road north from Odin to the county line. The county line location is the site of the community.

ROME
Ellis County

By 1867 the line of settlement in Kansas had reached as far west as Ellis County, and the first town to cross that line was Rome, once called the Pioneer of Western Kansas.[1] One of Rome's cofounders was William F. "Buffalo Bill" Cody, the noted scout and buffalo hunter, who thought he was going to make thousands of dollars selling lots in the new town. William Rose, a railroad contractor, was the other cofounder, and it was he who had asked Cody to be his partner in building the town.[2]

When the community was surveyed in May 1867, 500 were already living on or near the townsite, and a general store had been established by the Lull Brothers of Salina.[3] By mid-June Rose and Cody were giving free lots away to anyone willing to build a house or erect a tent on the site. A canvas-covered store was erected by Bloomfield, Moses & Company; Joseph Perry built the Perry Hotel; and Rose and Cody opened another general store.

William F. "Buffalo Bill" Cody led a varied and colorful career. Among other things he was the cofounder of Rome, an unsuccessful competitor to nearby Hays City.

The Union Pacific employed 1,200 men in its construction crews in the area, and they were busy surveying, grading, and laying the track during the summer of 1867. These workers were a ready-made clientele for the restaurants, saloons, gambling houses, and general stores in the town. Rome became the place to buy fresh buffalo and antelope meat; firewood from

Big Creek; hay for the livestock; and buffalo robes. By the end of July, Rome had over 2,000 citizens, some were permanent and some were not, but nevertheless the town was booming.[4]

The well-established citizens in Rome were far outnumbered by soldiers, railroad workers, gamblers, hunters, "cut-throats," and prostitutes. The saloons were the biggest moneymakers in town, and one glance down Main Street revealed such names as the Lone Star, Dewdrop Inn, the Occidental, Grader's Retreat, and The Last Chance. Rome recorded no fatal gunfights or hangings and had no "boot hill" during its short history, but since it was a rendezvous for many plainsmen, a quiet night was no doubt a rarity. One early settler wrote in his memoirs, "The saloon business was thriving and continuous all day, all night; no halt, no intermission."[5]

Trouble for Rome began when Dr. W. C. Webb arrived and asked to be included as a partner in the townsite venture. Bill Cody and William Rose refused his request, but unknown to them, Dr. Webb had the authority to locate townsites for the railroad. Spurned and angered by Rose and Cody's rejection, Dr. Webb and Phinneas Moore organized the Big Creek Land Company in June 1867 and laid out a townsite known as Hays City (Hays) just one mile east of Rome.

Webb and Moore advised the residents of Rome that Hays City would be the location of the railroad depot. Because of the danger of floods from Big Creek, the railroad men decided that the grade to the bridge at Rome would have to be raised three and a half feet higher than originally planned, and Rome essentially became a "walled city," surrounded on the south by the high railroad grade and on the other three sides by Big Creek. In spite of these problems, however, Rome boomed from June to August 1867, at least until the railroad depot was completed at Hays City.[6] Despite the competition between the two towns of Rome and Hays City, there was little violence, except when "Judge" M. E. Joyce, a peculiar plains character, got a bullet through his shoulder in the course of an argument in which he was speaking in defense of the town of Rome.[7]

When a cholera epidemic hit Rome in late summer of 1867, most of the remaining residents, including Cody and Rose, became frightened and fled. Trade from the railroad workers ceased as they moved farther west, and the only business left in town was from the soldiers at Fort Hays. The Perry Hotel moved to Hays City where it became known as the Gibson House, and the other businesses soon followed. By 1868 Rome had disappeared, and today not even ghosts remain in the town that was once known as the Pioneer of Western Kansas.[8]

Today the town of Hays reaches west to the Rome townsite. A marker near Fort Hays State College indicates where Rome once stood. Inquire at the college regarding access to the site.

CHETOLA
Ellis County

Kansas has had its share of mining booms, from coal, lead, and zinc to oil, but gold strikes have been practically unknown in the state. One of the best-known gold discoveries involved the town of Chetola, which had an actual gold rush in the 1890s.

Chetola, a small rural hamlet, was established in 1886 by a Topekan named Thomas Fulgum, who was involved in a number of land investments in Ellis County. In 1887 Richard Rogers, a carpenter from McCracken in Rush County, helped Fulgum construct a hotel in Chetola, and a store, two dwellings, an elevator, and two large barns were also built. Fulgum was an avid fan of horse racing, and he fashioned a racetrack between the two barns and made money from the sport. But Fulgum eventually lost money on his investments, and after renting his land to A. W. Copeland of Topeka, he left Ellis County for good.[1]

In the late 1880s the town promoters had hopes that a railroad would build through the community, but no matter how they schemed, two factors over which they had no control dictated otherwise. First, the Smoky Hill River would have to be crossed several times, and when this river was at flood stage, it would threaten the tracks and bridges along its banks. Second, an agreement had been made between the Union Pacific and the Santa Fe railroads which stated that neither would cross the other's territory for a century; if Cyrus K. Holliday's railroad ran from Smoky Hill to Denver, it would infringe upon the territory of the Union Pacific. When it became clear that Chetola had no chance of acquiring a railroad, most of the townspeople began to leave, although the old hotel and grocery store stayed open for the benefit of the local farmers and the occasional travelers who drifted through Chetola.

Suddenly, in 1893, Chetola was rejuvenated by the discovery of gold. The man who ignited the spark was H. P. Artz, a miner who had pitched a tent along the bluffs of the Smoky Hill River to look for a tin mine that was supposed to exist somewhere in the valley. Although Artz had a tent at his remote diggings, he roomed at night with the Enoch Nelson family and had his evening meal with them. When Artz failed to appear for dinner several evenings in a row, Mr. Nelson became concerned and went to investigate. Failing to locate him near his tent, he went over to the diggings and looked down the shaft. There was Artz sitting at the bottom smoking his pipe. His rope had broken, leaving him stranded in the mine. Artz remarked, "About time you got here. I'm about out of tobacco."

One day while Artz was digging he found a trace of gold in the dirt and rocks. Unkempt, unshaven, and greatly excited, he rode into town and spread the news that gold had been found in Kansas.[2] The rush began. Colonel Fred Close, a Civil War veteran, leased most of the land with the financial backing of Cyrus K. Holliday. A tent town sprang up on the banks of the Smoky Hill River, and gold seekers began pouring into Chetola. A gold mill was built as well as a blacksmith shop, another grocery store, and a post office. Frank Motz, publisher of the *Hays Daily News*, recounted that his father, Simon Motz, "was interested in some degree in the gold mining venture. I remember we visited it often. The region was thick with rattlesnakes and my father used to lift me in his arms to keep me from being bitten."[3]

The Close and Holliday gold mill operated for three years but showed little profit. The gold was found in blue shale that had to be crushed and washed by a steam-driven machine, then this substance was run through two large vats and baked in an oven. When this material was crumbled, it might yield a few small particles of gold, but the cost proved to be too great, and in 1896 the operation ceased production.[4]

For a few more years miners scratched the bluffs up and down the river searching for the mother lode, which was never found, but the madness for gold that had obsessed the people had finally passed. During the last days of the gold rush, a New York reporter came to Chetola to cover the story of the mines in Kansas, but all he found were disappointed settlers. Being an experienced miner himself, he decided to do a little panning before he left the state, but just as he was starting to pan, news came of a gold strike in the Klondike, and he left immediately for Alaska. After he had spent a few years there, the Klondike gold rush made him rich and famous—this reporter was the novelist Rex Beach.[5]

Chetola gradually became a ghost town. The lumber from the gold mill and the hotel was hauled six miles to help build the church at Antonino. In 1907 the townsite was sold to Peter Hauschild, and his descendants still own the land. The only remnant left on the townsite today is the abutment of an old bridge located in the brush near a contemporary bridge. The only major gold rush in the state left no one rich and many poor on the Kansas prairie.

6

SOUTH CENTRAL
KANSAS

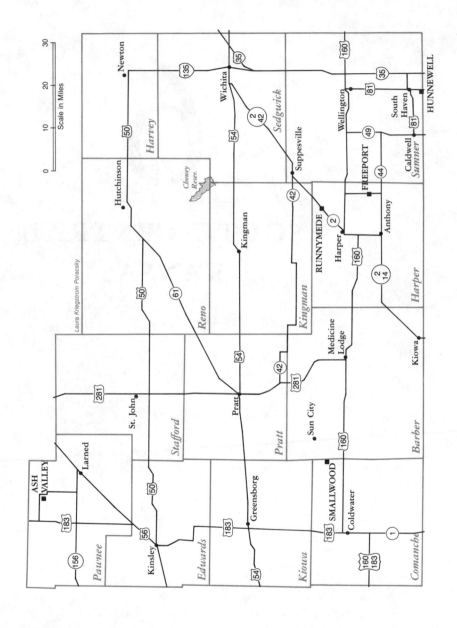

Scale in Miles
0 10 20 30

Laura Kriegstrom Poracsky

Cowboys in Hunnewell were always able to keep busy in their spare time. Here they have gathered in front of the town hotel for a mock hanging, circa 1890.

HUNNEWELL
Sumner County

The first "singing cowboy" of any prominence in western Kansas was a whiskey-tenor named Darling Dan who married a girl from Hunnewell, and for a time the couple delighted frontier audiences with their singing. The cowboy's real name was Bill Cox, a versatile entertainer who operated on a wide circuit ranging from schoolhouse pie suppers to rodeos. Bill was able to oblige in any department—he could cheerfully bust the meanest bronco, flip a steer on its tail, and then top off the performance by singing a song of his own composition. Bill wrote all of his own songs, and fortunately, all but a few have been lost.

When Maggie married Bill, her family in Hunnewell was appalled. They could not understand what she saw in that bow-legged, partially bald man who made his living as a singer; nevertheless, the duets that came from this team captured the hearts of many. But one night Bill got drunk, and after something provoked him, he drew one of his pistols and shot at Maggie. The bullet took a chunk off the top of her left ear. Bill felt guilty about this, especially since it gave Maggie such a lopsided look when her hair was tied back, so the next time he got drunk, he took his bowie knife and cropped her other ear to balance her appearance. Maggie did not appreciate this, and she left him for good. This just about ended Bill's singing career, and he spent the rest of his life in Canon City, Colorado, the owner of a livery stable. Maggie went back to Hunnewell where she married a farmer and lived a more quiet life.[1]

Such was life in Hunnewell back in the days before the opening of the Cherokee Strip, a stretch of land three miles wide that marked the boundary of Kansas with Indian Territory. Hunnewell had its beginnings as a terminus of the St. Louis, Kansas & Southwestern Railroad, which ran through Sumner County, and the town was named in honor of the president of the railroad.

The nearby settlement of South Haven first aspired to be the terminus of the railroad, but its proposals were too high, so the Hunnewell Town Company took advantage of the situation, and when the railroad arrived on June 16, 1880, a full-fledged town was in the making. The first store building was the outfitting place of Ford & Leonard, and within a matter of days, the town became the site of many other places of business, some of them operated from wagon beds and hastily erected tents. There was Hocker & Phelps, druggists; Roland & O'Neil, hardware; Dr. Dobbins, physician; and P. M. Judd, attorney-at-law.

In 1880 the most imposing structure in town was the Hunnewell House, a large thirty-three-room hotel that was completed on August 20 at a cost of $5,000.[2] The hotel was frequented by trail hands, railroad employees, and cattle buyers since it had the best reputation of any hotel for over a hundred miles in any direction.

In the early 1890s Hunnewell benefited greatly from being an "end-of-the-track" town. After the government had ordered all cattle removed from the Strip, thousands of head were driven to the stockyards at Hunnewell for shipment to market or to other grazing grounds. The town was at its peak during this time.[3]

Hunnewell had a business directory that was larger than that of many of the neighboring towns, but unfortunately, along with economic growth, there came a period of lawlessness.[4] The town was jammed with cowboys, cattle buyers, railroad workers, horse thieves, dance-hall girls, whiskey peddlers, and those who just wanted to make a fast dollar. Groups of cowboys

A rare glimpse of the Cherokee Strip Run, September 16, 1893. After the shot was fired and the crowds stormed onto the strip, Hunnewell began a decline that never ended.

would often become boisterous after drinking too much liquor, and they would ride up and down the streets whooping and hollering and firing their guns. Although most of the rowdyism was "meant in fun," and defined by locals as cowboys "letting off steam" from being too long on the trail, there were often acts of real violence, and some of the wild sprees ended in killings. Sometimes men killed each other for their money or for their stock certificates, but most often they fought over gambling and women, and now and then they even fought when another man attempted to crash the waiting line at the registration booth for Indian Territory.

Hunnewell had only 250 permanent residents, but there was a large itinerant population, and waiting lines were everywhere—at hotels, restaurants, stores, and at the post office.[5] Despite the rowdy behavior of some, the vast majority of "boomers" (people awaiting the Oklahoma land boom) were honest, hard-working, and well behaved—at least until the Oklahoma land run started.[6]

Once the Strip was opened for settlement in 1893, most of the people in town left as fast as they had come, and Hunnewell was nearly deserted. The town declined even further in 1912 when robbers entered the Hunnewell Bank and used dynamite to blow up the safe in an attempt to get the cash. Not only did they destroy the vault, but they also damaged the building and its contents. When the surprised citizens realized what had happened, they lost no time in pursuing the outlaws. One was eventually captured but the other members of the gang were never found.[7]

A *Kansas City Star* article depicted the town's decline in a description of Hunnewell House in later years: "Its weatherbeaten sides still show the pockmarks of bullets, put there by drunken cowboys who came at intervals to 'shoot up' the pioneer town. . . . Once the liveliest spot in a border cow town, the building now stands almost forgotten. Its service for anything other than as a private dwelling has long since ended."[8] When the hotel was finally torn down in 1939, over seventy pounds of lead was extracted from the pine boards on the sides of the building—proof of the number of guns fired both "in fun" and for other reasons in earlier days. Also found was a "blind tiger" (a bootlegging term), that is, a trap door cut in one of the stair steps through which bottles of whiskey were passed from a closet underneath to someone on the stairway during the height of the hotel's popularity.

Hunnewell never regained the momentum it lost when the Cherokee Strip opened, and only a few houses are left in the area today. Like the cowboys, bootleggers, and outlaws, much of Hunnewell too has disappeared. You can reach Hunnewell by taking U.S. Highway 81 south nineteen miles from Wellington. The town borders the highway and is adequately marked.

RUNNYMEDE
Harper County

No one enjoyed life more on the rugged Kansas prairie than some British settlers in the now vanished town of Runnymede, which was planned by Francis J. S. Turnley. Turnley first came to southern Kansas in 1885 and purchased the Box T Ranch near the Cherokee Strip, but in 1887 he bought 1,700 acres of land in the Chikaskia River valley in Harper County and decided to try his luck at establishing a town.[1]

"Ned" Turnley, as he was nicknamed, made a trip to England to sell the idea of his new town to some wealthy Englishmen, who just happened to be fathers of restless, unmanageable sons. Turnley's proposed town had three special attributes that appealed to these parents: There would be no violence or crime and no "riff-raff" in the town; the young men would be taught responsibility and have occupations that would entail plenty of hard work; and no liquor would be available as Kansas was noted for its prohibition laws. Of course, naming the town Runnymede no doubt also struck a responsive chord in the hearts of these Englishmen since the original Runnymede in England was where their charter of liberty, or Magna Charta, was signed.[2]

Tennis on the plains? The Runnymede Tennis Club after a match, 1891. Some English traditions, such as tennis and fox hunting, were brought to the plains of southern Kansas.

On May 29, 1889, Turnley set sail for the United States with sixteen young men aboard the ship *Britannic,* having agreed with their fathers that for $500 a year he would teach these young men the business of stock raising and farming and help them purchase their own farms. After the *Britannic* landed in New Orleans, the group traveled most of the way by rail to the small community in Kansas.[3] The young colonists were eager to settle in the "Wild West," and they immediately started to help build the town.

They soon realized that to be successful, Runnymede needed to become a railroad center. Politics stood in the way of this happening, however, because the people in control of the Kansas legislature were against foreign capital in Kansas, and they used their influence to keep the railroad from building through Runnymede.[4]

In the 1890s life in Runnymede for these young men did not exactly conform to the scene that their fathers back in England had visualized. For instance, prohibition was not a part of their lifestyle as liquor was often readily available. One day two of the young men were riding home on a wagonload of hay when they met some local farmers who had been drinking heavily. These men challenged the young Britishers to a wagon race. The Englishmen eagerly accepted the challenge, but during the race, their wagon overturned and the hay spilled into a ditch. Everyone began laughing and drinking, and after a few hours of this conviviality, the colonists decided to burn the hay rather than take the time to pitch it back on the wagon. Then they rode blissfully home.[5]

The British held horse races at Runnymede, which were well attended by both the colonists and the residents from other towns in the area. On one occasion, the Englishmen's love for their homeland caused a commotion at one of the races when they hoisted the Union Jack above Old Glory. Spectators from the nearby town of Danville led an angry outcry, and the flags were quickly taken down and Old Glory hoisted back in its proper position on top. Turnley apologized for the "oversight," but news of this incident spread across the state. For a short time many Kansans thought the Runnymede colonists should be deported to England, but they were not, and the incident was soon forgotten.[6]

Fox hunting was another popular sport among the young colonists, and foxhounds and Irish setters were imported to chase, not foxes, but coyotes. What did the western Kansas cowboy think when he saw these men from Runnymede riding on the plains, wearing pink coats and white breeches and following dogs chasing an unlucky coyote?[7]

By 1892 Runnymede was a flourishing town of 500 people. A three-story hotel, with rates higher than those in Kansas City, had been built and did a thriving business. There were also several stores, two stage lines, a club house, and a number of fine homes.[8] On January 1, 1892, a correspondent of the *Wichita Eagle* reported that Runnymede colonists were prospering in spite of the hard times, and that one farmer had gathered over sixty bushels of apples from his trees and had sold them for $1.25 a bushel. This correspondent also noted that the cattle and horses bred at Runnymede were of better stock than those in other areas of the state.[9] An Episcopal church was also constructed at Runnymede, and it was the setting for the town's one and only marriage when Capt. Percy Wood married Sophia Turnley, a sister of the town's founder.

But the prosperity and lighthearted fun came to an end. A number of reasons have been given for Runnymede's demise including the lack of female companionship; the fact that the Kansas, Mexico & Orient Railroad laid its tracks two miles south of Runnymede, not through town; the depression and "panic" of 1893; the dry seasons that ruined crops; and the death of Richard ("Dick") Whatmough, one of the most beloved characters in Runnymede, shortly before he was to leave for England to marry his fiancée.[10]

For whatever reason, or combination of reasons, Runnymede was abandoned in 1892, and most of the Englishmen returned to England. All that remains today is the headstone of Thomas Sharp Hudson who died on January 3, 1890. The church and other buildings were moved to nearby towns in Harper County or across the line into Oklahoma.

The Runnymede Arms Hotel. When the town began to decline, several buildings were moved. The Runnymede church was moved to Harper; this hotel was moved across the border into Oklahoma.

Capt. Charles Seaton summarized Runnymede's existence best when he stated, "Runnymede . . . was a combination of British inexperience, credulity, some money, considerable cockneyism, but withal a jolly lot of men . . . transported to a bold Kansas prairie, where the immigrants expected to grow rich in a day and a night and then return to England."[11]

You can visit Runnymede by taking state Highway 2 northeast from Harper. After you cross the Santa Fe Railroad tracks, you are in the vicinity of the townsite.

FREEPORT
Harper County

There was a time in Kansas history when town developers welcomed all settlers because more residents meant more money in the community. In the early newspapers, headlines advertised that certain towns were the "Queen of the Southwest," or "the Up and Coming Wonder of Kansas." Freeport was once one of these towns, but today travelers who stop too long in this southern Kansas community may receive more than just a suspicious glance. The slogan of the town now is "No outsiders, please."

In 1976, the mayor told a reporter, "We just don't want to be in the newspapers. We're here and we're doing all right. Let's just skip it this time." The postmistress also refused to talk about the town. "Every time we've gotten into the paper, it's brought us trouble," she remarked. "It has attracted undesirable people."[1] All is quiet these days in Freeport, and folks want to keep it that way.

The words "peaceful and quiet" are not often used to describe Freeport's early years. "It used to be a hell of a town," remarked a Freeport resident. "At one time it had two or three hotels, a livery stable—it had the works here. That's what they tell me."[2] He had been told correctly.

The first settlement in the area originated in 1878 when a small trading post and post office named Midlothian was established by B. H. Freeman, three miles southeast of present Freeport. In 1885 when the St. Louis, Fort Scott & Wichita Railroad built a line to Anthony, Freeman moved his post office to the current site of Freeport, and on February 27 the town plat was filed consisting of forty-six acres located on Joseph Haun's farm.

The town of Midlothian received its charter eight days after Freeport, and its tract adjoined that of Freeport; only Grand Avenue separated the two rival towns. Several incidents of violence occurred, but the first major disagreement between the citizens of the two towns was over the placement of the railroad depot. To restore order, a fence was built down the middle of Grand Avenue. Finally on March 18, 1886, the *Freeport Tribune* noted that the citizens had settled their differences, removed the fence, and Midlothian was to be known as West Freeport.

After this competitive spirit between the two towns had been subdued, Freeport boomed, and in 1886 the following businesses were built: two grain elevators, three coal yards, two hotels, three lumberyards, nine grocery stores, five dry goods stores, two implement shops, three drugstores, two meat markets, two hardware stores, four blacksmith shops, a millinery store, a harness shop, a billiard hall, a bank, two land and loan offices, and two barber shops. In 1887 there were 300 residents; by 1892 there were between 700 and 1,000. During this period, Freeport was a "hell of a town"—several illegal saloons provided the townspeople with a source of recreation, and the town's proximity to Indian Territory made it an easy mark for rowdies and outlaws, who could shoot up the town and readily escape across the border.

Just before the Cherokee Strip was opened for settlement, the town reached its peak. However, when the Strip was opened on September 16, 1893, this growth came to an abrupt halt, and by 1895 Freeport had only

The Freeport Bank and Adams Department Store as they appeared around 1900. This was one of the largest buildings in Freeport.

54 people. By 1910 the situation had improved somewhat as the town reported a population of 161 citizens that year.

The Freeport Bank was chartered on January 7, 1902, with a capital stock of $5,000; by December 31, 1967, the bank had total assets of $854,992.62. Despite the town's gradual decrease in population, the bank has always prospered, even during the depression years. "We never did have any trouble to speak of here with our depositors," said one of the cashiers. "When Roosevelt declared the Bank Holiday and people could only withdraw a certain per cent of their money, we had customers that would come in and ask if they could withdraw their allowable. When we told them 'yes' then they would say they didn't want it but just wanted to know if it was available." The cashier said that the bank had few foreclosures during the 1930s, though some farming operations in the area failed. "We always tried to walk down the row with a man if we knew he was trying. We would rewrite notes and ask the borrowers to keep up the interest payments to keep the bank examiners off our necks."[3]

Freeport can boast of a police force and a fire department, but a jail was never erected, and the fire equipment is far from elaborate. In fact, through the years there have been a number of fires in town that destroyed a lumberyard, five cafés, a general store, hotel, pool hall, bank, newspaper office, two schoolhouses, and a church.[4]

Many abandoned buildings have been moved away, leaving Main Street

Freeport as it looks today. Most of the businesses have been abandoned, but the town still stands after ninety years of decline and depression.

nearly empty. In a plowed field near the railroad tracks, the skeleton of a frame house stands in the middle of a clump of trees and sunflowers. A pot-bellied stove and a chest are inside, but they too are rotting away.

Although the Freeport Presbyterian Church remains active and has about 120 members, the bank is actually the hub of the community today. The town has survived the ups and downs of nearly a century, and even though it lacks population, it does not lack civic pride. Freeport citizens are proud that their town is the smallest incorporated city in Kansas. You can reach Freeport by taking state Highway 49 east from Anthony. Follow the signs and turn north to Freeport on a marked county road.

SMALLWOOD
Comanche County

In the early days of county organization in Kansas, Smallwood, located near Mule Creek southwest of Sun City, was an imaginary town where a swindle was perpetrated on the legislature by the organizers of Comanche County, William H. Horner and A. J. Mowry. The latter was a former member of the legislature.

In the summer of 1873 a party of buffalo hunters in western Kansas met up with Mowry and four other men who were involved with the organization of Comanche County, an area that really had only two bona fide residents.[1] The men tried to convince J. S. Cox, one of the buffalo hunters, that he would make a good county attorney. Although Cox protested that he was not a lawyer, Mowry assured him that his lack of legal knowledge would not be an obstacle but an advantage. (Mowry was aware that having a county attorney who was actually a lawyer could prove to be embarrassing.) When Cox finally agreed to the plot, Mowry's scheme to swindle the state legislature was progressing as he had planned. Comanche County was too far west for government officials to investigate, and Mowry figured he would be gone before any scandal was discovered.

In order to hold any type of county election, at least 240 voters were needed. These names were found by Mowry in an old city directory of St. Joseph, Missouri, and he made certain they were all registered as voters in Comanche County. When the "election" was held, Mowry and his friends were easily elected to all the county offices by a "unanimous vote." The county seat was supposedly located at a town called Smallwood, which existed in name only.[2]

In order for everything to look official, Mowry and Horner appointed a census taker, A. Updegraff, who was easily persuaded to take the job for a certain amount of money. For ten days Updegraff walked or rode several hundred miles on the prairie, gathering the names of 600 people, which he sent to the governor's office in Topeka. On October 28, 1873, a governor's proclamation declared the county organized.

The county "commissioners" then issued $29,000 in bonds to C. C. Beemis to build a courthouse at Smallwood, but all he constructed was a frame cabin. The commissioners also issued $23,000 in bridge bonds, $20,000 in general expense bonds, and an unlimited amount of school bonds. A total of $126,593 in bonds were issued before any inquiry was made by state officials.[3] By that time Mowry and Horner were gone, and so was the money.

In 1874 the governor appointed a commission to investigate the irregularities in the organization of Comanche County, but the commission reported that it had been legitimately organized. The fact that so few people were living there at the time was explained—the families had left because they were afraid of the Indians.

Attorney General John Williams conducted a more extensive investigation that same year, and his findings led to the discovery of the scandal. According to Williams:

Comanche County has no inhabitants and never had. Testimony is unnecessary as there is no one living there. I camped upon the townsite of Smallwood and feasted upon wild turkey, with no white men to molest or make me afraid. In Smallwood there are two cabins without doors, windows, sash or blinds; about a mile off is another deserted ranch, and these compose the houses of the "householders" of the county. . . . Its organization is, and always has been, a fraud.[4]

A post office was supposed to have opened in Smallwood on January 9, 1874, and was listed as discontinued on May 21, 1875. The only other mention of the town was on July 18, 1880, when a town charter for Smallwood was filed by F. E. Gillett. After the secretary of state returned the charter for certain corrections, nothing more was heard. A town called Smallwood never existed.

ASH VALLEY
Pawnee County

On February 13, 1967, the *Larned Tiller and Toiler* sadly reported in a special article that "Ash Valley . . . is losing its last vestige of urbanity. The old Pawnee County Grain and Supply Company Elevator is being razed." This article was a good epitaph for Ash Valley, a ghost town on a railroad that went from boom to bust.

Ash Valley was established in 1916 along the Anthony & Northern Railroad, which had extended its line through Pawnee County. The town was first named Ely in honor of D. A. Ely, a Larned real estate man and landowner. By 1919 Ely was a trading point for a territory that reached out eight or ten miles in all directions. It was the only town north of Larned on the Anthony & Northern Railroad, and most lines of business were represented—a bank, two garages, a lumberyard, an elevator, two general stores, and a restaurant.

By 1925 Ely had changed its name to Ash Valley, after the rich agricultural region that surrounded the community. Bank officials boasted, "Kansas grows the best wheat in the world—the Ash Valley territory grows the best wheat in Kansas."[1] The local railroad also did some name changing and became the Wichita & Northwestern, which had thirty-three miles of main track in Pawnee County, more than the Santa Fe, and Ash Valley became the busiest wheat shipping point on the line. In 1924 alone 250 carloads of wheat had been shipped.

A prosperous future was predicted for the little railroad town. The *Tiller*

A Wichita & Northwestern locomotive stopped for water at Ash Valley circa 1920. The railroad helped to boost town businesses but was also responsible for the town's decline twenty years later when the railroad went into receivership.

and Toiler noted that "with its favorable situation in a wide, fertile territory, its substantial growth from year to year is a foregone conclusion."[2] In addition to the Ash Valley Bank, there were Vale's Cash Store, the Ely Garage, J. B. Wagner General Merchandise Store, and the Pawnee County Grain & Supply Company and Elevator.

Unfortunately, Ash Valley's "substantial growth" did not become a reality. Neither the town nor the railroad fulfilled the glowing predictions of their promoters. In 1940 the railroad went into receivership, and all the equipment was abandoned. In 1942 the rails were torn up and sold as scrap iron to aid the war effort.

Ash Valley's downfall was not quite so abrupt as that of the railroad. In the 1940s the bank was liquidated and the building torn down. One by one most of the stores closed, but the grain elevator continued in operation for many years after the railroad had been abandoned, the wheat being trucked to Larned, the closest shipping point on the Santa Fe. The schoolhouse closed in 1962 and became a private residence. Finally in 1967 the grain company failed and the elevator was razed, which almost removed

Ash Valley from the map. The Pleasant Hill Methodist Church was one of the few remaining structures left on the townsite.

Perhaps the *Larned Tiller and Toiler* summarized the passing of Ash Valley best: "Sometimes late at night when the wind blows across the wheat fields and moans around the farm house old timers can imagine they hear the whistle of a steam locomotive on the A & N pulling a long train of wheatladen boxcars out of Ash Valley—a ghost train and a ghost town."[3]

You can reach Ash Valley by taking U.S. Highway 156 west from Larned. At the intersection with an unmarked county road at the west edge of the Fort Larned Historic Site, turn north. Stay on this road for several miles until it borders Ash Valley.

7

NORTHWEST KANSAS

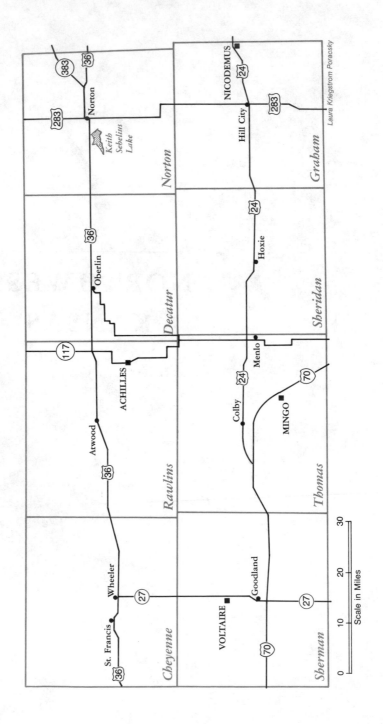

Laura Kriegstrom Poracsky

NICODEMUS
Graham County

In the late 1870s thousand of blacks, many of them destitute, fled the South and came to Kansas hoping to improve their fortunes. They established as many as eleven colonies in the state, one of them being Nicodemus. In time, lack of capital plus the rigors and vicissitudes of the Kansas climate discouraged the majority of these emigrants, and they drifted on westward, but Nicodemus survived, its citizens overcoming every obstacle that arose—both natural and man-made.[1]

Nicodemus was founded in 1877, and the colony received its initial inspiration for growth from a white man named W. R. Hill, a pioneer settler of Graham County who had arrived from Indiana the summer before. Hill had laid out Hill City, which was destined to become the county seat, and began to consider settling a colony of freedmen within the county. He presented his idea to a group of prominent blacks in Topeka, whose financial help and moral support were necessary, and they were enthusiastic about the plan.[2]

Hill traveled throughout the South in an attempt to persuade blacks to settle on the government land in western Kansas, and he must have presented some highly appealing arguments when he talked to them, both individually and collectively. Nearly 500 blacks from the states of Kentucky, Tennessee, and Mississippi decided to risk their meager savings and buy railroad tickets to a land where they had been assured of finding "game in abundance, wild horses, free for the taming, and marvelously fertile land."[3]

The group of black supporters in Topeka, who organized a company to help bring these emigrants west, were capable, intelligent, and far-sighted former slaves from Kentucky. W. H. Smith, who was selected as president of the Nicodemus Town Company, had lived in Kansas since 1874 and was no stranger to the hardships and dangers of frontier life. Simon P. Roundtree, selected as secretary, was an ordained minister and a skilled lecturer who reportedly had been "branded" for being taught to read and write by his master's son.

Hill took no active part in governing the colony, but he did select a site for the proposed town, about a half-mile from the eastern border of the county at the junction of Spring Creek and the Solomon River. Hill selected the site in June 1877, and by July 20 thirty exodusters—black emigrants escaping the collapsed economy of the post–Civil War South—had moved into the area. By September several hundred emigrants had arrived from Kentucky.

In the Nicodemus colony, money was almost nonexistent as the majority of the people had spent their savings on railroad fares to get to Kansas. Determined to hold onto their land, the men wandered near and far in search of work—some walked as far west as Colorado—while their wives eked out what they could from the land and held down the claims. The town company, in two circulars dated April 16 and July 2, 1877, had promised "plenty of provisions" for the settlers, but whatever meager supplies were furnished failed to meet the needs of an ever-increasing population, and soon it became necessary to appeal to white settlers in eastern Kansas for assistance. This appeal was fairly successful, and the supplies collected were transported free of charge by the Kansas Pacific Railroad, but by April 1879, the demoralizing effects of this aid were clearly evident in Nicodemus. Certain settlers were becoming dependent upon relief and disinclined to work, and it was feared that if the support continued, more exodusters might be attracted, people who were not only destitute but also largely inexperienced in working the harsh plains of western Kansas. For this reason, the Nicodemus Town Company was abolished in April 1879, and the town was left on its own.

Even so, the population of Nicodemus flourished. A federal census taken in June 1880 reported 484 blacks in Graham County: 260 of these in Nicodemus Township and 224 in Hill City and Wild Horse Townships. Although a large number of settlers had left the colony between 1877 and 1880, their decision was comprehensible in the face of the unyielding, demanding Kansas frontier.[4]

Most of the Nicodemus colonists did not succumb to charity. One of the hardest workers was R. B. Scruggs, who had found work driving a freight wagon from Nicodemus to Stockton, a distance of twenty miles, as well as work in the railroad towns of Bunker Hill, Ellsworth, and Salina. The years were hard but they paid rich dividends, and Scruggs eventually owned 720 acres of land.

By 1881, through a combination of courage and much hard work, other black settlers had also achieved a great deal. S. B. Welton, who owned suitable agricultural equipment, had broken fifty acres of land and had planted wheat as early as May 1879. Grant Harris had arrived penniless, but by 1881 he had forty acres in cultivation and owned sixty head of livestock. Anderson Boles, who owned the Douglas Hotel, was without means of support when he arrived, but by 1879 he had planted seventy-five acres in grain and owned a cow, a calf, and nineteen hogs. The progress of these men was impressive: Starting with little, they were doing almost as well as their white neighbors, and they were winning the respect of the people of Graham County.

A Nicodemus baseball team poses for the camera in 1921.

Nicodemus was the only black colony in Kansas that was not torn by internal dissension, and much of this cohesiveness was due to its leadership.

During the 1880s three of these exceptional leaders were John W. Niles, A. T. Hall, and E. P. McCabe.

Although Nicodemus was not quite so prosperous as the other towns in the county, its growth was constant. Z. T. Fletcher was operating the general store and post office, which he had founded in the fall of 1877, and W. H. Smith and Louis Welton had opened stores in town in 1878. Nevertheless, by 1881 the rest of the businesses that had lasted any length of time were in the hands of three white men: William Green, S. G. Wilson, and C. H. Newth. Green and Wilson, who had established general stores in 1879, erected two stone buildings in 1880 to house their businesses. Newth, an English emigrant, had opened a general store and a drugstore in 1879.

In the winter of 1878 Mrs. Z. T. Fletcher conducted school in her dugout, but by the spring of 1880, the town was vying with Hill City for the distinction of having the largest school in the county. The facilities did remain rather makeshift, however, until a four-room structure was erected in 1887. In the mid-1880s Nicodemus supported a baseball team, a literary society, and a benefit society—a kind of relief agency dedicated to helping the poor and needy. There was a town band, a music teacher, and for a short time, an ice cream parlor.

In 1887 the community had over 150 inhabitants. The most prominent new building was the St. Francis Hotel, operated by Z. T. Fletcher and his brother Thomas. Fletcher was still in the livery business and had added a line of farm implements, and his wife had opened a millinery store. By spring, Nicodemus could also boast of four general stores, a grocery, three land companies, a lawyer, another hotel, two livery stables, a blacksmith shop, and a harness and boot repair shop. S. G. Wilson and C. H. Newth, the town druggist and doctor, were the only white businessmen until A. G. Tallman established the *Nicodemus Western Cyclone* on May 13, 1887. Later that summer H. K. Lightfoot established a competing paper, the *Nicodemus Enterprise*. A. L. McPherson, another white man, established the Bank of Nicodemus, and with this addition the community became a commercial center of some importance in the county.

In the spring of 1888 the streets of Nicodemus were filled with new settlers—222 arrivals were counted in one week—and it was becoming increasingly difficult for them to find lodging. Some of the activity was due to the proposed extension of the railroad—the Missouri Pacific was supposed to be built to Stockton and then to Graham County via Nicodemus. The town had hoped for the Union Pacific, but those tracks were laid to Hill City rather than to Nicodemus. The editor of the *Cyclone* noted that

An abandoned building deteriorates on a street in Nicodemus circa 1940. Although Nicodemus was one of the most successful black communities ever founded in Kansas, the depression years of the 1930s severely affected the town.

"smoke of the engine" might be seen hanging in the southern sky, and the Union Pacific's railroad camp, which later developed into the town of Bogue six miles southwest of Nicodemus, was the subject of an ominous article: "We are sorry to see several of our businessmen making preparations to move to the proposed new town. We consider this a very unwise move and one they will regret. Nicodemus and her businessmen have nothing to cause them alarm. For everyone that goes now we will get ten wide awake men next spring. Don't get frightened, hold onto your property and be ready to enjoy the real boom that will surely come."[5] Unfortunately, however, the Missouri Pacific line was never extended beyond Stockton so Nicodemus had no railroad. But, although the town undoubtedly lost many of its most enterprising businessmen, there was no wholesale exodus of blacks. In fact, Nicodemus continued to grow slowly, reaching a peak population of 595 in 1910.[6]

The depression of the 1930s was particularly destructive in rural areas, and Nicodemus also suffered from the drought and the dust storms of the period. Like surrounding towns in the Dust Bowl, Nicodemus's population declined, from 429 in 1930 to 365 in 1940.[7] Massive outmigration from

A view of the almost deserted main street of Nicodemus circa 1940. Once this street was alive with activity.

the 1940s through the 1970s reduced the population of Nicodemus even more. An all-time low of around 35 was reached in the early 1970s. Many buildings in town were torn down or moved during this sad period in the history of the community. By the mid-1980s, however, the population had risen to around 80, thanks to a government-subsidized project for low-income residents. The First Baptist Church also completed a new replacement for their old building.[8]

A Kansas Historical Society marker along the highway tells the history of Nicodemus, and that history is celebrated every year at "Homecoming," which occurs during the first week of August. Originally it was called Emancipation Day, but now the more positive definition has taken its place. Each year, 400 to 500 descendants of Nicodemus residents come from all over the country for a week of festivities and remembering.[9]

To assess correctly the worth of Nicodemus, one might turn to the *Atchison Weekly Champion,* which, as early as 1883, predicted the future of the settlement and paid the blacks a fine tribute. The writer noted that someday Nicodemus might become only a name: "The waning and fading designation of a spot where men once lived; but to those who know the truth of history, the name will always recall the bravest attempt ever made by people of any color to establish homes in the high plains of Western Kansas."[10]

Nicodemus can be visited by taking U.S. Highway 24 west from Stockton. Immediately after you cross the border between Rooks and Graham Counties, you will be in the area of Nicodemus. Most of the townsite is south of the highway.

ACHILLES
Rawlins County

In 1868 a young man named Homer Wheeler went west in search of adventure and found it first at Fort Wallace, Wallace County, Kansas, where his cousin was the post trader. In the next few years Wheeler prospered by raising cattle and taking over his cousin's job. In time he would also be a major participant in the most violent confrontation in the history of the area surrounding Achilles.

A turning point in Wheeler's life came when his feelings toward the Cheyenne Indians changed considerably. On December 27, 1874, near Lake Creek, the Cheyennes killed a lone hunter named Charles Brown, looted his wagon, and stole his horses. In January 1875 a scouting expedition of infantrymen commanded by 2d Lt. F. S. Hinkle was sent against the Cheyennes. One member of this scouting party, which readily overtook the Indians and captured most of them, was Wheeler.

In April 1875 Wheeler was once again involved with the Cheyennes. He had been worried about the safety of his cattle scattered on the prairie, so he sent five men out to look for them. Not long after they left, he received word that the men had been attacked by Indians. Wheeler reported the news of the attack to the post commander at Fort Wallace, and on April 22 he sent out a detachment of the 6th Cavalry, commanded by 2d Lt. Austin Henely.

Led by Wheeler, Lieutenant Henely and his men came upon a party of buffalo hunters, who had noticed on the previous day that their unguarded camp had been pillaged by Indians camped about seventeen miles away on Sappa Creek. Wheeler and two other men were successful in locating the Indian camp before dawn the next day. After most of the Indians' horses had been rounded up by the men, and as darkness receded, the outlines of twelve tepees became visible. A sudden movement attracted Wheeler's attention—an Indian herder was sprinting to the lodges to give the alarm. Wheeler galloped back toward the command, shouting and waving his hat. Instantly, Henely ordered the attack.

As the soldiers crested the banks of the creek, a scene of utter confusion was being enacted on the opposite side. Several groups of Indians were aban-

Lt. Austin Henely was a young man when this photo was taken. Eager to make a name for himself, he led a brutal attack on a camp of Cheyennes near Achilles in 1875. His troops killed all of the Indians before the fight ended. Called the Battle of Sappa Creek, it was one of the most violent Indian battles fought in northwest Kansas.

doning their lodges and scattering toward two small herds of horses while another group prepared for a desperate defense. After a great deal of difficulty, because of clinging mud, the soldiers finally managed to reach the opposite bank, and Henely and Wheeler gave a sign to the Indians asking them to surrender.

When it became apparent that they would not do so, Henely ordered his men to dismount. He extended them in a skirmish line along a low ridge and gave the command to return the Indians' gunfire. Although they were ordered not to break ranks, Sgt. Theodore Papier and Pvt. Robert Theims charged to within twenty feet of the Indians' rifles. Both paid for their rashness with their lives.

One group of Indians was hidden behind the creek bank, and Wheeler decided to outflank them and force them into view. Suddenly a Cheyenne leading a spare horse rode boldly into camp and lifted a buffalo robe from the ground. Up jumped another Indian who leaped on the horse, and both galloped away. A carbine shot tumbled the rescuer from his mount, but the other Indian sped out of range unscathed. Three other Indians tried to escape, unsuccessfully.

Now, just one group of Indians was left, still concealed on the banks of Sappa Creek. Henely's men reassembled and readied for a final offensive. Soon these Indians were completely surrounded, and heavy fire from the soldiers succeeded in killing any that dared to peer over the bank. Most of the surviving Cheyennes died recklessly, firing to the last or leaping from cover as the soldiers came among them.

With "battle fever" still high, the soldiers began to search the camp for survivors and for booty. After the camp was set on fire, a Cheyenne child and a woman whose arm had been severed by a gunshot appeared out of the smoke. Henely ordered Sergeant Platten to throw her into a burning lodge, but he refused. Two other soldiers carried out the order.

As the camp was burning, Platten thoughtlessly laid down his carbine to search a tepee. Suddenly Chief Whirlwind appeared brandishing a knife. As Platten dashed for his gun, Chief Whirlwind was killed by a shot from Private Ayres, who had seen the incident from a distance. Among the items collected by the soldiers was a sketchbook which revealed conclusively that some of these Cheyennes had participated in the battle of Adobe Walls in Oklahoma and the massacre of the German family in Wallace County. Apart from the two deaths earlier in the three-hour fight, the command suffered no other casualties. The Indian dead numbered twenty-seven, including eight women and children. This skirmish became known as the Battle of Sappa Creek.[1]

The town of Achilles was not so interesting or so "famous" in the annals of Kansas history as the above incident that occurred on the site of the town before its founding in 1875, but three years after Achilles was built, a group of Indians came to the area to seek revenge for the deaths of their fellow warriors who had fallen at Sappa Creek.

In 1878 Little Wolf's band of Cheyennes were headed north through western Kansas when on October 13, they passed through the settlement of Achilles. The men who lived in the town at that time had had no part in the massacre of the Indians at Sappa Creek, but in the eyes of Little Wolf that was not important.

The Cheyennes attacked the little village and began burning houses. After the Indians had gone, eighteen men were dead, including William Laing, John Hutson, J. B. Smith, John Laing, Freeman Laing, Frederick Hamper, E. P. Humphrey, Moses Abernathy, George Walters, Marcellus Felt, Ed Miskelly, Ferdinand Westphaled, and three others whose last names were Wright, Lull, and Irvin. Other settlers on the outlying farms around Achilles were also killed—forty settlers in Rawlins County alone. This massacre was the last Indian uprising in Kansas.

After the Indian depredations had ended in northwest Kansas, more settlements began to appear. In late 1879 a post office was established at Achilles, with Armstead W. Morris as postmaster. It was Armstead's father, Achilles, a justice of the peace, for whom the town was named.

After Mr. and Mrs. J. W. Rush had laid out the town, several blocks and lots were purchased by Atwood businessmen who were certain that a railroad would be built through the area in a few months. The railroad never came, and most of the lots were sold to local residents.

The greatest population of Achilles was 30 between the years 1905 and 1910. Jim Mintier built the first frame building, which through the years was used as a post office, living quarters, and a store. Another store built by the Farmers' Co-op and a blacksmith shop operated by Jesse Lanning on the east side of Main Street burned down in 1905. The concrete dance floor that was constructed near the blacksmith shop is still there. A store built by J. L. Fields was moved to Atwood in the 1940s.

After the railroad missed Achilles, most of the residents moved away. The post office was discontinued on June 30, 1951. Today the building that housed it stands silent, as does the old schoolhouse.[2] To visit Achilles, take U.S. Highway 36 east about ten miles from Atwood. Turn south at the intersection with an unmarked county road where a cemetery borders the junction. Drive approximately nine miles. Achilles borders the road.

MINGO
Thomas County

Wishing to form a community that would be a center of commercial activity, settlers in southeast Thomas County submitted many town names to the Post Office Department. The name Mingo, of Delaware Indian origin, was chosen in 1894. In the 1890s the Union Pacific Railroad transformed Mingo from a small country hamlet into a major shipping center.

Most of the credit for the good fortune in Mingo can be attributed to Reuben Misner, nicknamed "Doc" because of his knowledge of veterinary medicine. Doc was a natural-born leader who often dabbled in politics. In 1893 he was successful in persuading the officials of the Union Pacific to move their station from Thurford, which was two miles south of Mingo, to Mingo, bringing not only shipping facilities to the town but also eleven section hands and their families, a welcome addition to the population.[1]

Doc Misner was always at the center of the community activities in Mingo, and one of the most fondly remembered events in the community was Doc's marriage on Christmas Eve, 1889. The community had prepared a special Christmas program at the Mingo schoolhouse, which was packed that night with most of the local settlers. After the program was over and the presents had been distributed, Santa Claus left the stage. Suddenly Fred Howard jumped up on the stage and asked everyone to be seated as Santa Claus was about to be married! Out stepped old "Saint Nick," or Doc Misner, and his bride, Belle Cain. Their marriage vows were taken while everyone cheered them on.

Doc Misner operated a store during the drought and depression of the 1890s, and while he was around no one in the community ever went hungry; he often donated sacks of flour and other foodstuffs to those who needed them. During this period, holiday celebrations in Mingo gathered the townspeople together and helped them to better withstand the loneliness that sometimes was a problem on the high plains. Independence Day was one of those times when everyone joined in and enjoyed each other's company. Ed Misner, the second son of Belle and Doc, reminisced about the first celebration he could remember in the late 1890s:

> The [Independence Day celebration] became an early occurrence in Mingo. Between sunup and sundown the town hummed; horseshoe pitching, sack races, several patriotic addresses, a ball game, horse racing, and a dance played a big part. A temporary shelter called a brush arbor served as shade for picnickers and visitors and as a platform for the dancers. Bill Wicke stirred up the lemonade—free for everyone—in a fifty gallon barrel. Ice had been cut the winter before from a pond back of the store.[2]

Bailey's Blacksmith Shop in Mingo circa 1930.

Mingo remained an important shipping point for grain and livestock along the Union Pacific for many years, but during the period following World War I, the emphasis on automobile travel changed the importance of the community as a railroad shipping center. During the depression years of the 1930s many businesses closed, and the farmers trucked their produce and stock to Colby or other larger towns, bypassing Mingo. By 1940 the business community had dwindled drastically, and the post office was closed.

Today the area is still called the Mingo community, although much of the community is gone. Unfortunately Mingo is another victim of the automobile, which accelerated lifestyles for the rural areas of the state during the 1920s and 1930s and was responsible for turning many small communities into ghost towns. You can reach Mingo easily by taking Interstate 70 about ten miles south of Colby. Mingo is immediately off the highway. Watch the signs for the appropriate exit.

VOLTAIRE
Sherman County

The town of Voltaire was founded in 1885 by R. W. Bradshaw, L. M. Harwood, L. H. Cromwell, and S. T. Lloyd, and a post office was opened there on September 10. Ira Garver was postmaster from April 1886 to September 1887 because the post office was housed in his general store, described as a "fine large business house." His stock of groceries, crackers, fruits, glassware, crockery, woodenware, and tobacco was unsurpassed, and his clothing department, which included ready-made suits, dry goods, and a large line of footwear, was outstanding. Garver's clerk, O. Campbell, was described as "one of the boys, very popular with the ladies and very much at home behind the counter." Maj. Rufus R. Edwards had "one of the finest grocery stores in the county, his mammoth stock of provisions—groceries, crockery, glassware, etc. makes an attraction for buyers who wish to purchase goods at a low price."[1]

Voltaire reached its peak in the summer of 1886 when it had a population of 143 and forty-five buildings and houses, all completed only a year after the townsite plat had been filed.[2] But the town of Eustis defeated Voltaire for the privilege of being the temporary county seat in the fall of that year. Inasmuch as Voltaire was established on government land, the government required that a certain number of individuals reside there and that general improvements to their properties be made before the land could be turned over officially to the townsite.

During 1886, there were enough people in the area to support a town, but they did not wish to remain there during the winter, so the promoters hired a man and his family to stay in Voltaire to hold the town until the next spring when the rush of settlers could improve the townsite and make it a trading point. After these arrangements were made, the townspeople went to Atwood where they could spend the winter in civilized comfort.[3]

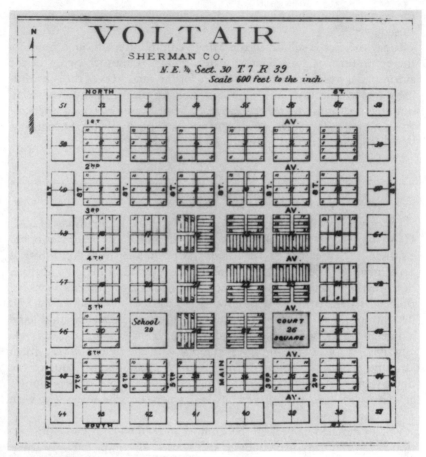

A plat of "Voltair" as it appeared early in 1886. That summer the town was at its peak. When it lost the county seat contest in the fall, the town began a rapid decline that was never reversed.

They proved wise to do so, for that winter there occurred an event that affected all of Kansas, and many pioneers related everything as either before or after this incident: the Great Blizzard of 1886. For the early settlers in Sherman County, the blizzard was a deadly one. O. P. Byers remembered what it was like around the town of Voltaire:

Fred Boyd, aged about 23, who came there from Saginaw, Michigan, and Jacob Koeningheim, aged 22, formerly from Lancaster, Ohio, left

Gandy Wednesday afternoon, the 6th [Jan. 1886] in a one-horse sled to go to Voltaire, a distance of 6 miles. Returning in the evening, they were overtaken by the storm. They stopped at the house of Mrs. Douglas not far from Gandy, and were urged to turn the horse loose and stay, as it was not safe to proceed. This they refused to do, and, having obtained a lantern, set out for Gandy. They soon lost their way, however, and went adrift with the storm. The horse has been found, some distance from the road, in a creek, where he had broken through the ice and froze to death, standing with the harness and the lines stretched behind as if the driver had dropped them sometime before. Koeningheim, who owned the horse, has not been found. Boyd drifted with the storm almost due south about 12 miles, when he succumbed, and was found yesterday, lying on his back with his hands and feet thrown up. His features are so deformed and swollen that he could not be recognized, but papers on his person told who he was. . . .

Three men left Voltaire the day before New Years to go to Colby and have not returned or been heard from. . . . They are Bert Hendricks, Monte Brashier, and John Vandeveer.[4]

Perhaps partially because of the storm, perhaps not, Voltaire began to decline. By 1889 the post office had been discontinued, and the town was vacated by the legislature. Eustis, Voltaire's biggest rival, lost to Goodland in the final county seat vote, and it, too, became a ghost town.

Today the townsite of Voltaire is only an empty field about five miles north of Goodland.[5] Voltaire can be reached by taking state Highway 27 north from Goodland.

8

WEST CENTRAL KANSAS

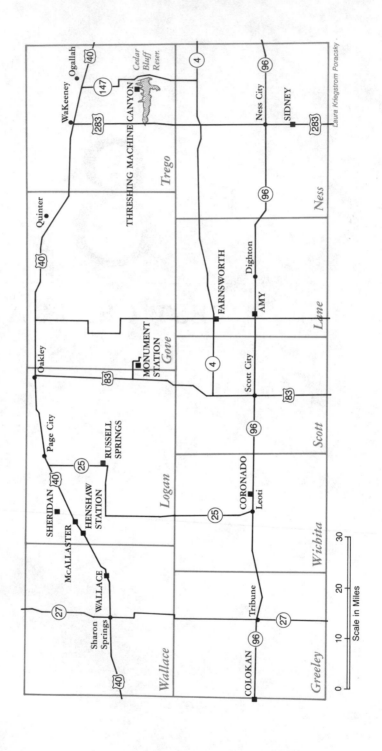

Scale in Miles

0   10   20   30

THRESHING MACHINE CANYON/BLUFTON
Trego County

The history of the Blufton stage station has been overshadowed by an incident that took place near there in 1867, which gave the surrounding canyon its unusual name, but in 1844 John C. Frémont first blazed a trail down the Smoky Hill valley through what later became known as Threshing Machine Canyon. In 1865 a more direct route was found that ran from Fossil Creek Station west for fifty miles until it reached the Smoky Hill River.[1] After Fossil Creek, the stage stations through this area were Forsythe's Creek, Big Creek, Louisa Springs, Blufton, Castle Rock, Grannell Springs, and Chalk Bluffs. In 1867 Forsythe's Creek was abandoned in favor of Fort Fletcher (later Fort Hays), and Blufton was abandoned without a replacement.

The Blufton stage stop then became a campground for emigrants heading west. In 1867 one traveler gave this description of Blufton and the nearby canyon: "A picturesquely located station. What strange convulsion caused this strange crag-like mass? It rises from the plains like a vast castle, fashioned by the most ancient architects."[2]

Many inscriptions on the bluff and canyon walls date from the 1850s, alluding to another stage stop there in 1859, when Butterfield ran a stage line to the Colorado gold fields. Some of the names found were C. N. B. Boston, 1859; O. Kelly, 1859; J. G. Carnahan, 1859; and W. W. Spencer, 1859.[3] The bluff itself once was seventy-five feet high and had more writing on it than any other formation of similar size in the West. Many of the names were actually cut across or over others in a jumbled manner. Immense sections of the cliff broke off and tumbled down, and even these were covered with writings. The earliest name found was that of T. R. Hunt of New Jersey, dated 1849, probably a member of a government surveying party. Many of the names that dated from 1865 were carved there by members of the 3d Wisconsin Cavalry who were assigned to protect a member of the Topographical Corps sent by the government to survey the route. At least one of the dates found, however, was a little more than suspicious. When Elihu Allman of Garden City visited the canyon in 1948, he found that one "man gave his name and town—some place in Missouri—and the date was 10 B.C."[4]

A tragedy that occurred at Blufton in 1867 gave the canyon its name. A party of freighters transporting a threshing machine bound for Salt Lake City camped in the area, and instead of placing their tents on the open prairie, they camped close under the bluff opposite a deep rocky ravine.

Indians had been watching the freighters for hours, and at the right time they crawled down the gulch without being seen and killed and scalped all of the men. Then, as a parting gesture, the Indians set the threshing machine on fire. For years afterward, people hunting souvenirs in the area picked up metal parts from the threshing machine that had been scattered about the canyon, and some of the gears from the machine are on display at Fort Hays State College.[5]

Long after the Butterfield trail had been abandoned, Threshing Machine Canyon still served as a popular camping place for cattlemen, and during the early 1900s the canyon was considered "a good place for a picnic" by local youths. In 1932 when Howard T. Raynesford and his son Kirk surveyed and mapped the station site, they found that the flat area between two creeks was covered with buffalo grass, and the ditch marks of many tents could still be seen.

During the mid-1930s the dry summer winds blew the dust to a depth of several inches over the grass, and the many weed seeds in the dust grew into a veritable jungle after the rains came. When a flash flood filled some of the deeper places in a nearby creek with rock and debris, the area no longer looked the same, and the bluff itself has changed in appearance over the last century due to wind and surface erosion.[6]

In 1948 the area was threatened by the construction of the Cedar Bluff Reservoir, but today Threshing Machine Canyon is located one mile west of the north end of Cedar Bluff Reservoir, and the normal water level comes up only to the base of the bluff.

SIDNEY
Ness County

Sidney, one of the first towns in Ness County, was located on the south fork of the Walnut River. On August 24, 1877, the *Hays Sentinel* made a reference to the townsite, stating that the "Sidney post office west of here is in full blast." Sidney was officially platted on June 6, 1879, and John R. May was appointed president of the town company.

In 1880 a conflict arose between the towns of Sidney and Ness City as to which one would be the county seat. The town promoters of Sidney offered the settlers a new stone courthouse as an inducement to vote for locating the county seat there; Ness City offered the settlers free lots. According to Gilmore Kinney, a Sidney resident, water was scarce in Ness City—there were only two wells. Therefore, Kinney reported that "I cast

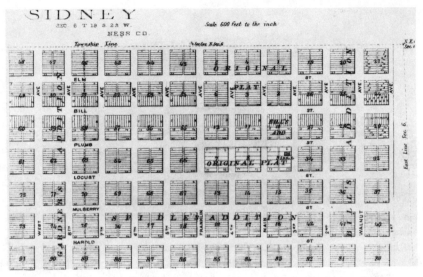

A plat of Sidney in 1886. By this time Sidney's fate was sealed with the loss of the county seat to Ness City. By 1890, most of the town was gone.

my lot with Sidney because I considered it the best location by far, as it had an abundance of good water."[1] But Ness City won the election; apparently the offer of free lots was the more popular option for most of the voters.

In 1882 Robert Findlay still strongly favored Sidney when he compared the two towns in a local newspaper. "Sidney has the best business houses and best improvements and does the best business of any town in the county. Mr. Linville in Sidney carries a store four times as large as Ness City merchants combined. Able and Spile's store house is also located in Sidney and is equal to any in Ness City. There is in Sidney a Masonic and Odd Fellows hall, a large two story building and two large stores and two hotels besides a large schoolhouse."[2]

By the late 1880s, however, the residents in Sidney realized that the county seat controversy was finally over, and most of the houses were sold and moved away. The stone store and Masonic Hall were torn down; only a few stones remain today to mark the spot where they once stood. To reach the vicinity of the Sidney townsite, take U.S. Highway 283 south from Ness City approximately seven miles.

The Boltz Store at Amy circa 1908. C. H. Boltz, the owner, induced customers to shop at his store by building a bandstand nearby and a merry-go-round for the children.

AMY
Lane County

In 1887 when the Atchison, Topeka & Santa Fe Railroad was building across Lane County, switch sidings were placed about every ten miles to hold the work trains while the next section of track was being laid. One particular switch siding, located four and a half miles east of the western boundary of Lane County, was named Ellen after a local resident, Ellen Patterson. In 1905 a farmer named Nolan Yates moved his residence by steam engine to Ellen and established a post office there. Since the name Ellen was similar to names of other Kansas communities, the U.S. Post Office Department requested that Yates change it in order to prevent a mix-up in the mail. Yates sent the government ten names of women in the area, and the name Amy (for resident Amy Bruner) was the one chosen.

In a short time other businessmen were attracted to the community. George and C. H. Boltz bought a tract of land from J. W. Herndon and built a store building and a two-story house on the site. C. H. Boltz was in charge of the general store, and he built a playground to keep the children amused while their parents shopped—one piece of equipment was a merry-go-round propelled by the riders who pumped it up and down like a railroad handcar. Boltz's progressive ideas and promotional schemes soon paid off as customers from all over western Lane County came to Amy to do their weekly trading at his store.

Amy began to resemble a thriving community. The men organized a baseball team and played against teams from other towns in the area. The local musicians put together a thirty-five-piece band which became so popular that Boltz had a bandstand built near his store. In the summertime the townspeople would gather each Saturday for a ball game and a band concert, and many families came to Amy in wagons and buggies from as far as twenty miles away just to hear the band play. Boltz was certainly no greenhorn—he knew that on those particular Saturdays, his store would do land-office business.[1]

Henry Sharp moved his flour mill from Leoti to Amy, and later he opened a grain and coal business near the railroad spur. A blacksmith shop and farm implement store also opened on Main Street.[2] But, unfortunately, despite these new businesses, the community was never very large, and when Nolan Yates sold out in 1911 and moved to Dighton, many of the townspeople followed him. Good roads and better automobiles also led people to trade in the larger towns, but this change took its toll on many of the small towns, including Amy. Amy was built for the days of the horse and buggy, not for the days of mechanized transportation, so the town dwindled in size and population until on May 31, 1954, the post office closed its doors after nearly fifty years of service to the community.

Today a few residences, a church, schoolhouse, grain elevator, and fire station still remain in Amy, but the days of the band concerts and ball games are over.[3] You can reach Amy by taking state Highway 96 west of Dighton approximately eight miles. The town is marked and borders the highway.

FARNSWORTH
Lane County

The town of Farnsworth was named after Ransom K. Farnsworth, an entrepreneur of sorts who liked to speculate in townsite investments. In January 1880 he established and operated a post office, store, restaurant, and hotel in Farnsworth. However, one man alone did not constitute a town, so Farnsworth promoted his settlement by writing a weekly column for a newspaper at Dighton. His colorful descriptions of Farnsworth and the surrounding area were responsible for inducing a number of settlers to choose the community as their home. In August 1881, after the settlement had been officially surveyed and platted, Ransom Farnsworth's town became a reality.

In August 1882 the Smoky Hill Cattle Pool, composed of cattlemen from all over the county, was organized at Farnsworth. Since the cattle pool's territory was twenty-four miles wide and extended thirty miles along the Smoky Hill River, sixty-eight miles of fence had to be built to prevent the cattle from going astray. Each member of the pool had his own brand so that the cattle could be separated when the herd reached the eastern markets.[1] Eventually, the organization grew so large that its headquarters had to be moved to Grainfield in Gove County.[2]

The cattle pool had been in existence for four seasons when the Great Blizzard of 1886 swept through western Kansas and caused whole herds to be wiped out by blinding snow and sub-zero temperatures. When the wind and snow finally abated, dozens of cattlemen were reduced to bankruptcy, and the Smoky Hill Cattle Pool was disbanded.

The blizzard did not wipe out the town of Farnsworth, however. Businesses in 1886 included a hotel, restaurant, lawyer's office, two general stores, a land agent, a drugstore, and the post office. Ransom Farnsworth and the other businessmen thought they had planned carefully for the future of their town, but in 1887 the Missouri Pacific Railroad built its tracks through Lane County and missed Farnsworth by several miles. The town continued to exist for several years, but a number of the townspeople left for other nearby towns, such as Healy and Shields, that were already established on the railroad.

But the citizens had organized a community in the spirit of friendship, and this camaraderie continued. The celebrations held every Fourth of July were times for Farnsworth family reunions, and settlers from Lane and Gove counties came to join in the festivities with the townspeople. Activities included band concerts, ball games, horse races, and a splendid variety of colorful fireworks.

In December 1891 Farnsworth was officially vacated by the state legislature, and although the post office was reestablished for a few years beginning in 1900, the community never regained the momentum it had lost when the railroad chose another route.[3] Farnsworth is north of Amy approximately four miles via a county road that bypasses Amy to the west.

MONUMENT STATION
Gove County

The Smoky Hill Pyramids are located twenty-two miles south and four miles east of Oakley in western Kansas. Only a few of the travelers who come to view them realize that about a mile to the south are deep ruts that mark the old Smoky Hill trail, which so many pioneers traveled on

A sketch of Monument Station drawn by J. Stadler, a member of Company G, 5th Infantry, circa 1865. A portion of the station was apparently underground, and some depressions can still be seen where the station once stood.

their way from Leavenworth to Denver or Salt Lake City. Nor do they suspect that a mile west of where the trail crosses the current road is the site of Monument Station. Actually they could stand on the ground of this old military post and not know that it was once considered a fort.[1]

Monument Station was established in 1865 as a stage station and received its name from the pyramids, which were referred to as "monuments." The first mention of Monument Station was in a letter dated September 12, 1865, from Isaac E. Eaton of the Butterfield Overland Dispatch to Thomas Carney, the mayor of Leavenworth. At that time the Smoky Hill route was used by Eaton's company when transporting freight and passengers from Leavenworth to Denver. Stations were located between nine and twenty-one miles apart along the trail, and every third one was a "home" station where passengers were fed and kept overnight by a local family.

Promoters of the Smoky Hill route claimed that it was better than either the Santa Fe or the Oregon trails because there was a sufficient water supply along its entire course. What they failed to mention was that it cut across the hunting grounds of the Indians and that trouble with them was not an uncommon occurrence.

The first Indian attack on a Butterfield stagecoach occurred near Monument Station on October 2, 1865. The passengers managed to fight the Indians off for a short time, but they finally had to abandon the coach, jump on the horses, and head back east. The Indians drove off the mules at the station, then plundered and burned the coach and the station house. Before the year ended General G. M. Dodge placed troops on the road at Big Creek, Monument Station, and Pond's Creek, and soldiers were at Monument Station at least by November 20, 1865.

On January 14, 1866, Lieutenant Bell and twenty men of the 13th Missouri Cavalry were sent to Fort Fletcher (later Fort Hays) for supplies, and the commander of the post at Monument Station reported that they had rations for only fifteen days. Evidently the necessary supplies never reached Monument Station because the records show that the post was temporarily abandoned. On March 1, 1866, Companies A, E, and I of the 1st U.S. Volunteer Infantry were ordered to march to Monument Station to reestablish the fort.

Root and Connelley, in their "Overland Stage to California," related an incident that was supposed to have taken place at Monument Station. According to their report, Enoch Cummings was a driver of one of forty wagons belonging to Powers & Newman of Leavenworth, and on August 2, 1867, the train was encamped on the Smoky Hill River at Monument Station. Several hundred Indians surprised the caravan about 5:00 in the morning and made a charge from the west just as the sun was rising. Cummings described the early morning rays of the sun striking the Indians' painted bodies and polished shields and guns as one of the most magnificent spectacles he had ever seen. The wagon train was under siege for thirty-two hours, but when the Indians finally withdrew and the travelers counted the casualties and losses on both sides, they found that only one Indian pony had been shot and one mule belonging to the travelers had been run off.[2]

A check of this account revealed that either Cummings was farther from Monument Station than he thought or this entire episode evolved in his imagination at a later date, for the post records show that Company I of the 38th Infantry was stationed there at the time; yet no mention was made of the troops or of the travelers seeking help from them during the siege.

By the spring of 1868 the railroad had reached as far west as Antelope Station, which was later renamed Monument. This town is located thirty-five miles northwest of the original Monument Station, nine miles west of Oakley. Because of a decrease in travel on the Smoky Hill trail and an increase in Indian attacks on the railroad workers, Company I of the 38th Infantry was ordered to abandon the old Monument Station on June 24, 1868, and march to Monument to guard government stores and protect the Union Pacific Railroad. (The troops were only there until August 23, 1868, however, before they were ordered to Fort Wallace.)

Today all that is left of Monument Station are a few scattered rocks that once were part of the foundations of the buildings and a long L-shaped trench that reaches out to the bluff on the river and might easily be mistaken for a wash-out except that both ends are closed. Several holes, some almost covered, still can be seen and denote the position of the dugout of the early post. An occasional rusty tin can and a few square nails may be found near a depression that served as a trash pit. Except for these scanty symbols of the past, the area looks just like any other part of a Gove County ranch.[3]

MCALLASTER
Logan County

It took a strong will and plenty of hard work for the pioneers to carve a living out of the western high plains of Kansas. A classic photograph that best depicts this tenacity is of a pioneer woman and her child standing next to a wheelbarrow full of cow chips they have gathered to use for fuel. Behind the two nothing can be seen but barren bleak prairie fading toward the horizon. This picture was typical of the desolation and loneliness that awaited many settlers when they came to western Kansas. However, for a brief time, at the outset of county development, a number of communities dotted the landscape and broke up the harshness of the prairie. These towns boomed briefly, then they either declined or were abandoned. McAllaster was one of these towns.

The founding of McAllaster was directly related to the arrival of the Union Pacific Railroad in Logan County. On February 12, 1887, B. McAllaster, who was the land agent for the Union Pacific, laid out the village and named it after himself. J. P. Israel appeared in McAllaster soon after it was platted and became the town's staunchest promoter. Although Israel was officially an employee of the Union Pacific, his name appeared in connection with other early townsite developments in western Kansas—most of them

Little remains of McAllaster today except a couple of buildings. This wind-swept stucco structure probably dates back to the days (1880s–1920s) when McAllaster was an important stop on the Union Pacific Railroad. (Photo courtesy of Don Miller.)

failures. He founded a newspaper, the *McAllaster Herald,* in June 1887, and 1,500 copies of the first issue were printed and mailed to prospective land buyers all over the United States in an attempt to lure settlers and investors to the area.

The town company had great expectations for McAllaster that first year because the population of the town increased rapidly. McAllaster was on the main line of the Union Pacific, and plans were formulated with the railroad for a north-south branch with the town at the junction. Streets were laid out from First to Eighth, with perpendicular streets named Grand, Garfield, Sherman, Grant, Logan, and Sheridan.

The town company and Israel spared little expense in promoting McAllaster. A $6,000 hotel was built, and it became the location of the post office—Israel was both the hotel proprietor and the postmaster. During the summer of 1887 a number of general stores, a blacksmith shop, a restaurant, a drugstore, and a livery stable opened for business. Early in

December 1887, the Union Pacific depot was completed and ready for business.

McAllaster prospered for a few years as an active shipping point on the railroad for local farmers and stockmen. But the projected north-south rail connection never materialized, and unfortunately, several other towns, such as Oakley, Page City, Monument, Winona, and Wallace, offered the same advantage of having a railroad. This competition with other towns, and the fact that McAllaster was unable to secure the county seat, cast a shadow on the prosperity of the community.

During the 1890s, J. P. Israel left McAllaster for greener pastures, and the town began to decline, but in 1906 McAllaster was revitalized by the possibility of an oil boom. For a short time the "smell" of oil was so real to the townspeople that they drilled a well in the eastern part of town, but it turned out to be a dry hole. By 1912 the population had dwindled to 50, but the town still had a post office and a few stores. The depression of the 1930s came with its dust storms and drought and dealt the final blow to the economy of the entire area. Many farmers were forced to leave McAllaster, and most of the businesses closed down. The town never recovered.

Today McAllaster is an impressive ghost town along U.S. Highway 40. In the field to the south of the road stands an imposing ruin of what was once a schoolhouse. There are several stores and homes located just off the highway, but for the most part, McAllaster is history.[1] You can reach McAllaster by taking U.S. Highway 40 about thirty miles west from Oakley. The remains of the community are on both sides of the road.

RUSSELL SPRINGS
Logan County

The town of Russell Springs was the county seat of Logan County for over seventy years. In 1865 the site was known as Eaton Station—named for Col. Isaac Eaton, leader of the Smoky Hill trail surveying party. Two years later the station was renamed Russell Springs for the springs found in the area and William Russell, a local cattleman.[1] The site was occupied for only a short time before it was abandoned in 1868, and until 1886 there is no evidence that anyone lived there.[2]

In the fall of 1886 three men—R. H. Morgan, James Armstrong, and J. E. Hilts—founded a community with the hope that it would become the county seat of Logan County. The town was platted by the Pioneer Townsite Company, and its efforts were quite impressive. In March 1887 a Topeka reporter commented:

The town company [is] now putting in a first class system of water works. . . . The company has pledged and will build at once a $5,000 hotel, also a $5,000 schoolhouse which will afford ample school facilities at once. They will also build a $5,000 courthouse. . . . The men [who compose the town company] are live, enterprising businessmen of sound judgement and men that will do all in their power for the good of the place. . . .

Sixty days ago not a house was built in town, today there are thirty houses complete.

The article also noted that there was a bank, a restaurant and boardinghouse, and one newspaper, the *Logan County Record*.[3]

In 1887 there were four principal candidates involved in the county seat contest—Oakley, Logansport, Winona, and Russell Springs—but Winona and Oakley withdrew from the race. Logansport promised the voters a big hotel, and Russell Springs built a $25,000 courthouse and a $10,000 school in order to attract votes. It was rumored that men from Logansport were planning to come to Russell Springs to dynamite the courthouse, so men armed with Winchester rifles guarded the courthouse night and day until the election was over.

By that fall many local men were employed in the construction of the water works system for Russell Springs as well as a reservoir outside the town, which transformed Spring Creek into a seven-acre lake and pleasure resort. The town was booming with an estimated population of 800, although one source placed it as high as 2,000.[4]

The election was held in the fall of 1887, and Russell Springs was the victor with 520 votes, a few more than all the other competitors combined. On the day of the election, Carl Forney, editor of the *Russell Springs Record* (renamed the *Logan County Record*), was offered $1,000 cash for the four lots he owned in town. As he found out later, it was a once-in-a-lifetime offer.[5]

Becoming the Logan County seat did not mean immediate success for Russell Springs; indeed, the town actually began to decline. In 1889 a severe drought caused many of the settlers to leave, and Forney's four lots sold for 10¢ each in the 1890s. More than 100 houses were placed on wheels and hauled to other towns,[6] and only a year after it was completed, the dam, along with the reservoir, on Spring Creek was washed away by a heavy spring rain, and no money was ever collected to rebuild it.[7] In the 1890s three separate fires destroyed the restaurant, a store, and a church. One of the fires also caught the bank and hotel on fire, but fortunately those buildings were saved.[8]

In 1887, Russell Springs had a reservoir that transformed Spring Creek into a seven-acre lake and pleasure resort. In 1888, it was washed out by a heavy rain and never rebuilt. Here is a rare glimpse of the short-lived lake.

In 1911, when the Garden City, Gulf & Northern Railroad was building northward from Garden City, Russell Springs was one of the proposed stopping points, so people began returning to Russell Springs and land values increased. A number of new stores and houses were built, a railroad depot was constructed, and another waterworks project was planned. Unfortunately the railroad was only in business for about six years, and when it ceased operations, troubled times were in store for Russell Springs residents.[9]

In the 1920s there was talk among the commissioners about moving the county seat as the residents of Oakley and Winona, both prosperous communities, had to drive to Russell Springs to conduct county business, and sometimes they had to stay overnight. At first this was not a problem as there was a boardinghouse that could feed and house forty or fifty people.[10] However, when the boardinghouse finally closed down, there was no place for anyone to stay overnight except in the jail. Sometimes when a court case was being tried, the attorneys, plaintiffs, and defendants all slept in the jail for lack of better sleeping quarters, and as time went on the discussions concerning the moving of the county seat to Oakley became more than just talk.

The Logan House Hotel at Russell Springs flanked by townspeople, 1894. For many years, this served as the town's only hotel and boardinghouse. When it finally closed its doors, visitors to town on overnight business had the option of sleeping in jail or out on the prairie.

On March 23, 1937, a bill was introduced in the state legislature to permit Logan County to move its county seat to Oakley upon a favorable vote of 55 percent of the electorate because Russell Springs was not on a main highway and had "no telephone service, no bank, church, waterworks, sewage, or public electricity."[11] Oakley "sweetened the pot" by offering to build a new courthouse free of charge.

But at the election held in November, Oakley still lost to Russell Springs, as it did again in 1945.[12]

By 1960 the population of Russell Springs had fallen to 93, and the town's businesses were down to a service station, grocery, restaurant, post office, and lawyer's office. Oakley had a population of 2,248, which was a sizable percentage of the population of the entire county. Special petitions were circulated by both Oakley and Russell Springs citizens, and it was a case of eastern versus western Logan County, each side charging the other with undue pressure and threats in order to muster support. A special election was held October 18, 1960, and when the vote was counted, Oakley had finally won the privilege of being county seat with 1,441 votes out of 2,398, two more votes than the required 60 percent now needed to move the courthouse.[13]

The election was contested by Russell Springs citizens, who took the case to the Supreme Court where it dragged on for over two years.[14] Finally, on July 11, 1963, the Supreme Court upheld the ruling that the election was legal. On August 13 the official records of Logan County were moved from Russell Springs under guard by five sheriff's deputies, and five months later, the transition was complete when the bonds were voted for a new courthouse at Oakley.[15]

Today Russell Springs is still on the map, but it is not nearly the town it was 100 years ago. The old courthouse is now the home of the Butterfield Trail Historical Museum where visitors learn about the county seat conflict through excellent displays and photographs. Although the bitterness of the controversy has lessened with time, local citizens walking down a hallway in the old courthouse remember how it looked when the town was the county seat.

You can reach Russell Springs by taking U.S. Highway 40 about eighteen miles west from Oakley. Follow the signs and turn south at the junction with state Highway 25; drive twelve miles. Russell Springs borders the road.

SHERIDAN
Logan County

Sheridan was the terminus of the Kansas Pacific Railroad for nearly two years, and during that time over 2,000 people congregated there. The town was host to every bad element on the Kansas plains including gamblers, horse thieves, buffalo hunters, murderers, and prostitutes. Often it was not an exaggeration to say that Sheridan had a "dead man for breakfast every morning."

Harper's Magazine reporter W. F. Webb was on the scene when Sheridan was first established in 1868 and noted the following:

Sheridan is situated on the side of a desolate ravine. The everlasting plain embraced it. Two solitary buttes, named "Hurlbut" and "Lawrence" have been placed on guard over the region by nature and looked as wretched and dismal as sentinels in a penal settlement. A months [*sic*] hammering and the new town was built. Before one street had been surveyed, however, the engineer was called upon to locate a graveyard. This he did upon a ridge overlooking the town. "I'll give you a high lot," was a threat in Sheridan for it meant 6 feet of soil on the hillside. During the first week three of the inhabitants moved into that quarter, all going, as the phrase has it in that country, "with their boots on." During the winter the number increased to 26.[1]

Sheridan was located on a hillside on the east bank of the Smoky Hill River, and was named for General Philip Sheridan, who dined in the first sod house on the townsite.[2] It became an end-of-the-track town on July 25, 1868, and it was also a stage station for a Santa Fe stage line and the Butterfield Overland Dispatch.

After the Kansas Pacific reached the North Smoky Hill, it ran out of funds and was unable to build farther west for several months. Thus, Sheridan had a longer life span and a larger population than other temporary end-of-the-track towns. All freight for Colorado, New Mexico, and Arizona was transported from there to other points in the territory by mule and ox train, and on the return trip, when the ox trains brought wool, hides, and valuable ore from the mines, as many as 1,000 wagons would be camped at Sheridan at one time.

Once the saloons, gambling houses, and dance halls had been built and were flourishing, fights and shootings were common. When the conditions in town became intolerable, a committee composed of the local businessmen was organized for the safety of the citizens, and they notified some of the "characters" by letter to leave town within forty-eight hours. On the night following the issuance of this letter, three of the outlaws were hanged. When Miguel Antonia Otero, the former governor of New Mexico, was a young boy he lived in Sheridan with his father who was the owner of a large warehouse. In a two-volume work, *My Life on the Frontier,* Otero related many of his experiences in the wild and boisterous town of Sheridan and told about the mornings he and other boys would go out to the railroad trestle east of Sheridan to see if they knew any of the ruffians hanged there during the night. Indeed, throughout Sheridan's turbulent history, more than 30 men died by hanging, and nearly 100 died either in Indian raids or in shootouts among themselves. For convenience, the town cemetery was situated just 100 yards north of the Sheridan railroad station.

During 1868 and 1869 Indians were a constant threat to the settlement. The town was located thirteen miles northeast of Fort Wallace, which was the closest fortified stronghold in the area. On one occasion several hundred Cheyenne warriors raided a ranch near Sheridan and were intercepted later in the Arickaree Valley of Colorado by a detachment of soldiers from Fort Wallace commanded by Col. George A. Forsyth. A battle ensued that is known today as the Battle of Beecher's Island.[3]

Sheridan was the subject of several national articles as one of the wildest towns in the West. This sketch, "Attack of Indians on Bull Train near Sheridan, Sept. 10, 1868," appeared in Harper's Weekly Magazine.

The citizens at Sheridan were always anxious about the possibility of an Indian raid, and a report made by De B. Randolph Keim after a stop there in 1868 describes the situation:

> Owing to the dangers of travel on the lines of communication with points farther west, I found myself booked for the night at Sheridan. . . . The prospect was anything but agreeable. . . .
> At the time of my visit, Sheridan was in a state of siege. Several days before, a large war party of savages had appeared up on two buttes near the town and opened fire upon the inhabitants. Everybody rushed to arms, and for the larger part of the day a spirited fusilade [sic] was kept up. The people of the place at once organized a regular corps of defenders, and detachments were on the watch day and night. . . . At night the guard was doubled so as to completely encircle the town.[4]

For two years Sheridan was considered the "black-eye" of Kansas. Journalists came from great distances to report the everyday happenings of the railroad boom town, and some reports were slightly more favorable than others:

> Sheridan is a lively, stirring place. The customs and ways of the town are rather on the free and easy, high-pressure order and there is but little danger of the citizens dying from ennui. Whiskey, tents, gamblers,

roughs, and "soiled doves" are multiplying at an astonishing rate and all things are lively indeed.[5]

The "end of the track" is a gay village with fine wide streets and a general air of thrift. . . . Gayety seems to be the principal occupation of a large majority of the denizens of Phil Sheridan. Most of them dance a good deal. I observed "dance halls" so called where the "light fantastic toe" was considerably exercised. A "dance hall" means various things. It means faro, monte, and whiskey, together with some revolver and a large amount of knife. A man is always safe here in attending strictly to his private concerns. Delicate inquiries into matters which belong to your neighbor are not healthy.[6]

By reports from Sheridan, the present western terminus of the Kansas Pacific Railway, we should charge that the town should at once be placed under martial law for the protection of well disposed people who may wish to tarry at that questionable portion of God's bountiful heritage. Human life is there at a discount. The scum of creation have there congregated and assumed control of municipal and social affairs. Gamblers, pick-pockets, thieves, prostitutes and representatives of every other class of the world's people, who are ranked among the vicious, have taken possession of the town and reign supreme. . . . Government troops should be sent there to protect the innocent and respectable who dwell there. . . . "Let us have peace."[7]

Perhaps the best description of the town itself was written by Nathan Meeker, who founded Greeley, Colorado, for the *New York Tribune*, December 11, 1869:

Sheridan is composed of two half streets, some 300 feet apart, the railroad track being in the center. There are large commercial houses engaged in Santa Fe trade having heavy stocks of stable goods. . . .

Besides these houses, there are a few hotels and several buildings belonging to the railroad, and the rest are saloons and gambling establishments, more then 50 in number, all open and apparently doing good business. In almost every one there are women. Fiddles and accordeons [*sic*] are playing, glasses jingling and there are billiard and roulette tables and other gambling devices. The men are able-bodied and strong; few are more than 35; the majority are less than 30 years old; their faces are flushed, their necks red and thick and they speak good English as any people in

View of unidentified buffalo hunters cleaning rifles at their dugout at Sheridan sometime during the 1870s. After Sheridan's decline around 1870, only a handful of people were left in town, and it became a rendezvous point for transients and buffalo hunters.

the United States. But they have a restless, uncertain look and a quickness of movement both strange and suspicious and this more so because they are connected with much that is homelike and familiar.

Plans to build the Kansas Pacific Railroad from Sheridan to Denver were made during the latter part of 1868, and the decision to build to Denver was ratified at the annual meeting of the stockholders on April 5, 1869. On May 12, the final survey of the route from Pond Creek to Big Springs, 133 miles west of Sheridan, was made and construction began. It proceeded at the rate of 2 to 4 miles a week, and after a period of three months, the track reached Kit Carson, Colorado.[8]

Once Kit Carson became the end-of-the-track town, the tents, shacks, and buildings were moved there just as quickly as they had been built in Sheridan. Businesses flocked to the Colorado town, and in May 1870, the railroad moved most of its equipment there. When a local census was taken in Sheridan on July 3, only eighty people were left, and within a short time only the section house, pumping plant, and cemetery remained.

W. E. Webb's impression of Sheridan in 1875 is a fitting epitaph for the short-lived town: "The passengers of the plains today will find at the station of Sheridan, a solitary house, that of the railroad section hands. There

This sketch of a child escaping an angry buffalo at Sheridan appeared in Harper's New
Monthly Magazine, *November 1875. Sheridan never lacked excitement.*

are no streets and no other vestiges of former habitation, except empty
cans and old boots. The position of any former block could not be found
without a new survey. . . . No title deeds of the town property were ever
recorded and an air castle could not have faded out more completely than
has this air town."[9]

Today the townsite of old Sheridan is a pasture, and only a few depressions mark the location of some dugouts. If anything is left, it is the
memory of a wild town on the high plains of Kansas. Sheridan, now private
property, is north and east of McAllaster and north of U.S. Highway 40.
Inquire with local residents regarding access.

WALLACE
Wallace County

The town of Wallace was founded in 1865 shortly after the establishment
of Fort Wallace, a military outpost maintained by the War Department
to protect the settlers from Indians.

In the 1870s Wallace was a thriving city of 1,800 people and a division

The Peter Robidoux store at Wallace claimed to be the largest store between Kansas City and Denver. This is a view of the store during Wallace's heyday in the 1880s.

point on the Kansas Pacific Railroad, which maintained a roundhouse, an office building, a station, and a hotel there. Wallace was a place where two large general merchandise stores supplied everything to the settlers within a radius of 100 miles, a place where Indians hid in the shadows on the outskirts of town, and a place where a quiet moment was hard to find.

The history of the "Harvey Girls," waitresses in railroad eating houses along the Kansas Pacific Railroad, began at Wallace when Fred Harvey drifted into town and opened a hotel and restaurant for the railroad. Cowboys, soldiers, railroaders, and businessmen were catered to by the Harvey Girls at the Wallace Hotel, which was said to offer the best accommodations and food in western Kansas.

The history of the town parallels the lives of two influential men—Peter Robidoux and Thomas Madigan—who were the "master builders" of a merchandising empire in Wallace that grew along with the railroad.[1]

When the Kansas Pacific was building westward across Kansas, Peter Robidoux was a boy of sixteen who drove mules with one of the construction gangs. He was from Canada and a member of the prominent Robidoux family that founded St. Joseph, Missouri. In the same construction gang was Tom Madigan, an Irishman who sold whiskey and beer to the railroad graders at 25¢ a drink. Robidoux watched Madigan and the money he was making, and he decided to go into the same business. He sold whiskey from an old army tent in Wallace until he had enough money to buy lumber and put up a small building opposite the one that had already been built by Madigan. From that time on, the two men were friendly rivals in business at Wallace.

The Thomas Madigan General Store at Wallace, circa 1880. During the boom years of Wallace, Madigan was a tough competitor to Robidoux. It was, however, a healthy fight. Both men won—and lost—several fortunes.

Within a few months of being established, Wallace was a typical frontier town with dancing and gambling halls, cowboys and bad men. Robidoux used an empty beer keg for a safe in his first saloon, and money was so plentiful that his usual income for one day was a keg full of silver.[2]

Madigan had become accustomed to the wild frontier life. One night Buffalo Joe, a black, was drunk, and he came into Madigan's store in a belligerent mood. He drew his gun and shot at Madigan; the bullet grazed the shopkeeper's arm and became imbedded in the wall. Madigan tried to sober Joe up, but he only drank more and ended up killing Buffalo Jones, another black man. On the night before Christmas when the temperature was 10 below zero, friends of Jones marched Joe to the edge of town where they hanged him from a tree. He was wearing a heavy overcoat with a fur collar, which the hangmen neglected to turn down when they adjusted the noose around his neck, and the next morning when Buffalo Joe was cut down, it was discovered that he had not been strangled but had frozen to death. In a jovial mood, the hangmen took down the stiff body and carried it to the railroad station and stood it upright, a startling sight for the passengers on an early morning train passing through Wallace.

Madigan and Robidoux vied with each other for favorable locations for their general stores. The railroad company gave Madigan a location close to the roundhouse, and Robidoux secured one near the depot. Business for each thrived.[3] Madigan added groceries to his stock; Robidoux added groceries and general merchandise. Both built newer and bigger stores two or three times in competition with each other. Among some of the goods they handled were handmade boots from France that sold for $20 a pair and Stetson hats for $10 each, which could have been bought much cheaper in Kansas City or Leavenworth. Both men became wealthy.

During the boom years at Wallace fourteen men were killed at different times in brawls and gunfights, and all of them were buried in one place at the edge of town. Around the turn of the century, the townspeople hired J. H. Barrett to dig up the fourteen bodies and move them to a graveyard at Fort Wallace. Barrett claimed that when he dug down to the bodies, he found a pair of high-heeled cowboy boots in each grave, and one of the bodies was wrapped in the remnants of a buffalo coat.

In the 1880s Wallace became known as the Metropolis of Western Kansas and was the central freighting point for the entire area. As many as 150 freighters, with their wagons and teams, often camped there at one time. For a few years the teams hauled goods from Wallace to points as far as 100 miles away, but the extension of the Kansas Pacific westward and the building of the Santa Fe, Missouri Pacific, Rock Island, and Burlington railroads ruined the freight business.[4]

Thomas Madigan homesteaded a claim near Wallace and went out of the merchandising business to become a rancher. After he filed a tree claim the government required that he plant 10,000 young trees on it. Half of those trees still survive even though a severe hail storm in 1896 almost destroyed them. The range was open so Madigan fenced thirty-six sections on which to run his cattle. Not to be outdone, Robidoux, also a landowner, fenced fifty sections, running his cattle on lush pastures studded with ponds and creeks. At its peak, Robidoux's empire ranged over 32,000 acres. Unfortunately, the Great Blizzard of 1886 nearly ruined him when his stock drifted more than fifty miles with the storm, reaching the right-of-way of the Santa Fe Railroad where they piled up and perished along the snow fence. Men sent to skin the dead stock recalled that they could have walked from Garden City to the Colorado line on the bodies of dead animals bearing the Robidoux brand—the loss was estimated at 4,000 head.[5]

In the 1890s business in Wallace was no longer booming. First the government abandoned Fort Wallace and moved the soldiers away, then the railroad moved its division point and shops to Sharon Springs, twelve miles west of Wallace, which meant that the town was now just a whistle-stop. After several extremely dry years the settlers in the area could not grow wheat, so they abandoned their claims and moved back East and the town dwindled even further.

The Robidoux General Store abandoned and falling into disrepair, circa 1910. One day no one came into Robidoux's store. Disgusted, he closed it down, leaving several thousand dollars worth of goods to rot on the shelves.

For twelve years the doors had never been locked on Robidoux's store and saloon. His store building, typical of the frontier days, boasted the legend "P. Robidoux, Dealer in Everything," and he sold it all, from wagons to tablecloths to prunes. During its peak years, the store was the largest establishment between Kansas City and Denver. Despite their business rivalry Robidoux and Madigan met in friendship when Robidoux's daughter Aline married Madigan's son Frank. This celebration was the last of their happy times in Wallace,[6] as business declined along with the town, and whatever business was left went to Madigan, who had reopened his store and lowered prices. One day Robidoux sat from morning until night in his store and not one customer came by. He realized that he must either lower his prices or close up, so with bitterness in his heart against the fate that had befallen his once prosperous business, he decided to close the store. The next morning he boarded up the windows, locked the doors, and he and his family moved out to his ranch.

Once he had closed his store, Peter Robidoux never opened it again, nor would he permit anyone else to enter. He was so filled with disgust at the town and the loss of business that he declared his store would remain closed until his death. The merchandise he left in the establishment was estimated to be worth at least $20,000. A newspaper account of the store, written around 1915, stated:

Peering through the cracks in the boards covering the windows one can see the shelves filled with goods, showcases full of expensive cutlery, kegs of tenpenny cut nails that have been out of fashion for years, piles of clothing upon long counters, harness, boots, and cowboy outfits hanging from the ceiling, and buggies, rows of barrels, tiers of boxes and hundreds of tin cans.

Moths, mice, rust and decay, unchecked for 18 years, have done their work. . . . Through the window cracks one can see wheat flour spreading out over the floor from the rotted sacks; the men's clothing is a pile of lint that eighteen generations of moths have rested in. The seams in the harness, gloves and saddles have sprung apart, the handsaws are red with rust, the labels on the rows of canned goods are falling off. A musty smell comes out of the closed store. Peter Robidoux has never been in it since he closed it 18 years ago.[7]

By 1915 there were only twenty houses left in Wallace. Nearly all the buildings in town had been moved either to ranches, Kit Carson, Colorado, or Cheyenne Wells, fifty miles away. George Bowers, a homesteader the year Wallace was established, was one of the few pioneers left in the area. From the door of his dugout he had seen the town grow and then die a slow death.

By the 1920s the beautiful Harvey House and hotel were gone. Madigan's saloon building was moved two miles west of Wallace where it became a country school. Robidoux, however, was destined to leave his mark on thousands of acres of short-grass country, some of which is still referred to as part of the Robidoux Empire.[8] Thomas Madigan also left his impression on the countryside in the form of trees that survive today. In certain respects, therefore, the legacies of Madigan and Robidoux continue. Wallace is accessible by taking U.S. Highway 40 east from Sharon Springs approximately nine miles. The townsite is immediately north of the highway.

HENSHAW STATION
Logan County

Henshaw Station, a military post founded shortly after the Civil War, was located about nine miles east of Fort Wallace on Turkey Creek, not the best place for a small command post because of the frequent Indian attacks in the area. The first recorded attack there was on June 5, 1867, when the Indians killed four men and stampeded the horses. At the time the station was guarded by only ten soldiers and two stock traders, so pursuit of the Indians was out of the question. By the time a force arrived from Fort Wallace, the Indians had dispersed.[1]

There was more trouble in 1868. On May 8 twelve Indians attacked a Union Pacific train near Henshaw Station. They stretched wire across the tracks to stop the engine, burned three cars, and pulled down the telegraph poles. On May 26, the Cheyennes attacked the contractor camp of Giddings and Kessee, shot Herbert Bray, and stole eleven mules. On the same day at Henshaw Station, one man was killed during a surprise attack, and D. P. Powers, who supplied the station with hay, had sixteen mules stolen. Several settlers in the area reported that a band of Indians had been seen only four miles west of Big Timbers, another camp near Henshaw Station, but those Indians withdrew without attacking.[2] Because Indian attacks were so frequent, Henshaw Station finally had to be abandoned in 1869, but the ruins of the station existed long after the soldiers had gone. In the 1880s a buffalo hunter reported the following in his journal:

> We camped in the old building which had been used by the stocktender in the early days. This house was dug into the bank on the east side of the creek and walled up with rock, but there was no cover over it. We afterwards covered it with canvas and made it our home all winter. This was on a creek called Turkey Creek and put into the Smoky Hill River from the north side. There was a little valley right in front of the door on the west side of the house about a mile wide.[3]

Nothing remains at the Henshaw Station site. However, a similar station—known as Pond Creek Stage Station—is part of a local historical museum at Wallace.[4]

CORONADO
Wichita County

In October 1885 the town of Coronado was incorporated with John W. Knapp as president of the town company, and W. D. Brainerd as secretary. The first building, the Hotel Vendome, was completed in February 1886, and by March 1887, there were over 100 stores and residences in the town. Coronado grew so rapidly that it became a business rival of the nearby settlement of Leoti, and the two towns became fierce competitors for the county seat of Wichita County. Both towns had progressive newspapers, whose editors rarely missed a chance to promote their respective towns or to condemn the opposition, and during 1886 and 1887, the editors indulged in some of the most invective journalism ever printed in Kansas. Each accused the other of lies, forgery, trickery, fraud, intimidation, and finally murder.[1]

The trouble began in the spring of 1886 when the townspeople of Leoti sent a representative to Topeka with a charter for the organization of the county. Before approving the charter, Gov. John A. Martin appointed W. D. Brainerd of Coronado to take an official census of the county. Both Leoti and Coronado officials asked that another agent be sent with him in order to protect their respective interests, but Governor Martin refused their requests. The Coronado newspaper remarked, "As a public official Mr. Brainerd intends to do his work impartially, but as a citizen of Coronado he is for his town first, last and all the time."[2]

On November 8, 1886, a delegation from Leoti, headed by C. W. Garland, arrived in Topeka to meet with Brainerd, charging him with delaying the organization of the county until Coronado citizens could get enough voters on their charter to make Coronado the county seat. On November 12 Brainerd reported to the governor a total population of 1,095 householders in the county, 817 voters, and $510,572 in taxable property.

During the last week of November 1886, Governor Martin agreed to appoint an impartial commissioner, T. B. Gerow, to canvass the county for votes for the county seat; the town with the most votes was to have two county commissioners and the title of temporary county seat. Gerow, accompanied by men from both Leoti and Coronado, began canvassing the county on December 7, and on December 22 he completed his poll: 451 votes for Leoti and 285 for Coronado. The *Coronado Herald* of December 23, 1886, wrote: "No doubt Leoti has a majority of the votes polled. Four townships north and northeast were intimidated from voting by the presence of 72 teams loaded with rifles, shotguns and imported bulldozers [hired guns] from Wallace, Greeley, and Hamilton counties, 242 [bulldozers] in number put there by Leoti agents." The *Leoti Standard* retaliated by charging that Coronado men had said they would win if it cost them $50 per vote, and that they had employed a U.S. marshal, without authority, to guard the polls. The *Standard* also claimed that the polls at Coronado had been guarded by 300 armed men stationed in stairways and second-story windows.[3]

On December 24, Wichita County was officially organized by a governor's proclamation. Leoti was named as temporary county seat, but an election was scheduled for February 8, 1887, to decide whether Coronado or Leoti would become the permanent one. Nearly all of Leoti voted at this election, but over 400 Coronado citizens refused to vote, claiming that the election was illegal and should be postponed until March 10. The Leoti townspeople claimed that postponing the election would be unconstitutional and that Leoti had been legally chosen as the county seat.

The climax of the controversy came on February 27, 1887. According to a report made by Commissioner Frank Jenness, Sheriff John Edwards, and Commissioner S. E. Gandy, a messenger from Coronado invited Charles Coulter and other Leoti residents over for a "good time."

About 1 P.M. Mr. Coulter, Frank Jenness, William Raines, Albert Boorey, George Watkins, A. Johnson, and Emmet Deming went over to Coronado in one rig. They met a few of the boys at the drug store of Dr. Wright, and after a half hour visit got in their wagon to return, when Coronado men began an abusive tirade. Coulter and Williams got out of the wagon, and the fight began. Several volleys of shots were fired into the Leoti boys, killing Charles Coulter and William Raines and mortally wounding George Watkins, who died later. The other four men were sitting in the wagon unarmed, but none of them escaped without four or five severe wounds from large Winchester balls. They all fell out of the wagon at the first volley except Albert Boorey, who with Frank Jenness escaped to Leoti with the runaway team.[4]

The men at Coronado claimed that the group from Leoti announced they had come to "round up" the town and offered free drinks to everyone. They forced a visitor from the East to "dance" to the spatter of bullets and started a fist fight with two Coronado men. Then the Leoti men climbed back into the wagon and started shooting at them, which forced the Coronado men to return the gunfire in self-defense.

No matter which account was correct, Albert Boorey was so filled with bullet holes that his escape from death was considered a miracle. A. Johnson got hit in the head with a bullet that physicians were unable to locate. After he had suffered in agony for weeks, the bullet suddenly dropped into his mouth, and he improved from that time on. Emmet Deming was shot in the leg, and the limb had to be amputated below the thigh. Frank Jenness was badly wounded, and the other three members of the Leoti party were killed.[5]

General A. B. Campbell of the 2d Kansas militia was notified at once of the situation, and he instructed Col. J. H. Ricksecker to ready the Larned and Sterling militia for marching. On February 28, 1887, when Campbell and Ricksecker arrived at Leoti, they found it closely guarded and a large rifle pit dug near the center of town.[6] General Campbell and Sheriff Edwards proceeded on to Coronado in an attempt to bring about justice and some degree of military discipline. The sheriff arrested twenty citizens who were involved in the murders, including the town banker and the president of the town company, who swore they had nothing to do with the shootings. Eventually the prisoners were all released, eight on $3,000 bail and the others for lack of evidence. On December 12, one more Coronado man was arrested and lodged in the Leoti jail, and he was nearly lynched by a mob of angry masked men.

The trials of the nine defendants were held at Great Bend in February 1888. The jury acquitted the man who was nearly lynched, and the other eight were released due to lack of evidence. Not long after these trials, another fight occurred on the streets of Coronado when men from Leoti arrived and started shooting. This time two Leoti men were killed, and five Coronado men were wounded.

Since Leoti had received the most votes in the election of February 8 and the one held on March 10, 1887, the county commissioners declared Leoti the permanent county seat. The newspaper at Coronado bitterly fought this decision, claiming that Coronado had actually won the election because the votes for Leoti included 500 that were illegal and that the small number of votes cast at Coronado was caused by the presence of Leoti's armed ruffians entrenched in rifle pits around the polls. As late as September 1888, Coronado was still fighting to set aside the county seat election held in March of 1887.[7]

The dispute between the two towns finally came to an end when businessmen at Leoti offered free lots to any Coronado citizen who wanted to move to the county seat. This proposition was gratefully accepted, and by 1889 nearly all of the buildings at Coronado had been moved to Leoti. The previous violence was so quickly forgotten that John Knapp, who had been president of the Coronado Town Company, was elected to the Leoti city council the following spring.

The feud between Coronado and Leoti is an extreme example of county seat rivalry in Kansas, whih unfortunately was frequent because the victorious town almost always prospered and the defeated one often became a ghost town. Victory was seldom gained easily or without leaving hard feelings in its wake because too often these conflicts led to bloodshed.

Today the site of Coronado is on private property, and there are no noticeable surface remains. Actually more remnants of the town can be found in Leoti—many of the older structures there were once fine buildings in Coronado.[8] You can reach Coronado by taking state Highway 96 about

The Missouri Pacific depot at Coronado boarded up with no one left to take tickets, 1941.

three miles east of Leoti. The townsite sits immediately north of the highway.

COLOKAN
Greeley County

Colokan, which was so close to the Kansas-Colorado border that its name was derived from both states—COLOrado and KANsas—was one of the last communities established in Greeley County.

In 1886 forty-two Civil War veterans from Murphysboro, Illinois, arrived in the region and founded a soldiers' colony for the purpose of establishing claims in the West. Officials of the colony were R. H. Morgan, president; R. Q. Thompson, vice-president; W. A. Rogers, secretary; and C. J. Childs, treasurer. In the spring of the same year, C. M. Rogers and Dr. J. C. Kilgore from Iowa were looking at land in the area, and they decided to establish a Presbyterian colony near the same site. They returned to Iowa where they packed their household goods, farm implements, and stock on twelve railroad cars, and headed to their new homesteads just south of the soldiers' claims.

In August 1887 the Denver, Memphis, & Atlantic Railroad was constructed through the area between the soldiers' settlement and the Presbyterian colony, and both groups decided that it would be wise to combine the two settlements. In September the Colokan Town Company was formed, and a plat for the town was filed on September 26, 1887, just a half mile from the Colorado state line. Colokan, known as the Star of Western Kansas, was born.

A newspaper, the *Colokan Graphic*, was published and edited by O. Q. McNiel, and the first issue, on November 10, 1887, contained advertisements for Robert Rockwell's new hotel and restaurant with "meals at all hours," S. S. Williamson's real estate and notary public office, and the building partnership of Morgan & Thompson. By spring several more businesses had opened including a feed store, a general store, and a blacksmith shop run by Charles Holmes.

In 1888 competition began between Colokan and Towner, Colorado, just across the state line. Since the two towns were only a mile apart, the trains were not going to stop at both places. Although Colokan had originally been given a siding, it had been removed by the railroad, and the *Graphic* editor was angered: "The D. M. & A. [Railroad] is the greatest fraud we every saw. . . . It refuses to stop at Colokan, haul lumber there, put in a crossing and culvert over the wagon road and it tries to build up Towner."[1]

An effort was made by the citizens of Colokan to relocate the Towner depot. One report noted that some men from Colokan went to Towner one dark night and stole the depot, but they were embarrassed the next morning when it was discovered that they had taken the wrong building. The railroad proposed that Towner and Colokan be combined, but this recommendation was not acceptable to either town. In March 1888, when the Colokan residents seemed to be losing the battle, the railroad began stopping there again; however, by mid-summer the trains had discontinued their stops, and the situation was at an impasse once more.

Some of the settlers, tired of the long-running dispute, moved to the state line to start a new community, but others opposed the state line compromise because of the obvious problems such a community would encounter when dealing with two sets of state laws. The situation was described in the *Graphic*: "Colokan . . . we . . . found making faces at its neighbor and rival Towner. . . . They are engaged in a friendly contest just now trying to see which can strike blue shale first. . . . Like man and wife the two are one, but the question is which one."[2] Evidently Towner struck "blue shale" first, for that town is still on the map.

Colokan eventually lost the railroad, and by 1889 only three businesses were left in town: a notary public, a lawyer, and a blacksmith. The post office remained open until December 5, 1892, when it was discontinued.[3]

In 1897 Colokan was officially vacated by the legislature,[4] and Towner, Colorado, became the dominant community in the region.

To visit the Colokan townsite, take state Highway 96 east from Tribune approximately sixteen miles. The townsite was virtually on the Colorado-Kansas line next to the Missouri Pacific Railroad tracks. Little remains to mark the site today.

9

SOUTHWEST KANSAS

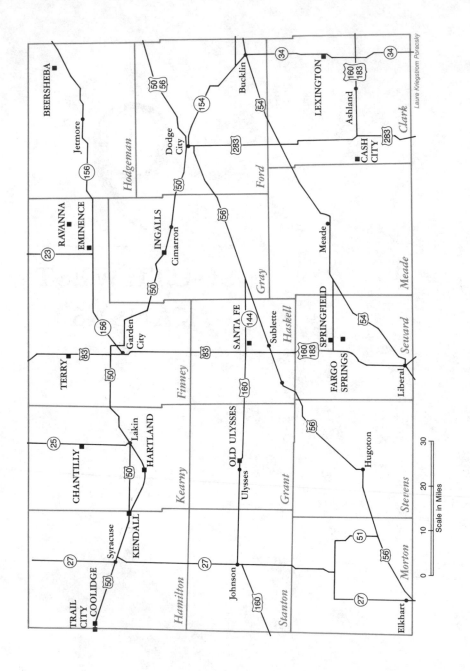

BEERSHEBA

Jetmore

50
56

154

Bucklin

34

LEXINGTON

160
183

34

Ashland

Hodgeman

Dodge
City

54

283

Clark

156

283

CASH
CITY

50

Ford

23

RAVANNA
EMINENCE

INGALLS

56

Meade

Meade

50

Cimarron

Gray

SPRINGFIELD

156

Garden
City

SANTA FE

144

Sublette

Haskell

54

Seward

83

TERRY

83

160
183

50

Finney

160

FARGO
SPRINGS

Liberal

Lakin

OLD ULYSSES

56

25

CHANTILLY

50

HARTLAND

Kearny

Ulysses

Grant

Hugoton

Stevens

Syracuse

KENDALL

51

30

27

COOLIDGE

50

27

Johnson

Stanton

56

20

TRAIL
CITY

Hamilton

160

27

Elkhart

Morton

10

Scale in Miles

0

LEXINGTON
Clark County

Lexington originated in the minds of nine men who formed the Aurora Town Company on November 2, 1885. Since there already was a town in Kansas called Aurora, the group chose the name Lexington, after Lexington, Kentucky.

By the spring of 1886 two newspapers, the *County Beacon* and the *Lexington Leader*, were advertising the community, and the editors told prospective settlers that all the necessities of life were easily available in Lexington. According to the local press, water could be found anywhere at 4 to 40 feet, coal had been discovered only three miles away, and a railroad was proposed that "cannot miss us."[1] Actually coal was discovered three miles west of town, and the first shaft was sunk by C. C. Jaens in December 1886.

During 1886 business was booming in Lexington, and lots were selling for $150 to $200 each. By the year's end, nearly forty buildings had been completed, including twenty-one residences and eighteen businesses. The business directory advertised a wide variety of services, such as a post office, butcher shops, drugstores, a hardware shop, blacksmith shops, a hotel, livery stables, restaurants, feed stores, general stores, a doctor, real estate agents, loan and insurance agents, carpenters, a justice of the peace, a constable, stone masons, and a grist mill.

The key to Lexington's prosperity was the proposed railroad, the Southern Kansas & Panhandle, which was building west from Wichita and was expected to build first to Coldwater and then to Ashland by way of Lexington. The *Ashland Journal* noted on April 22, 1887, that the plans had been finalized and the tracks were being laid through Clark County. Rousing speeches were made by both the businessmen and the railroad officials in Lexington and Ashland in order to sell railroad bonds, but even though enough bonds were sold, the Southern Kansas & Panhandle decided to alter the route. As a result, Lexington was left without a railroad, and the town's boom turned to bust. In late 1887 many businesses moved away, abandoning the town in favor of Ashland and other nearby communities.

The last time Lexington made the headlines was in 1891 when a Lexington family was the victim of arson and robbery. According to the *Ashland Journal* of February 27, Mrs. M. J. Borman was arrested for burning down the residence of the L. G. Pike family and stealing grain from their barn. An investigation further revealed that Mrs. Pike had had some prized quilts,

The Henry Rogers home in Lexington circa 1900. By this time, only seven buildings re-mained to mark the townsite. All the rest had been moved elsewhere.

which she had brought with her from North Carolina, and since no rem-nants of these quilts were found after the fire, it was assumed that Mrs. Borman, who had openly admired them, had stolen the quilts and burned the house to cover the theft. While Mrs. Borman was in the Clark County jail facing charges of larceny and arson, an inquest was held into the mysterious death of her husband because it was rumored that he had been poisoned. Even though she was charged with that crime but not convicted, Mrs. Borman would never walk the streets of Lexington again.

By 1896 only seven buildings were left on the townsite—six stores and a residence. When these buildings became unoccupied, they were either moved to local farms or the lumber was used in the construction of other buildings. By 1900 most of the lots in Lexington had reverted back to the county, and four years later the town was a true ghost town.[2] You can reach the Lexington site by taking U.S. Highway 160/183 east from Ashland to the junction with state Highway 34. Go north on 34 until you reach a second four-way intersection. Turn right at the intersection and drive about two miles to the townsite.

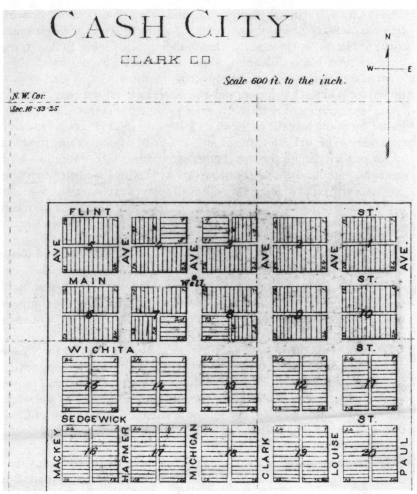

A plat of Cash City during its heyday, 1886. In spite of its promising name, the town rapidly declined, and within nine years it was a ghost town.

CASH CITY
Clark County

Cash City was founded by—and named after—Cash Henderson, who purchased a section of land in Clark County in 1885, had it surveyed and laid out into thirty square blocks, and built a large hotel, the first business in town.

Cash City's growth was phenomenal, and in less than a year the population was over 500. Besides the hotel, there was the large mercantile establishment of Harmer & Grimes, the Otto Building, the *Cashier* Building, the lumberyard, a blacksmith shop, a shoe shop, and a livery stable.[1]

An advertisement on October 29, 1886, in the *Cash City Cashier* promoted town lots at low figures and offered free lots for sixty days to those going into business, and the November 19 issue noted that within a year Cash City would have the choice of no fewer than three railroads. However, the reality of life in Cash City without a railroad was something the local editor pondered in his column on that same day in 1886: "We must have railroads, without them what can we do? At present the farmer draws his products fifty miles to market, endures all sorts of exposure, sleeps under his wagon, fries his own bacon, makes his own coffee, and eats his meals in the snow and rain. Does he want the railroad at his door? Most assuredly he wants railroads."

In 1887 J. M Mackey found a three-inch vein of coal instead of water while digging a well in the hills surrounding Cash City, and for a few weeks the townspeople held a contest to see who could bring in the largest lump of coal. A number of back-breaking chunks were entered in the competition, but most of the men were farmers who were too busy with their crops to mine coal.

Cotton was another unique local product. The February 4, 1887, issue of the *Ashland Herald* reported: "O. H. Harrison of Cash City presented to the Ashland Herald office on Wednesday, a sample of cotton grown on the farm near Cash City this last season. The cotton is clean and white and the fiber nice and long. If cotton can successfully be grown in Clark County, it will add greatly to the wealth of the county by adding to the variety and diversity of her products."

Neither the cotton nor the coal was all that important to Cash City's citizens, as their hopes for prosperity were centered on the railroad. But when the Chicago, Kansas & Western Railroad built through Clark County, it went through Ashland instead of Cash City. As a result the town declined rapidly. In 1888 the newspaper was suspended, most of the businesses were closed, and many of the residents moved to Ashland. In 1893 Cash City was abandoned; by 1895 the townsite was officially vacated by the legislature.[2]

To visit the site of Cash City, take U.S. Highway 160/183 west from Ashland to the junction with U.S. Highway 283. Go south on 283 approximately one mile to a four-way intersection. Turn west and go about three and one-half miles. This route places you in the area of the townsite.

BEERSHEBA
Hodgeman County

In June 1882 several eastern European Jewish immigrants left Cincinnati, Ohio, and traveled to southwest Kansas where they selected a tract of land twenty-two miles from the railroad at Cimarron for a Jewish agricultural colony. During that summer and fall Rabbi Isaac Wise's newspaper, the *American Israelite* (Cincinnati), printed articles in every issue describing the colony, and appealing for charitable contributions to aid the endeavor.

The first party of colonists, consisting of twenty-four Russian-Jewish families, departed from Cincinnati on July 26, 1882. Their journey to Kansas was followed closely in the *Israelite* as the rabbi's son, Leo Wise, accompanied the emigrants. Rabbi Wise called this group "martyrs" because they had clung to their Jewish religion during the anti-Semitic pogroms in Russia, and the rabbi was confident that "in a very short time they would feel at home. Uncle Sam has a farm for everyone and the land must be carefully selected. The implements and livestock should remain the common property of the colony. . . . These things are loaned to them and they must in the end pay for all they receive."[1]

Another man who departed with the colonists was Charles K. Davis, who was to help them on their journey westward. Davis discovered on the way to Kansas City that the Jewish emigrants were fair game for prejudiced train agents and hotel managers. The Russian Jews were denied first-class rail accommodations even though they had paid for first-class tickets, and in Kansas City, one hotel manager tried to evict them until Davis talked him out of this discriminatory action. Davis became apprehensive, however, when he heard so many discouraging remarks about living in Kansas from the visitors and workers at the hotel.

After spending a week in Kansas City, Davis received a telegram from Rabbi Wise telling him to proceed with the group to join Wise in Larned. They arrived in Larned the next day, and Rabbi Wise explained to Davis why there was so much criticism of western Kansas. He pointed out that since the western counties of Kansas were new and the railroads paid no taxes on their lands, it was to the interest of these counties to keep the emigrants farther east where the counties were organized and taxes are being paid. In addition, he told Davis that the large number of cattle being driven up from Texas grazed on the land and it was no easy job to keep the cattle from destroying the crops.

On August 6, 1882, Davis arrived in Cimarron and saw his first cowboy. He wrote, "Every man, almost, in this section carried his shoot iron as they call it and many of them lay down to sleep the night with these little trinkets on their persons." Davis was shocked to see all the wide-open saloons with their gambling, liquor, and "wild women."[2] After picking up the colony's supplies on August 10, Davis reached the Beersheba site the following day and spent the first afternoon tramping about the area in 110 degree temperatures.

In October 1882 Rabbi Wise noted that houses had been built and wells sunk and that every family had 160 acres of land with a dwelling on it. That fall Joseph Baum was appointed superintendent of the colony, and Rabbi Wise predicted that Beersheba would expand to "500 souls" by the next spring; even the hard winter that followed did not diminish Rabbi Wise's spirit or his hopes.

Religion and education in the colony were not neglected inasmuch as the settlers erected a sod synagogue and by December they had constructed a sod schoolhouse. "An educated American lady" had promised to be the colony's teacher.

In the summer of 1883 H. M. Marks left Cincinnati for Beersheba to conduct a personal inspection of the settlement. His report, published in the July 20 issue of the *Israelite*, stated that "eleven happier and more independent families would be hard to find and I doubt if any reasonable sum of money could induce any of them to leave their land and return to the city. . . . God's poor were on Government land. . . . Jews can become successful farmers."

During the spring of 1884 the settlers needed some ready money so they leased part of their holdings to a livestock syndicate that wanted to increase the length and number of cattle trails. Upon hearing of this action in Cincinnati the committee, with the approval of Superintendent Joseph Baum, ordered that all farm implements and livestock be taken from the settlers and sold to a neighboring community. This action severely crippled the colony as the colonists now had no way to work the land. Their one friend, Charles Davis, investigated the lease of the land to the cattle syndicate and wrote a bitter article in the *Israelite* in which he justified the colonists' action:

The matter was entirely misrepresented. The transaction was legitimate and had the full sanction of the neighbors. This arrangement leaves them as much land as they can possibly cultivate and gives them the means to fence it and replace stock and implements taken from them. . . .

Under this contract made for one year with the privilege of 5, eight families received $200 per year, a living in itself. . . . If there is any indignation, it is against Joseph Baum who induced the Committee to take back the stock, implements, etc., that had been advanced to the colonists.[3]

Unfortunately Davis's article did not change the situation, and the Beersheba colony collapsed. After 1886 there was nothing left since most of the disappointed settlers had returned to Kansas City, St. Louis, or Cincinnati.

This attempt to establish a Jewish agricultural colony at Beersheba was only one of several such endeavors in Kansas. But the Beersheba colonists set in motion new forces in American Jewish life inasmuch as Jews were called upon to help other Jews through community action and concern. This concern was but one redeeming quality of the colony.

INGALLS
Gray County

In 1887 Asa T. Soule, a millionaire promoter from New York, laid out a town in Gray County and named it after Senator John J. Ingalls. Ingalls was more centrally located in the county than the town of Montezuma, and it was only six miles from Cimarron, the nearest business rival.

Soule immediately began a campaign to secure the county seat for Ingalls, and if successful, he planned to spend $100,000 on public improvements in the town. In a "People's Convention" held in September, Soule promised a railroad to the townspeople of Montezuma if they would vote for Ingalls for county seat. In the first election, the citizens of Montezuma voted overwhelmingly for Ingalls, so Soule built a railroad from Dodge City to Montezuma and named it the Dodge City, Montezuma, & Trinidad Railroad. Soule also bought a section of land north of Dodge City and laid it out into lots. On forty acres of this land, Soule built a college and a dormitory that cost $50,000. As an endowment he turned the administration of the college over to the Presbyterian Church, along with an additional gift of $10,000.

The main focus of Soule's attention was the Eureka Irrigation Canal Company. The sources of water supply for the canal were the Arkansas River at Ingalls and Coon Creek at the lower end of the canal, forty-five miles east of Spearville in Ford County. To divert the water into the canal, Soule built a dam out into the river and extended it upstream 2,000 feet. When it was finished, the total length of the canal was an impressive ninety-six miles.

Workmen digging the Eureka Irrigation Canal, circa 1886. An optimistic plan that was perhaps ahead of its day, the canal, which was dug through Ingalls, might have worked had it been able to hold a significant amount of water.

When the irrigation company issued stock in the amount of $1 million, Soule bought it all. He also furnished $250,000 for the construction of the canal and had it bonded for $1 million. After securing enough water contracts to make it look like a good investment, Soule sold the bonds in London at a handsome profit. Unfortunately the irrigation project failed because similar canals upstream were draining too much water from the river. In fact, the only time the canal was full of water was when Soule was concluding the deal in London.

In the fall of 1887 the question of the permanent county seat location was to be settled. The county commissioners, who were in favor of Cimarron, ordered an election for October 31, only eight days before the regular election day, November 8. When the commissioners met to canvass the vote after the election, they were served with an injunction issued by Kansas Supreme Court Judge Jeremiah Strang, who instructed the citizens to vote again on November 8. The October vote had resulted in the election of Cimarron as the county seat; that in November, Ingalls. Judge Strang finally held that the November 8 election was the one that was legal, and the county records were moved to Ingalls on February 21, 1888. Soule had said before the election, "If any man will tell me how to buy the county seat, I will freely pay for it."[1] He had also paid several troublemakers to stand

A view of the Eureka Irrigation Canal full of water at Ingalls circa 1890.

by the polls, and no doubt their presence was felt by the voters.

All was quiet until March 14, 1888, when an alternative writ of man-damus was issued by the Supreme Court ordering the county offices moved back to Cimarron. This action, however, was postponed.

On January 12, 1889, a few of Ingalls's finest citizens, including Bat Masterson, decided to go after some county records that were still being held in Cimarron. The men, armed with Winchesters and six-shooters, slipped into Cimarron at 10:00 in the morning. They rushed into the county building, seized the records, and placed them in a wagon, but by this time the Cimarron men had gathered, and shooting began between the two factions. One Cimarron man, J. W. English, was killed, and two others were seriously wounded. After the fight was over, the raiding party returned to Ingalls with the county records and three slightly wounded men. When he heard of the incident, Gov. John Martin ordered two com-panies of militia to Cimarron to keep the peace.

The county seat controversy had dragged through two years of litiga-tion in the district and supreme courts, but on October 6, 1889, the *Topeka Daily Capital* noted that a decision had been made: "The Supreme Court handed down an opinion yesterday in the famous Gray County seat con-test, between the towns of Cimarron and Ingalls for permanent county seat, which settles the question for a least five years. The case was decided for Ingalls."

But Ingalls remained the county seat for only three years. During 1891

A view of Ingalls circa 1890. In the foreground stands the church and school, with a business building under construction in the background.

the population of Ingalls declined to 120 despite the building of a new county courthouse. Cimarron, on the other hand, was the most prosperous town in the county. The commissioners had no other alternative but to order the county seat moved to Cimarron.

Today Ingalls is still on the map and is increasing in population, although it is only a shadow of its former self.[2] The deep ditch left from the Eureka Irrigation Canal can still be seen, a forgotten legacy to Asa Soule. Soule's college, one of his last surviving philanthropic ventures in southwest Kansas, existed until 1907. You can reach Ingalls by taking U.S. Highway 50 west from Cimarron about six miles. The town is immediately south of the highway.

RAVANNA
Finney County

In 1882 Ravanna was called Bulltown after John Bull, the man who established the town and operated the post office. The name of the town, not all that appealing to the settlers, was changed to Cowland, which pleased the cattlemen, but the merchants thought the name sounded too "dirty." After a great deal of discussion among these groups, the merchants won out and Cowland was changed to Ravanna, a more respectable name.[1]

During Ravanna's formative years, Reverend H. S. Booth, a Methodist minister, arrived from Boston to preach in Ravanna, and since there was

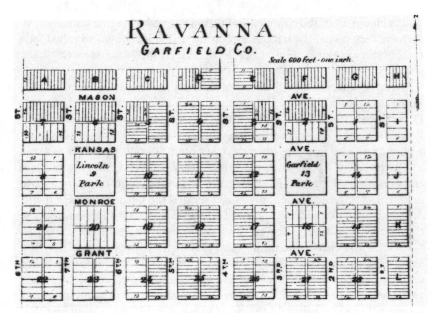

A plat of Ravanna, 1886. The question over which town—Ravanna or Eminence—would be county seat of Garfield County was finally settled when Garfield County was annexed to Finney County, leaving both towns losers.

no church, a billiard hall was chosen as the place of worship. On one occasion, a bunch of drunken cowboys filed in and began creating a disturbance. A man in the congregation, B. L. Stotts, politely asked them to be quiet, but he had hardly sat down when the disturbance started again. Mr. Stotts walked to the front, faced the cowboys, and remarked, "If you fellows want to remain here, you are welcome, but if you stay, you will have to behave like men. The first fellow who makes a disturbance will have to be carried out that door." Then he sat down by the preacher, took out his six-shooter and laid it across his lap. The preacher finished his sermon without interruption.[2]

A county with the name of Garfield was organized in July 1887, and by that time Ravanna was a flourishing trade and recreational center for the ranchers who came to town for supplies and for the cowboys who rode in for whiskey. There were sharply defined lines between the western Garfield County voters, who were led by "Buffalo" Jones and wanted the county seat at Eminence, and the eastern county voters, who were led by John Bull and were in favor of Ravanna. Gov. John Martin named John

Bull as chairman of the county commissioners, and when the commission-ers met, they placed the temporary county seat at Ravanna and called for a county seat election in November. In that election, Ravanna received 467 votes to Eminence's 432.

After the election new businesses opened in town: the Bank of Ra-vanna, the Buffalo Town Company, the Grand Central Hotel, Crow's Department Store, John Bull's store, the Eagle House and Hotel, the *Ravanna Record,* Hoffman's Bakery, a livery barn, a blacksmith shop, and a physician. The Ravanna townspeople voted $10,000 in bonds to build a courthouse of native rock, the same material used in the schoolhouse and in many of the stores and residences.[3] When the courthouse cost $2,000 more than the bonds issued, it was nicknamed the Great White Elephant. All the country records were moved to the Great White Elephant where they were to be housed for all time, or so everyone thought.

Some of the citizens at Eminence started an investigation of the elec-tion, which Ravanna had won by only 35 votes. They discovered that a construction crew had been allowed to vote, using the names of dead men, and that none of these men were residents of Ravanna. According to one account, "In 1887 they held the election to establish the county seat. Ra-vanna got the most votes—but they were not all live ones, as the story goes. In 1892 when I worked for a construction company in Colorado, I met a man who said he was in Ravanna on election day and got paid for every one of the nine times he voted."[4] After an order from the attorney general's office 60 votes were deducted from Ravanna's count, which gave the county seat to Eminence.[5] But the Ravanna commissioners refused to hand over the county records, and the Eminence citizens were furious. There were two versions of what happened next. According to the most widely cir-culated account, the Eminence men split into two groups with the first group marching down the main street into Ravanna and the second group circling around and entering from the back alleys. While the first group was fighting the Ravanna men, the second group entered the courthouse and took the county records. As they left the Great White Elephant, they set it on fire, totally gutting it. The fire broke up the fight but not before a number of men were either killed or injured.[6] The other version of the incident was simpler: One evening at dusk two men in a light rig drawn by fast horses drove quietly into Ravanna, seized the county records, and slipped quickly back to Eminence.[7]

The state adjutant general was sent to Eminence to soothe the people's tempers and to postpone further hostilities until a September session of the court. The final judgment in the matter declared Eminence the county

The expensive Garfield County courthouse at Ravanna. Dubbed the Great White Elephant, the building was destined to hold court over tumbleweeds and prairie dogs, but not before costing the county thousands of dollars.

seat.[8] For Eminence, this was victory, but for Ravanna it meant an unsure future.

In the fall of 1892 the citizens of Ravanna hired a competent surveyor to make another survey of the county, and he presented evidence to the court indicating that the county was shy the required acreage for its legal organization. The county had the lawful number of sections—432—but the survey showed that a number of these sections were short the 640 acres required of all conventional sections. The court upheld the law and declared that Garfield County lacked the required acreage. At the regular meeting of the county commissioners in January 1893, the officers-elect were sworn in, but that spring the state legislature made a present of Garfield County to Finney County.

That action had a devastating effect on both Ravanna and Eminence because neither town was to be the county seat. People began moving away, and when the Kansas Pacific Railroad changed its plans for a line through Ravanna to Dodge City, the merchants boarded up their shops and left town. In 1922 Ravanna lost the post office, the last business in town.

All that was left of Ravanna in 1941 was a main street and some old foundations. Christine Shiwise, a Hoisington widow, filed a deed in the Garden City courthouse for the 795 acres scattered on three sections of land where old Ravanna once stood. She purchased all of Ravanna including the old schoolhouse and the shell of the former courthouse. When the owners prepared the title to transfer to Mrs. Shiwise, they had to notify hundreds of former owners that their lots were being purchased. It was one of the largest law suits ever filed in Finney County. Included in the list of former owners were 14 Smiths and more than 100 John Does, unknown husbands of women claimants. Every letter of the alphabet was represented in the list of 648 names except "U" and "Z." Hundreds of owners had left without trying to sell their lots, so they had title in name only for the years through 1941.[9]

Today there are few people living within the bounds of Garfield Township in Finney County because there are no major towns in the area. In Ravanna itself only a few foundations remain as a reminder of the county seat conflict that left two towns deserted.

To visit Ravanna, take U.S. Highway 156 west from Kalvesta about six miles to the junction with an unmarked county road. Take this road north about seven miles to the junction with an east-west road. Turn east and drive about one mile to the area of the townsite.

EMINENCE
Finney County

Eminence was first known by the post office name of Cuyler, but in 1886 the post office was moved two miles east along the Pawnee River. Relocated on land belonging to "Smith and Quick's" school near the center of Garfield County, it was renamed Creola. Since there was already a town in the state by that name, Lyman Naugle suggested the name Eminence, and that name became official on June 3, 1887.[1]

As Eminence began to prosper, some men from Garden City became

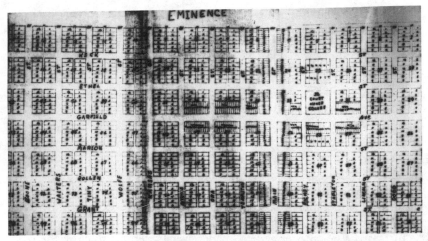

A plat of Eminence as it appeared around 1890. On paper, Eminence resembled a large community; in reality only a few buildings were built on some of the lots illustrated here.

interested in the town and built several large two- and three-story buildings there. Frederick Finnup owned the building that later became the Garfield County courthouse. A newspaper, the *Garfield Call,* was first published on July 1, 1887, and every week thereafter the editor supported Eminence for county seat and belittled the town's rival, the nearby town of Ravanna. At the same time other town promoters in the western part of the county were also working diligently to win votes for Eminence.[2]

In the summer of 1887 Eminence had a population of nearly 300.[3] New businesses included three hotels and three general stores, all of them drawing the biggest share of the local trade. The optimistic townspeople voted city bonds for a sugar factory, but like other similar speculative ventures, the factory never materialized.[4]

Originally Ravanna was designated to be the temporary county seat, but the governor appointed a census taker who was a Ravanna supporter, and after a poll of the county, he recommended that Ravanna be named the permanent county seat. The governor ordered an election held in November 1887, and Ravanna received the most votes for county seat.

This choice was not upheld after an investigation by the court revealed that Ravanna had tried to win the election by stuffing the ballot boxes with names of sixty voters who were deceased. On November 15, 1887, the attorney general ordered the clerk of the district court of Garfield County to move his offices from Ravanna to Eminence, and a year later on

December 11, 1888, Eminence was officially declared the county seat of Garfield County. Ravanna appealed this decision to the state Supreme Court, but on July 5, 1889, the court upheld the decision that the Garfield County seat was Eminence, not Ravanna.[5] The victory celebration at Eminence was short-lived, however, for Ravanna went to the courts again. Some Ravanna citizens had discovered that Garfield County was too small to be a county since it contained less than the 432 square miles required by Kansas statutes. A new survey revealed that it did indeed lack the required area, and soon thereafter Garfield County was annexed to Finney County.[6] (On the current map of Finney County, the large block of land that protrudes to the northeast was once Garfield County.)

In 1893 when the annexation of Garfield County was final, Ravanna and Eminence and other small towns in the area were doomed. By 1910 Eminence had a population of only 92.

In 1933 the postmaster general made several attempts to close the post office at Eminence, which would have removed the town from the map, but a few local politicians with some influence in Washington succeeded in keeping the post office open and saving the town for another ten years.[7] But in 1943 the post office was finally closed, and today little remains to mark the townsite.

You can visit Eminence by taking U.S. Highway 156 west from Kalvesta about fourteen miles to the junction with an unmarked county road. Turn north on the road and drive about five miles. Not much remains of the site, although a rural cemetery is only two more miles to the northwest.

TERRY
Finney County

Terry, originally known as Terryton, was once a stage station located midway between Garden City and Scott City. The town was founded in 1885 by a real estate speculator from New York, Porter D. Terry. At one time four stages went through Terry every day, and one of the stages, named the Cannon Ball, held the record for going from Scott City to Garden City, a distance of thirty-six miles in five hours.

In 1886 businesses were booming in Terry. Young & Jeffrys owned a grocery store, George W. Morse advertised provisions and glassware, Porter Terry operated a real estate office and livestock exchange, and J. M. Dunn had a general store. There was also a comfortable hotel, a drugstore, a livery stable, and a lumberyard. A newspaper, the *Enterprise,* was published by

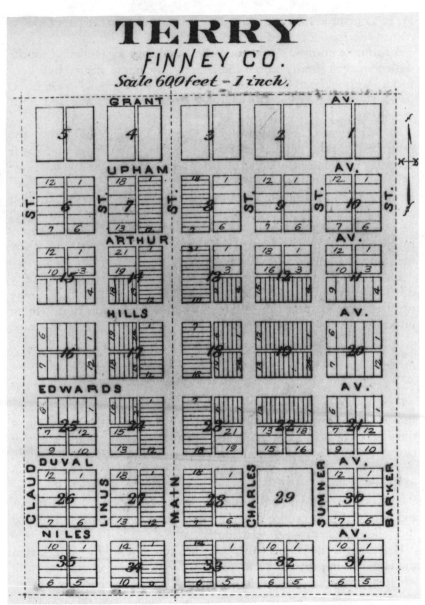

A plat of Terry, 1886. Today few artifacts remain to mark this impressive townsite.

W. E. Coutant in 1886 and 1887; during 1888 and 1889 the paper was re-named the *Eye* and edited by B. L. Stephenson.

A half mile north of Terry stood the Old Kentucky Home where the settlers went to Sunday school and church. The home, named by a Kentuckian who sold it to Porter Terry in the 1890s, was later sold to Dr. L. H. Johnson, an eastern speculator, who bought several sections of land in the vicinity in 1895.[1]

For three years Terry flourished. Then a drought that drove the homesteaders from this area of Kansas also ruined any hopes that Porter Terry had for the town, and the following ad appeared in the *Hatfield News:* "For Sale. A one-horse railroad boom, broken in the middle and without head or tail. It might be repaired to suit emergencies, as its constitution and plan were constructed with that end in view. A quit-claim deed will be given. Will be sold very low, as I wish [to] (or rather people wish me to) give place to a more able man, and hie myself back to Yankeedom where my real estate interests are. Porter D. Terry."[2]

Today a careful search of the area reveals only rocks, bricks, and a few other remnants of the town. You can visit Terry by taking U.S. Highway 83 north from Garden City about twelve miles to the junction with an unmarked county road. Turn west about one mile to reach the townsite.

HARTLAND
Kearny County

Hartland was founded in 1885 and became a destination for homesteaders, the end-of-the-line on the railroad, and the gateway to the beginning of the great cattle drive and feeding area of the Southwest.[1] In the spring of that year the town company bought a section of land at Hartland Station from the Santa Fe Railroad and began platting the town lots. The location of the town was ideal as it was only a mile from the Arkansas River; to the south there was wide open country dotted with cowboys' work camps and homesteaders' dugouts; and to the north the prairie, sometimes termed the "short grass country," seemed endless.

That summer the Hartland Town Company advertised for businesses in the Hutchinson papers and had special pamphlets printed and sent to all adjoining states for distribution. The people began to come in droves: speculators, land seekers, businessmen, and laborers arrived on every train. Since no place in town was large enough to accommodate such numbers, Mrs. McFarland built a big barn and let the people sleep in the stalls and the loft. By the fall of 1885 the town had more than 500 residents.

The Reynolds Stage Line in front of a business building in Hartland, 1887. This stage ran between Hartland and Hugoton for several years.

An offer of a free lot to anyone who would build a hotel was made by the town company. When Mrs. S. E. Madison from Carthage, Missouri, heard about the offer, she accepted and immediately ordered a carload of lumber, hardware, windows, and doors—enough to build a small hotel. With the assistance of her son-in-law, H. H. Cochran, the Madison House hotel was soon ready for business.[2]

In 1886 the town continued to grow rapidly. Kirtland & Flash were the first bankers; H. H. Cochran was the postmaster and express agent; Richard and Gabard were the first physicians; and B. D. Williams and Dr. Gabard operated the dry goods store.[3]

Charles Smith visited Hartland early in 1887 and noted the following:

We found Hartland a thriving little city of perhaps one thousand population. All lines of business seemed to be well represented. There were 3 hotels, 2 newspapers, a bank, 3 hardware stores, 1 wholesale grocery store, feed stores, livery stables, harness shops, barber shops, a millinery store and 5 lumberyards. . . .

Grant and Stevens counties were being settled and new towns were springing up every few days. . . . As Hartland had the only natural pass through the sand hills much of the freighting was done from there. It was a common sight to see 50 or 60 wagon loads of lumber start out of Hartland in the early morning. . . .

A daily stage line from Hartland to Ulysses . . . was a real Western stage drawn by 4 horses, and the driver was just the kind of man you would expect to see in the box if you read Western stories. He boasted that he could drive from Ulysses to Hartland in three hours and 75 minutes. . . . It was a wonderful experience to live in this country at that time.[4]

In January 1887 county lines were changed so that Hartland was switched from Hamilton to Kearny County, a decisive factor for the town as on February 19, Hartland was selected as the first county seat of Kearny County. Although the issue was controversial, the court decided that there would be no more county seat elections for five years.[5] William H. Heirgood later recalled that county seat "fight":

I bought a pre-emption four miles east of Garden City. Lakin, Hartland, and Chantilla which was six miles north of Garden City and now a ghost town, were having some fun at the time and some serious moments as well, about the matter of where the county seat should be. I hired out to a group to help them in this little enterprise, for the excitement and money consideration. . . .

Hartland was determined to get the county records which were then at Lakin. A man, named Pearce, in Chantilla, and his hired gang made things lively for us at times. . . . Always Pearce rode with his men. . . . But our gang didn't care, for we got the county seat records to hold anyway until the next election. . . .

It was thrilling backing up to the courthouse at Lakin, taking the books, galloping away to Hartland and stopping at the Leland Hotel to turn the records over to the future custodians. . . . Our gang consisted of Frank Lence, Warren Pierce, Bill Smith, Bill Jay, and myself. The Lakin group were "I Bar" Johnson, Jack Tully, Jim Murphy, Frank McCallister, Ira Duckworth, and Joe Duckworth. . . . Some men even came from as far as Syracuse, stayed 30 days and voted and finally Hartland got the county seat settled there by the greatest number of votes.[6]

Business was thriving in the 1890s. Joseph Dillon purchased a printing press and hired Ed Watt to edit the first newspaper, the *Hartland Times*. The Kearny House, built just north of the railroad station, was used later as a courthouse. A free bridge was constructed over the Arkansas River by the town company, and hundreds of wagons loaded with supplies were sent over the Bear Creek route to other counties to the south.

Hartland was one of the few western Kansas towns devoid of saloons. A young man named Delemater tried to operate one, but his bar and rooms for gambling were always empty. When Delemater died of typhoid fever, his building was sold and moved to another town.

In 1894 another county seat election was held, and again it was a political contest between Lakin and Hartland. Since Lakin received the most votes, the county seat was moved to Lakin from Hartland. All the county commissioners moved too, and unfortunately most of the townspeople and businessmen followed. The Madison House was moved to Lakin and rebuilt as a residence.[7] Before the election Hartland had 1,500 people; by 1920 it was a ghost town.

Today there is nothing left to indicate the town's existence except for the name L. H. Carter on a mailbox at the farm that was once the homestead of John H. Carter, the first resident in the area in 1878. A lush growth of trees and brush between the fields on the south side of the old river road off U.S. Highway 50 are especially noticeable as the Hartland site is approached. Across an old canal on this road looms an Indian mound, and at its peak is a marker erected in 1936 by the Kearny County Historical Society. The marker designates the site of Chouteau Island just south of the mound and near the Hartland townsite.

Hartland, the "rose of the valley," is gone, but the site is still a picturesque spot, marked by the highest mound between Pawnee Rock and Bent's Fort in Colorado.[8] You can reach Hartland by taking the county road south and west of Lakin that parallels the Arkansas River and the Santa Fe Railroad. Hartland is on a road about six miles from Lakin.

CHANTILLY
Kearny County

Many settlers secured claims in the newly formed counties in the southwestern portion of the state under the Homestead and Timber Acts of 1886. In 1887 Gov. John Martin appointed a census taker, S. S. Prouty, to count the inhabitants of Kearny County and find out their preference for the location of a county seat. Settlers in the northern part of the county decided that Carolina V. Pierce, a ranch owner in the area, should plat a town that they could enter as a county seat contender. The town was to be named Chantilly in memory of the Civil War battle in which Gen. Phillip Kearny, after whom the county was named, was killed.

It was with a great deal of determination and enthusiasm that Mrs. Pierce planned the town and built the first hotel. The other businesses that soon opened were the Schmiezer Brothers and W. F. Hazard general stores; Charles and J. W. Palmer blacksmith shop and livery stable; and the first newspaper, the *Kearny County Coyote,* edited by Lon Whorton.

In the summer of 1887 the town supported a school, several churches, an active literary society, and dances at the hotel. The largest community gathering in Chantilly was the Independence Day celebration that year. Settlers from Lakin and Hartland even drove in the day before and camped overnight in order to enjoy all the festivities.

Securing an adequate water supply became one of Chantilly's biggest problems. As it was necessary to go as deep as 200 feet to find water, most of the settlers had to haul it from the Arkansas River, a task that occupied much of their time and labor. A familiar sight on the prairie was a wagon rolling along with several barrels covered with burlap to keep the water from splashing or evaporating.

In 1887 Chantilly was a contender for the county seat, but Lakin and Hartland were also in contention because the Santa Fe Railroad had built through those settlements. After the election was held and the votes were counted, Hartland became the county seat. Chantilly had lost not only the election but also its chance for survival.

In addition to that disappointment, the late 1880s were extremely dry years, and the general economic conditions became unfavorable at Chantilly. Sod houses and dugouts were abandoned, and buildings were moved away.[1] When the Cherokee Strip was opened for settlement in 1893, more people left the county and never returned. Chantilly became a ghost town, and today nothing remains to indicate the location of the townsite.[2]

COOLIDGE AND KENDALL
Hamilton County

Coolidge was established as a railroad stop on the Atchison, Topeka, & Santa Fe Railroad in 1883. It was named for Thomas Jefferson Coolidge, former president of the Santa Fe. The producers of western movies could use Coolidge in Hamilton County as an example of historical authenticity as it was probably closer to being a typical western town than the celebrated Dodge City. Since Coolidge was located almost on the Colorado border, it was a target for robbers and gunfighters from both states.

On October 3, 1883, a train robbery occurred at Coolidge, and the *Dodge City Times* reported that "a gang of roughs" attempted to rob the westward bound trains, and that the engineer and fireman had been killed before the masked men were driven off.[1] Four suspects were arrested and tried, but they were released for lack of evidence.[2] Coolidge was also a typical wild border town in its early days. The *Dodge City Times*, October 4, 1883, reported that "on Monday a lot of drunken cowboys had another hurrah for Coolidge, shooting through doors, windows, etc., and making things lively generally. Under-sheriff Fred Singer and Jack Bridges arrested one of the leaders and placed him in jail Tuesday morning."[3]

The first newspaper at Coolidge was appropriately called the *Border Ruffian* and was in business until 1900. From 1883 to 1884 Coolidge had a successful merchandising and cattle trade through the firms of Otero & Sellers, and Chick, Brown & Company.[4] In 1886 the town was at the end of the track for a Santa Fe division, and railroad officials claimed that the company's improvements there represented an outlay of $432,000. At that time Coolidge had a population of 800 to 1,000, but within five years those numbers decreased drastically. The "Mighty Hunter" Charles Youngblood noted a few interesting facts about Coolidge in his recollections:

The Peck Water Works Co. furnishes the city and the railroad with the finest quality of water in the state and a fire protection next to none. Its location on the western edge of Kansas is almost identical with that of Kansas City on the eastern and 20 years from now may find it as large a city. . . .

Coolidge is situated on the Main Line of the Santa Fe R. R. which has here its division Round House, Workshop, and Eating House and pays out monthly about $8,000.[5]

Kendall was first platted in 1885 by the Arkansas Valley Town and Land Company. A building boom hit the town almost overnight. In February 1886, there were only 10 houses on the townsite; by May, this number had risen to 200.

Three towns were competing for the county seat of Hamilton County from December 1885 to November 1888: Coolidge, Kendall, and Syracuse. In an election in April 1886, Coolidge had Kendall's votes, but Syracuse still won. The other two towns then filed a petition on May 25, 1886, through their attorney B. F. Simpson of Topeka, asking the court to oust the alleged county officers at Syracuse. The court issued an order summoning the officers to appear in court June 24 and to show by what right they held office. The petition set forth the following: that the judges and clerks of the election board in Syracuse Township had refused to tell the number of votes polled there, which had delayed the count; that before the election, it had been the plan of the county commissioners to declare

The Kendall Hotel as it appeared around 1890.

in favor of Syracuse regardless of the actual results; and that the commissioners had delayed their counting of the votes until the Coolidge and Kendall votes were returned, then they had placed over 800 ballots in the box in favor of the Syracuse candidates and for Syracuse as county seat, enough to win over the competing towns of Coolidge and Kendall.

It was established that fraudulent names had been used to pad the election returns of Syracuse Township: the names of dead persons; the names of 133 voters of Silver Lake Township, Shawnee County; the names of residents of Topeka including two well-known lawyers; and the names of 43 voters of Mills County, Iowa. Even old William Penn was made to do duty as a voter. One man openly admitted that he had voted three times, once under the name of Penn. After hearing the facts, the state Supreme Court, on October 5, ordered the county commissioners to move their offices to Kendall, which had been designated as the temporary county seat.

Kendall soon called a meeting to devise ways and means to continue the fight against Syracuse. It asked the support of citizens from Coolidge, promising in return to vote for that town as county seat. On April 26, 1887, the Kendall county commissioners ordered a special election for the permanent county seat to be held on May 31. Syracuse officials opposed the election, but it was held anyway. Kendall, Coombs precinct, and Coolidge

A street scene in Coolidge around 1910 shows several impressive buildings of native stone. Coolidge survived losing the county seat but never became the town of which the founding fathers dreamed.

voted and Coolidge received a majority of 419 votes for county seat. Kendall citizens voted solidly for Coolidge.

The Hamilton county seat cases were continued in the Kansas Supreme Court until February 1888. During this period, Kendall remained the temporary county seat despite the other election results. The decisions of past elections were not effected until April 7, 1888, when the court maintained that Kendall was still temporary county seat and no town had been legally chosen county seat because of fraudulent elections.

Then things began to happen for Kendall. On April 10, the Syracuse county officers agreed to move their offices to Kendall. The date of June 20 was decided upon to hold another special election for the location of a permanent county seat. The result of the election was canvassed by two boards—one at Kendall and one at Syracuse. Syracuse claimed a majority of 178, having received 698 votes according to the canvass made at Syracuse, which did not include the canvass of votes at Coolidge, Kendall, or the other precincts. The latter were canvassed by the Kendall board, which claimed a majority of votes for Coolidge as county seat.

In 1888 Joe Borders, the county treasurer at Syracuse, removed his records and funds from Syracuse to Coolidge. However, in July 1888 the U.S. Land Office issued a document recognizing Syracuse as the permanent county seat and directing that final proofs on land grants be made there. On November 9 the district court ordered Borders to return all records, funds, and office furniture from Coolidge to Syracuse and to deliver them to his "duly elected and qualified successor," W. F. Reed. Borders obeyed this order on November 16, 1888, and Syracuse was designated the permanent county seat. This decision ended one of the longest legal battles ever waged in Kansas over the location of a county seat.[6]

Coolidge continued to be a successful town for a few years, but in the early 1890s a severe drought in the area ended its hopes for survival, and by 1912 there were only 145 people left in the town. Today, Coolidge is still a small rural community with several business buildings that date back to the town's founding. Kendall survived losing the county seat, but it remains a small community with several buildings that were constructed during the town's heyday. You can visit Coolidge by taking U.S. Highway 50 about fourteen miles west of Syracuse. To reach Kendall, take U.S. Highway 50 about twelve miles east of Syracuse. Both ghost towns are along the highway.

TRAIL CITY
Hamilton County

In September 1883 the Western Central Kansas Stockmen's Association met and discussed the need for a trouble-free trail over which cattle could be driven safely from Texas to the ranges and markets to the north. The need had arisen because between the state quarantine laws against the Texas longhorns and the stream of homesteaders coming to western Kansas, the cattlemen were losing access to the railroad and their markets. In 1884 the cattlemen petitioned Congress to set aside a strip of land six miles wide along the Kansas-Colorado border for a permanent trail to be known as the National Cattle Trail. But since this strip was already being used by several hundred cowboys who camped with their herds near the Santa Fe tracks, Congress did not grant their request, and in 1885 Martin Culver, assisted by the firm of Smith & Bennett, laid out a town he called Trail City at this cowboy rendezvous point. Investors and speculators from southwest Kansas arrived at the site, including a few from the "queen of the cow towns," Dodge City. Two hundred shares of stock were sold at $100 a share, and the town was on its way to becoming an important cattle shipping point.

In September 1885, Print Olive built a stable, a wagon yard, and a saloon where prostitutes were forbidden—an oddity in Trail City. Other businesses included general merchandise stores, a large saddle and harness shop, and a trail outfitting store. Martin Culver built a large limestone hotel to accommodate the trail hands and the railroad workers, and the Santa Fe Railroad constructed a siding, stockyards, and loading chutes.[1]

Trail City was one long main street and had a distinctive layout: All the front doors of the businesses on the east side of the street opened into Prowers County, Colorado, and the back doors opened into Hamilton County, Kansas. This location on the border made breaking the law easy because all a cowboy needed to do was step into another room and he was in the jurisdiction of another state. One saloon even painted a stripe across the floor indicating the exact position of the state line. The cowboys—unhappy with Kansas because of the cattle quarantine and its laws prohibiting alcohol—would throw their empty liquor bottles out the back door of the saloon into "dry" Kansas and were often heard to remark, "toss 'em into Kansas, there's nobody there nohow but sunflowers and sons of bitches!"[2]

By the summer of 1886 Trail City was attracting cattlemen by the hundreds. A July 3 newspaper article from Trail City reported that 80,078 head of cattle had arrived, and that "this is a pretty dull place except when there are several herds near town, then, it is a lively place."[3] By July 29 over 125,000 head of cattle had passed through town, and on August 25 the Globe Livestock Journal announced that the town was "looming up" and was destined to become the best "rip-roaring Texas cattle town of the West." In 1886 the population of the town was over 500, but nearly 300 were transients.[4]

In the fall of 1886 Trail City reached its peak, and the town did its best to live up to its reputation of "the hell hole of the Arkansas," and "the Cesspool of Sin."[5] The saloon operated by Joe Sparrow was the worst in town. The front of the building contained a large bar, but in the back there were small private rooms where prostitutes, many of whom had come from Dodge City, took their "clients" for the evening.[6] In addition to cowboys and prostitutes, Trail City attracted escaped convicts and common criminals who took advantage of the town's position on the state line.

In spite of this rougher element, there were only two recorded murders in Trail City. One of the victims was Print Olive, and the other was a cowboy named Joe Redmond.[7] Olive's murder was the more unusual. After the Civil War, he had had a reputation for being a cold-blooded killer as he and his gang had committed robberies and murders from the Indian Territory to Nebraska. While in Nebraska, Olive took two settlers from the Kearney jail, where they were being kept for their own safety, and hanged them. After a trial, a jury that had been intimidated by Olive set him free, but Joe Sparrow, a relative of one of the victims, haunted him for months. Sparrow finally shot and killed Olive at Trail City, but when he was tried for the crime, a jury in Pueblo, Colorado, found him not guilty.[8]

The town of Coolidge, about three miles away, considered Trail City a nuisance, but the "dry residents" of Coolidge provided much of Trail City's business. Five hacks were often shuttled between the two towns, and they sometimes carried prostitutes as an added "inducement" to visit Trail City. The shaky relationship between the two towns was further strained by the Lady Godiva incident. A few cowboys, who were always looking for new ways to have fun, decided to ride over to Coolidge one day with one of the town's prostitutes, but they were taken by surprise when the lady, stark naked, rode down Main Street waving to passers-by. This incident led Coolidge officials to adopt an ordinance against public displays of nudity.[9] By the end of 1886 Trail City was so clogged with prostitutes that they overflowed the brothels and hotels and set up shops in tents along the city's streets.[10]

Trail City existed for three years but began to decline after 1886 because the railroad, which had helped the town to exist, also brought about its demise. The completion of the Denver & Fort Worth Railroad ended the town's importance because it was more profitable to ship cattle north from Fort Worth by rail than to drive them north on the trail. In the summer of 1887 only about 90,000 head of cattle were sold in Trail City, and the settlers began moving in and fencing the land, which blocked the passage of the herds on the trail. By 1890 only about fifty people inhabited the townsite, and most of the buildings had been moved away. Like many other cattle towns, Trail City went from boom to bust in a short period of time.[11]

The *Hutchinson News*, on December 16, 1962, printed the best epitaph for Trail City in an article recounting the town's sudden rise and fall: "Echoes of the last shot fired in anger on the western Kansas plains have faded away, the blood of the last bow-tied gambler has soaked down into the subsoil of the prairie and the tinkling of the last frontier saloon piano has been silenced. The turbulent frontier is gone."

You can reach the site of Trail City by taking U.S. Highway 50 about two miles west of Coolidge to the Kansas-Colorado line. Most of the community is now private property.

A tornado hit Ulysses around 1906, doing heavy damage. This view shows what was left of the R. R. Wilson barn after the storm passed. A buggy next to the barn was not even moved.

"OLD" ULYSSES
Grant County

The plat of the first Ulysses in Grant County—"Old" Ulysses—was filed on July 16, 1885, and signed by A. J. Hoisington, president of the town company.[1] By September 1886 the town had a population of nearly 1,500 and an opera house, a large hotel, and six saloons. To help raise money for public projects, the citizens held a bond election that year. The town company issued city bonds for $36,000, and the majority of them were sold to investors in the East.

In 1888 a county seat controversy that had been building in intensity between Ulysses and Cincinnati, which was five miles from Ulysses, reached a climax, and the emotions of the citizens became so volatile that the residents of one town would not enter the other. Two weeks before the election, some people became suspicious because there seemed to be plenty of money in Ulysses. Approximately 300 men were being fed and supplied with money, and individual groups of organized voters throughout the county were given as much as $1,000 for "advertising." There was little doubt in the minds of many citizens that most of the money that

Moving the hotel from Old Ulysses to the new site in 1908 was a challenge. Here workers have disassembled the building into three sections because the structure was too large to move in one piece.

had been collected from the sale of the city bonds was being spent on the county seat election. As it turned out, only one public well, a small frame courthouse, and a cheap school building were built before the bond money ran out. Ulysses did win the county seat election over Cincinnati, and most of its citizens moved to Ulysses.

In 1889 a disastrous drought ruined the crops and caused many of the farmers and businessmen to leave the community. Since there were fewer than forty individuals left on the townsite, Ulysses could no longer be considered an incorporated city with city officials and government. This downward trend in economic conditions continued throughout the 1890s.

In 1908 the city bonds were due to be paid. When the eastern bond holders were unsuccessful in their attempts to collect the principal and interest, they sent E. F. Foote, a Hutchinson attorney, to Old Ulysses to begin legal action against the city—when the citizens heard about Foote's mission, they became irate and had him jailed temporarily. A town meeting was hastily called when the residents realized that the city council would have to levy a tax to pay for the bonds, which could mean bankruptcy for the town. The only solution they could come up with was to move

The New Ulysses Hotel as it stood in 1909 after workers had moved the building and put all three sections back together at the new location.

the town outside the city limits and give the bond holders the land on which the town stood, but not the town.

Plans were made to move the town as quickly as possible. Men and teams from other nearby towns came to help, and they moved houses, stores, a bank, a hotel, the opera house, and a restaurant three miles across the prairie. The smaller houses were put on skids with a wagon under each corner, but the hotel was sawed in half and mounted on wagons. The opera house had to be cut into three parts in order to be moved. Every building except the school was transferred to the new townsite, which had been laid out free of debt.[2] Though most sources say that the entire move took only two days, an older resident, who was present during the move, stated that it took nearly two months.

By late 1909 the freshly painted buildings had been set up on both sides of a wide street, and the town of New Ulysses, population 90, was born. The eastern bond holders, who had no recourse against the new town, were forced to accept their losses. After an election in November 1909, New Ulysses became the county seat of Grant County. Within a short time the compound name was dropped, and the city became known by its present name—Ulysses.[3]

In 1970 a newspaper reporter visiting in western Kansas described Ulysses as the "cleanest, neatest, most sanitary town in Kansas . . . with streets of perfect cleanliness, two town pumps with water of absolute purity that sparkles like a diamond, and every house and store and barn in it is painted white or red. . . .

"Ulysses sits upon the top of a knoll on the prairie and, approaching it from any direction, it may be seen from 10 to 20 miles away, its immaculate buildings glistening in the sunlight."[4]

The new town of Ulysses is a prosperous western Kansas community of several thousand people today, but the old Ulysses site is in a wheat field and the foundation of the old schoolhouse is all that remains of the town. "Old" Ulysses is about three miles east of Ulysses on U.S. Highway 160. Much of the townsite is now on private property.

SANTA FE
Haskell County

Santa Fe was officially platted on July 31, 1886, "at 4 P.M." and was named after the Santa Fe Trail that passed five miles north of town.[1] The first newspaper, the *Santa Fe Trail*, took pride in reporting that several businesses had quickly been established—two grocery stores, one restaurant and hotel (with twenty-five regular boarders), one bakery, one laundry, and two lumberyards—and that arrangements for more businesses had been made.

When established, Santa Fe was in Finney County, but on March 5, 1887, Haskell County, named for Congressman Dudley C. Haskell, was established by the legislature. In July Santa Fe was chosen as the temporary county seat, and at the November 7 election the town was voted the permanent county seat.

Since the railroads had not yet reached Haskell County, the stagecoach line of Lee and Reynolds served the communities of Santa Fe, Ivanhoe, Loco, Old Spring, and Fargo Springs, carrying both passengers and mail.

On January 2, 1888, Santa Fe was incorporated as a third-class city, and according to the incorporation charter, its population then was "more than 350, less than 2,000." Since 1886 the town had added three banks, a brick kiln, two more hotels, two churches, a school, several grocery stores, a flour mill, two real estate offices, and five newspapers. The longest running newspaper was the *Santa Fe Monitor*, published from June 15, 1888, to July 18, 1918.[2]

The building of a railroad through the community was of prime importance, and the citizens' hopes were centered on the Kansas, Texas & Southwestern Railroad, which had made a survey through Santa Fe.

Students pose for a classroom photograph at the Santa Fe school around the turn of the century.

However, representatives of the Dodge City, Montezuma & Trinidad Railroad proposed that if the people would vote aid to the railroad at $2,000 a mile and an additional subsidy of $1,000 per mile to be paid upon completion of the grade through the county, the railroad could guarantee the track would be completed within thirty days. The citizens were excited about the offer, and it took them only a few hours to raise $10,500 for this purpose. Unfortunately both railroads decided to build farther south instead.

The 1890s were mostly good years. There were baseball games between the Arapahoe Baseball Club and the "Santa Fe Boys," Independence Day celebrations were conducted by the Methodist Episcopal Aid Society, and programs were given on Children's Day. The Haskell County Agricultural Society was organized and served for years as a social and political association for farmers.

In the late 1880s crop failures had affected the lives of the farmers at Santa Fe when a persistent drought had plagued the area. In the late 1890s the dry weather was even more severe, and between 40 and 60 percent of the county's population was forced to leave. The renewed possibility of a railroad through Santa Fe was encouraging, however, and this prospect kept most of the townspeople together during those troubled times.

The town did decline throughout the early 1900s because the Santa Fe Railroad built through Sublette, and two banks in town were forced to close, at great expense to the county.[3] But from 1903 to 1912 the town's most prominent citizens continued to meet with representatives of railway companies, and up until 1911 they were certain that Santa Fe would have a railroad. Even in February 1913 they believed there was a fair chance that the Wichita Falls Railroad would build through the county near Santa Fe. But that railroad, too, failed to materialize.

Because Santa Fe had lost population and was in a business slump, another county seat election was held on February 5, 1913. The choices on the ballot were Santa Fe and the thriving town of Sublette, but Sublette failed to get the necessary three-fifths of the vote. Not satisfied with the outcome of the election, the Sublette citizens took the case to the state Supreme Court, and the court decided in favor of Sublette.

During the next five years, most of the citizens left Santa Fe and moved to either Sublette or Satanta. On July 25, 1918, the *Santa Fe Monitor* moved to Sublette, and the editor, John Miller, wrote the following about the occasion: "We have published the *Monitor* in Santa Fe for twenty-eight years and three months . . . but as most of the town has moved away we thought it was to our advantage to move also and we believe time will fully justify our action."[4]

Today the site of Santa Fe, located in the exact center of Haskell County, is at the junction of U.S. Highways 83 and 160, seven miles north of Sublette. No buildings remain, and part of the land is now being farmed.

FARGO SPRINGS
Seward County

Fargo Springs, founded in May 1885, was one of the earliest communities established in Seward County. Although the town's name was changed in November to Harwoodville, the *Prairie Owl* (the first newspaper in Seward County) continued to call it Fargo Springs. By popular demand, the original name was officially restored after a couple of months, and the *Owl* reported on January 14, 1886, that "the mail leaving the post office was stamped Harwoodville Wednesday morning for the last time." Named for C. H. Fargo of the C. H. Fargo & Co. boot and shoe house in Chicago, the town was laid out in May 1885 by the Southwestern Land & Town Company of Emporia.[1] In 1886 Fargo Springs was at the peak of its development, and the only other notable competitor was a smaller town nearby called Springfield.[2]

This promotional bird's-eye view of Fargo Springs shows the town as it appeared around 1886. Violence between Fargo Springs and Springfield citizens over the county seat question was only narrowly averted on several occasions. In the end, Liberal was the victor.

On August 5, 1886, Seward County held its first election and Fargo Springs was chosen the county seat, which aroused bitter feelings among Springfield citizens. The *Topeka Daily Capital* of September 12, 1886, published this letter to the editor:

> Your mention of the lively times in Seward County don't say anything about the forged names on the petition for organization of Seward County presented by the Fargo Springs people. He probably doesn't know about that. He does not say anything about the formation of the election board in favor of Fargo Springs and against Springfield. He doesn't say anything about the 50 odd Fargoites taking armed possession of the room in Fargo designated as the polling place the night before the election, holding it all night and only opening it about a foot. . . . He probably don't know about it.
>
> He don't say anything about the windows of the room being closed up so that it was impossible to see who was therein or what they were about. He doesn't tell that the wagon-bed vote was at the suggestion of the sheriff of the county, he claiming he had no authority to force an entrance into the room designated. He doesn't tell that the voting was canvassed in the face of injunction from the proper court. . . .
>
> He doesn't tell that a certain Fargo precinct with 60 odd votes cast

130 votes, principally for Fargo. He did not tell of the intimidation and illegal votes. He probably doesn't know this. It is only Fargo stuffing.

Signed—Springfield

The controversy over the county seat continued, but in a November 1887 election, Fargo Springs once again won over Springfield.[3] However, after ten months of litigation in the Kansas Supreme Court, Springfield was named the county seat. The rivalry between the two towns was so intense that no businessman "in one town dared even to solicit business from the other town and so closely were the lines drawn that members of the church would have been ostracized had they dared attend communion services in the rival town."[4]

The tempers of the citizens finally reached the boiling point. The two towns were only a short distance apart, but the hills separated them so that one town was not visible to the other. One night word reached Fargo Springs that groups of men from Springfield were coming to "clean up the town." The Fargo Springs men lay at the foot of a rise near the town all night guarding it from attack. Little did they know that the same rumor had reached Springfield citizens, so while Fargo men lay at the foot of the hill on one side guarding it from Springfield men, on the other side of the hill lay Springfield men on guard against Fargo. Neither suspected the presence of the other.

A more important factor decided the fate of the two towns—the railroad. Had the Kansas Southern (later the Rock Island) built west to the Colorado coal fields, as it originally intended, either town could have become the county seat and an important railroad town or division terminal. But the railroad builders turned southwest and built through Liberal. As a result the Kansas Southern missed both Fargo Springs and Springfield by eighteen miles, and Liberal became the county seat.[5]

Within a year of losing the railroad, Fargo Springs was abandoned and by 1920 all that was left was a crumbling brick schoolhouse. Today there are a few surviving traces left of the town.[6] You can visit Fargo Springs by driving one mile west on the county road from Kismet. At the junction with another county road, go north two miles to a second junction with a county road heading west. Take that road about seven and one-half miles until it becomes a dead-end dirt road—the approximate location of Fargo Springs. Make local inquiries at Kismet before attempting the drive.

SPRINGFIELD
Seward County

Springfield was founded in 1885 by William Minton, E. Chute, J. F. Wetzel, Evan R. Wortham, Warren Ames, John Kauble, all of Springfield;

J. W. Madders, Meade Center; and F. J. Fulton of Garden City.[1] In the spring of 1886 the town of Carthage in Meade County was abandoned, and many of Carthage's leading citizens moved to Springfield. Although there were already two stores in town, Murry & Watson moved their building from Carthage and opened the first "general store" in Springfield.

In June 1886 Gov. John Martin declared Springfield the temporary county seat of Seward County. By 1887 the town had a population of 600 and had been incorporated as a city of the third class, but other "indications of permanence" were late in coming. For example, a school building and a church were not erected until the spring of 1888.[2]

The *Seward County Courant*, Springfield, November 11, 1887, was optimistic about the prospects of the town:

> Springfield has made astonishing progress. . . . It has laid the foundation for a city of several thousand inhabitants by the erection of a commodious and elegant hotel which cost the snug little sum of ten thousand dollars. . . . Another hotel costing the same amount is now enclosed and will be ready to open by January 1, 1888. Those two hotels . . . furnish accommodations second to no town in the West. . . . Twenty-seven two-story buildings have been erected during the past summer.

By late 1887 Springfield had four newspapers: the *Transcript*, the *Soap-Box*, the *Courant*, and last but not least the *Prairie Owl*, the oldest newspaper in the county.[3]

Both Springfield and Fargo Springs wanted to be the permanent county seat, so the commissioners arranged for an election to be held August 5, 1886, in Fargo Springs. The men on the election board at Fargo were sitting in a closed room, and when each person voted they had to prepare a ballot on the outside and pass it through a raised window. The blinds were drawn, which made it impossible for the voters to see who was in the room taking the ballots. The men from Springfield decided they were being cheated, so they pulled a wagon into the middle of the street in front of the voting place. Then they found a soap box, nailed it up tight and cut a hole in one end, put it on the wagon, and proceeded to place their ballots in it.

The county commissioners met the next day and canvassed the ballots according to law, and the ballots that had been cast in the closed room were the ones that were recognized as legal. However, the Springfield citizens were angry enough to take the case to the state Supreme Court, and after nearly ten months of litigation, the court declared that the "soapbox" ballots were the legal ones. Springfield was declared the county seat of Seward County.

Early in 1887 the county commissioners purchased $100,000 in stock in the Kansas Southern Railroad (later absorbed by the Rock Island), with bonds voted for that purpose, but the railroad built through Liberal instead. This unfortunate action by the railroad brought about a decline in Springfield's prosperity.[4]

One of the strangest incidents that occurred in Springfield's history was not associated with the county seat war or the railroads, but with the attempted assassination of Judge Theodosius Botkin in January 1892. Although Botkin was supposed to represent the whole county, his views were primarily pro–Fargo Springs, and many of his decisions had been made in its favor. These biased judgments so incensed a number of Springfield men that they planned to ambush the judge and kill him.

Certain members of the group found out that Judge Botkin was going to Springfield in his buggy on the morning of January 3. Plans were made to drop a package in the road near the spot where the assassins would be hiding, and when Botkin stopped the buggy to examine the package, they would kill him. However, an informer told Sheriff Samuel Dunn of the plan, and he alerted Botkin.

On January 2 Sheriff Dunn and six other men—E. S. Guymon, Sid Nixon, George Stein, W. A. Custer, and Joe and H. P. Larrabee—left Springfield and waited until dawn near the location where the killing was to take place. The sheriff encountered one group of troublemakers and ordered them to disperse and go home. When the rest of the posse rode on in the direction of Judge Botkin's house to tell him of the encounter, they accidently came across a second group of ruffians. Loud conversation between the two parties ensued, and Sid Nixon became so frightened that he turned and ran, which caused the gang to start shooting. When these shots were heard by the men talking to Sheriff Dunn, they opened fire on him and he fell backward into a ravine. The two Larrabee brothers ran to his assistance, but when they found that he was dying, they dropped their guns and fled to Springfield. The other officers with the second group ran for cover, but after about a hundred yards, Guymon's legs cramped, and he collapsed. When Stein and Custer saw him fall, they thought he had been shot, and they "lit out" for town.

After the shooting had been reported, a group of men with bandages and other medical gear went to the area where Sheriff Dunn and Guymon had last been seen. They found Dunn's body riddled with bullets, some

A view of Main Street in Springfield circa 1890. Today the buildings are gone.

inflicted after he had died. Guymon was found alive but unable to walk because of the cramps in his legs.

A few months later some of the men responsible for the murder of Sheriff Dunn were captured and tried, but the jury was unable to find any one person guilty, so they all went free.[5] However, from that time on, Judge Botkin became a little less biased in his decisions.

Due to the loss of the railroad and the resultant decline in business, the county seat was moved to Liberal in 1893, and that fall, officials from Liberal set out in wagons to transfer the county property from Springfield to the new county seat. As they loaded the official records, desks, and other paraphernalia into the wagons, there was little visiting between the stiff-necked partisans of the two towns. Soon only one matter remained to be settled. The old Windsor Hotel contained some furniture that was mortgaged in the amount of $235.11 to a Liberal hotel man. As he backed his wagon up and commenced to load the furniture, he was prevailed upon by the Springfield citizens to await their efforts to raise the mortgage money. Finally, the funds were raised, and after calling the mortgage holder into their midst, they counted the money into his hand. The four-poster bed and the rocking chair were unloaded from the wagon and returned to their customary places in the hotel's master bedroom. The Liberal party mounted their wagon seats, and when the signal was given, the caravan moved slowly out of town.

Along the road stood the last of the Springfield residents and businessmen—the holdouts, the tough, the stubborn, and the gallant men and women who had first settled the town and were determined to stay until the end. Their heads were held high, and their gaze passed right through the wagons that were removing the town's only claim to power— the county records. There was probably not a $10 bill left in the town, and there was not a dry eye among the Liberal men and women riding on the wagons.

An old pioneer told of a strange experience that happened to him several years later when the old town had finally accepted its ghost town status. On a moonlit night a few months before the old Windsor Hotel was razed, he rode through the streets that had once been Springfield. On the wind- swept porch of the hotel building stood a group of misty figures. The pioneer pulled up his horse and watched the tableau on the porch. The group stood perfectly erect, heads held high while one member counted out into the palm of another the exact sum of $235.11.[6]

You can visit Springfield by driving north on U.S. Highway 83/160 from Liberal to the junction with U. S. Highway 160. This junction places you at Springfield.

NOTES

FOREWORD

1. John J. Ingalls, *A Collection of the Writings of John James Ingalls* (Kansas City, Mo.: Hudson-Kimberly Publishing Company, 1902), p. 68.

2. John J. Ingalls to Elias Ingalls, October 5, 1858, in John J. Ingalls Collection, Manuscript Division, Kansas State Historical Society, Topeka (hereafter KSHS).

3. Reprinted in Charles Hurd, "The Story of Trail City," *Three Score and Ten: Lamar's First 70 Years on the Arkansas* (Lamar, Colo.: n.p., 1956), p. 28.

PREFACE

1. This quotation was taken from William Elsey Connelley's introduction to "Some of the Lost Towns of Kansas," *Kansas Historical Collections* 12 (1911–1912): 426.

CHAPTER ONE: NORTHEAST KANSAS

White Cloud, Doniphan County

1. *White Cloud Globe-Tribune*, January 30, 1931.

2. Cora Delbee, "July Fourth in Early Kansas," *Kansas Historical Quarterly* 9(1941):75.

3. James C. Malin, "Judge LeCompte and the Sack of Lawrence," *Kansas Historical Quarterly* 36 (1953):465–494.

4. *White Cloud Globe-Tribune*, January 30, 1931.

5. *Kansas City Star*, May 4, 1936.

6. George A. Root, "Ferries in Kansas," *Kansas Historical Quarterly* 2 (1931): 133–136.

7. A. Andreas, *History of Kansas*, 2 vols. (Chicago: Andreas, 1883), 1:483–484.

8. Ibid.

9. "From Atchison, Kansas, the Great Railroad Centre of the World, to Lincoln, Nebraska, the Great Political Capital of the West," promotional brochure by the Atchison & Nebraska Railroad, May 1873, p. 7, KSHS.

10. Andreas, *History of Kansas*, 1:483–484.

11. *White Cloud Globe-Tribune*, January 30, 1931.

12. *Kansas Country Living Magazine*, August 1978, contains a biography of Alex Poulet as well as an architectural history of his home.

Iowa Point, Doniphan County

1. KSHS, comp., "Doniphan County Clippings," vol. 1, n.d., p. 92.

2. "Iowa Point," Ghost Town Files, Manuscript Division, KSHS; Atchison & Nebraska Railroad, "From Atchison," pp. 5–7.

3. KSHS, "Doniphan Clippings," p. 92.

4. *Troy Kansas Chief, Illustrated Doniphan County History* (Troy, Kans.: *Kansas Chief*, 1916): p. 188.

Eagle Springs, Doniphan County

1. *Troy Kansas Chief, Illustrated Doniphan*, p. 116.

2. "Eagle Springs," Ghost Town Files, Manuscript Division, KSHS.

3. Ibid.

4. Ibid.

5. "Dr. W. W. Simonson, Palmer Graduate Chiropractor," promotional pamphlet in Library Division, KSHS., n.d., pp. 2, 3, 5.

6. *Kansas City Star*, June 26, 1969.

Geary City, Doniphan County

1. *Troy Kansas Chief, Illustrated Doniphan*, p. 219.

2. Ibid., special edition, November 23, 1893, p. 280.

3. Ibid., *Illustrated Doniphan*, p. 219.

4. *Atchison Globe*, November 25, 1919.

5 *Troy Kansas Chief, Illustrated Doniphan*, p. 219.

Doniphan, Doniphan County

1. *Atchison Globe*, December 11, 1949.

2. Ibid., July 26, 1919.

3. Ibid., December 11, 1949.

4. *Kansas City Chief*, November 26, 1914.

5. Atchison Globe. December 11, 1949.

6. Ibid.

7. Root, "Ferries," p. 121.

8. *Kansas City Star*, July 6, 1911.

9. Ibid.

10. *Kansas City Chief*, November 23, 1893.

11. *Troy Kansas Chief, Illustrated Doniphan, p.* 217.

12. *Kansas City Star*, July 6, 1911.

13. Atchison & Nebraska Railroad, "From Atchison," pp. 4–7.

14. *Kansas City Star*, July 6, 1911.

15. *Troy Kansas Chief, Illustrated Doniphan*, p. 217.

16. *Atchison Globe*, March 5, 1953.

17. Joseph G. Waters, "The Wyandotte Convention," *Kansas Historical Collections* 11 (1909–1910): 48.

18. *Atchison Globe*, April 7, 1918.

19. *Kansas City Star*, July 6, 1911.

Sumner, Atchison County

1. William Elsey Connelley, "Some of the Lost Towns of Kansas," *Kansas Historical Collections* 12 (1911–1912): 434.

2. John James Ingalls, *A Collection of the Writings of John James Ingalls* (Kansas City, Mo.: Hudson-Kimberly Publishing Company, 1902), pp. 37–38.

3. Albert D. Richardson, *Beyond the Mississippi* (Hartford, Conn.: American Publishing Company, 1867), p. 56; Daniel C. Fitzgerald, "Town Booming: An Economic History

of Steamboat Towns along the Kansas-Missouri Border, 1840–1860" (M.A. thesis, University of Kansas, Lawrence, 1983), pp. 180–181.

4. Connelley, "Some Lost Towns," pp. 435–436.

5. *Sumner Gazette*, December 12, 1857.

Four Houses, Wyandotte County

1. *Kansas City Journal*, January 2, 1879.

2. Louise Barry, *The Beginning of the West* (Topeka: KSHS, 1973), p. 88.

Rising Sun, Jefferson County

1. Root, "Ferries," 2:344–347.

2. "Rising Sun," Ghost Town Files, Manuscript Division, KSHS.

3. Ely Moore, "The Story of Lecompton," an address given at an old settlers' meeting at Lecompton, Kansas, 1907, Manuscript Division, KSHS.

4. Root, "Ferries," 2:344.

5. Ibid.

Hickory Point, Jefferson County

1. *Lawrence Journal-World*, September 11, 1946.

2. KSHS, comp., "Notes," *Kansas Historical Quarterly* 2 (1933): 328.

3. Charles W. Smith, "Battle of Hickory Point," *Kansas Historical Collections* 7 (1901–1902): 534.

4. George A. Root, "First Day's Battle at Hickory Point," *Kansas Historical Quarterly* 1 (1931–1932): 29.

5. Smith, "Hickory Point," p. 534.

6. KSHS, "Dr. Albert Morrall: Pro-Slavery Soldier in Kansas in 1856, " *Kansas Historical Collections* 14 (1915–1918): 128–129.

7. Smith, "Hickory Point," p. 534.

Arrington, Atchison County

1. Linda Mae Krogman Curtis, *Arrington Heights* (Holton, Kans.: Bell Graphics, 1977), p. 20.

2. Ibid.

3. Bruce Jones, "Arrington: A Health Resort," unpublished manuscript, 1971, p. 3, Atchison County Historical Museum, Atchison.

4. Ibid.

5. Ibid.

6. Ibid., pp. 4–5.

Kennekuk, Atchison County

1. *Kansas City Star*, October 17, 1977.

2. W. R. Honnell, annual address regarding the history of the Pony Express, given to members of the Kansas State Historical Society, 1935.

3. *Kansas City Star*, October 12, 1977.
4. *Horton Headlight*, June 22, 1967.
5. *Kansas City Star*, October 12, 1977.
6. *Horton Headlight-Commercial*, September 18, 1924.
7. *Ibid.*
8. *Kansas City Star*, October 12, 1977.
9. *Topeka Daily Capital*, August 13, 1922.
10. *Hiawatha World*, July 11, 1890.

America City, Nemaha County
1. "America City," Ghost Town Files, Manuscript Division, KSHS.
2. *Atchison Globe*, October 22, 1920.
3. "America City," Ghost Town Files, Manuscript Division, KSHS.
4. A. Andreas, *History of Kansas*, 2 vols. (Chicago: Andreas, 1883), 2:965.
5. *Atchison Globe*, October 22, 1920.
6. R. L. Polk & Company, *Kansas State Gazetteer* (Detroit: R. L. Polk & Company, 1878), p. 78.

St. George, Pottawatomie County
1. *Wamego Reporter*, January 2, 1947.
2. Ibid.
3. *Kansas City Times*, October 2, 1975.
4. Ibid.: *St. George News*, September 19, 1940.

Juniata, Pottawatomie County
1. James C. Carey, "Juniata: Gateway to Mid-Kansas," *Kansas Historical Quarterly* 21 (1954–1955): 87–94.
2. Connelley, "Some Lost Towns," pp. 426–427.
3. Carey, "Juniata," p. 91.
4. Connelley, "Some Lost Towns," pp. 426–427.
5. Carey, "Juniata," p. 90; George A. Root, "Ferries in Kansas," *Kansas Historical Collections* 3 (1934): 120–121.
6. Manhattan Centennial Committee, *The First One Hundred Years: A History of Manhattan, Kansas, 1855–1955* (Manhattan, Kans.: Manhattan Centennial Committee, 1955), p. 7.
7. Carey, "Juniata," pp. 89–90.
8. Ibid., p. 90.
9. Connelley, "Some Lost Towns," pp. 426–427.
10. Carey, "Juniata," p. 94.

Pawnee, Riley County
1. Winifred, N. Slagg, *Riley County Kansas* (Manhattan, Kans.: Winifred N. Slagg, 1968), pp. 124–125; KSHS, 26th Biennial Report (Topeka: KSHS, 1928), pp. 78–79.

2. Theodore Gardner, "Andrew H. Reeder: First Territorial Governor," *Kansas Historical Collections* 16 (1923–1925): 584–585.

3. KSHS, 26th Report, p. 83.

4. Slagg, *Riley County*, pp. 127–128.

Old Randolph, Riley County

1. Slagg, *Riley County*, pp. 202–215.

2. Ibid., pp. 210–211.

3. Ibid.; George A. Root, "Ferries in Kansas," *Kansas Historical Quarterly* 3 (1934): 131.

4. Walter A. Boles, *Randolph* (Randolph: Randolph Centennial Committee, 1954), pp. 210–211.

Irving, Marshall County

1. Andreas, *History of Kansas*, 2:926.

2. *Kansas City Times*, December 5, 1957.

3. *Blue Rapids Times*, May 16, 1957.

4. Andreas, *History of Kansas*, 2:926.

5. *Kansas City Star*, April 5, 1978.

6. *Blue Rapids Times*, May 16, 1957.

7. Frank W. Blackmar, *Cyclopedia of Kansas History*, 3 vols. (Chicago: Standard Publishing Company, 1912), 1:944.

8. *Kansas City Times*, July 24, 1959; *Topeka Daily Capital*, July 17, 1960.

Alcove Springs, Marshall County

1. *Topeka State Journal*, April 13, 1935.

2. Emma Forter, *Marshall County History* (Indianapolis: B. F. Bowen & Company, 1917), p. 426.

3. Alcove Springs Historical Association, "Alcove Springs Area: Why It Should Be a National Monument," pamphlet, 1961, p. 2, KSHS.

4. *Kansas City Star*, February 13, 1903.

5. Forter, *Marshall County*, p. 385.

6. Alcove Springs Historical Association, "Alcove Springs."

7. State of Kansas, *Compiled Laws of Kansas* (Topeka: Kansas State Printing Plant, 1941), p. 733.

8. *Marysville Advocate*, June 15, 1961.

CHAPTER TWO: EAST CENTRAL KANSAS

Trading Post, Linn County

1. Daniel Wilder, *Annals of Kansas, 1541–1885* (Topeka: T. D. Thacher & Co., 1886), p. 30; A. Andreas, *History of Kansas*, 2 vols. (Chicago: Andreas, 1883), 2:1,115.

2. *Fort Scott Tribune*, special anniversary edition, May 30, 1942; D. A. N. Chase, "Trading Post," original in Manuscript Division, KSHS.

3. *Fort Scott Tribune*, May 30, 1942.

4. KSHS, comp., "Linn County Clippings," vol. 1, n.d., p. 226.

5. Andreas, *History of Kansas*, 2:1,115.

6. *La Cygne Weekly Journal*, May 17, 1895.

7. KSHS, "Linn Clippings," 1:226.

8. Ibid.

9. Ibid.

Centropolis/Minneola, Franklin County

1. William Elsey Connelley, "Some of the Lost Towns of Kansas," *Kansas Historical Collections* 12 (1911–1912): 433–434.

2. Andreas, *History of Kansas*, 1:602, 603.

3. Ibid.

4. *Ottawa Herald*, December 22, 1916.

5. *Merriam News*, April 2, 1936.

6. Andreas, *History of Kansas*, 1:602, 603.

Silkville, Franklin County

1. *Topeka Journal*, June 19, 1939.

2. Ibid., September 28, 1952; Garnett Carpenter, "Silkville: A Kansas Attempt in the History of Fourierist Utopias, 1869–1892," *Emporia State Research Studies* 3, 2 (Emporia: Emporia State Teachers College, December 1954), p. 24.

3. *Topeka Journal*, June 19, 1939.

4. "Silkville," Ghost Town Files, Manuscript Division, KSHS.

5. *Topeka Journal*, September 28, 1952.

Black Jack, Douglas County

1. G. W. E. Griffith, "The Battle of Black Jack," *Kansas Historical Collections* 16 (1923–1925): 524.

2. Ibid.; *Wichita Morning Eagle*, September 20, 1903.

3. *Wichita Morning Eagle*, September 20, 1903.

4. Andreas, *History of Kansas*, 1:355–356.

5. *Wellsville Globe*, September 3, 1953.

6. Andreas, *History of Kansas*, 1:355–356; *Wellsville Globe*, September 3, 1953.

Franklin, Douglas County

1. William Stanley Hoole, "A Southerner's Viewpoint of the Kansas Situation, 1856–1857," *Kansas Historical Quarterly* 3 (1934): 54.

2. *Kansas City Star*, August 1, 1936.

3. *Kansas City Journal-Post*. October 30, 1927.

4. V. E. Gibbens, "Letters on the War in Kansas in 1856," *Kansas Historical Quarterly* 10 (1941): 374.

5. Elizabeth Williams Smith, "R. L. Williams: A Biographical Sketch," *Kansas Historical*

Collections 17 (1928): 559–560; *Topeka Daily Capital*, June 22, 1924; for a lengthy history of the Franklin community, read Josephine McGonigle, *Mankind Yields* ([Lawrence, Kans.]: Meseraull Printing Company, 1978).

6. *Kansas City Journal-Post*, October 30, 1927.

Lecompton, Douglas County

1. Mrs. Joseph Childs, ed., *Lecompton Centennial, 1854–1954* (Lecompton: Lecompton Centennial Committee, 1954), p. 12.

2. Ely Moore, "The Story of Lecompton," an address given at an old settlers' meeting at Lecompton, Kansas, 1907, KSHS.

3. Childs, *Lecompton Centennial*, p. 24.

4. Moore, "Story of Lecompton." Reeder fled the territory and never stood trial.

5. Childs, *Lecompton Centennial*, pp. 9–15.

6. Moore, "Story of Lecompton."

Big Springs, Douglas County

1. Lecompton Rural High School, *An Early History of Lecompton, Kansas and Vicinity* (Lecompton: Lecompton Rural High School, Class of 1933).

2. *Topeka Journal*, October 8, 1921.

3. Ruth Rankin, "Big Springs Unincorporated," original in Manuscript Division, KSHS.

4. Andreas, *History of Kansas*, 1:352.

5. Lecompton Rural High School, *Early Lecompton*.

6. Rankin, "Big Springs."

7. *Topeka Journal*, October 8, 1921.

8. "Big Springs," Ghost Town Files, Manuscript Division, KSHS.

Calhoun, Shawnee County

1. M. Tabor, *This Day in Kansas History*, clippings compiled by KSHS, 1932, p. 156.

2. James H. Lowell, "The Romantic Growth of a Law Court." *Kansas Historical Collections* 15 (1919–1922): 593.

3. Tabor, *Kansas History*, p. 156.

4. Lowell, "Law Court," p. 593.

5. Ibid.

6. Tabor, *Kansas History*, p. 156.

Indianola, Shawnee County

1. Connelley, "Some Lost Towns," pp. 427–429.

2. *Topeka Mail and Breeze*, May 22, 1896.

3. Connelley, "Some Lost Towns," pp. 427–429.

4. *Topeka State Journal*, November 16, 1901.

5. *Topeka Mail and Breeze*, May 22, 1896.

6. Connelley, "Some Lost Towns," pp. 427–429.

7. *Topeka Mail and Breeze*, May 22, 1896.

Sumner City, Shawnee County
1. "Sumner City," Ghost Town Files, Manuscript Division, KSHS.
2. Douglass W. Wallace, *Things Ended and Things Begun: A History of Tecumseh, Kansas, 1854–1974* (Topeka: Doug Wallace, 1975), pp. 5–6.

Uniontown, Shawnee County
1. Louise Barry, *The Beginning of the West* (Topeka: KSHS, 1973), pp. 737–738.
2. *Missouri Republican*, St. Louis, February 16, 1849.
3. Barry, *Beginning of the West*, pp. 795–796.
4. Ibid., p. 931.
5. Ibid., p. 937.
6. *Topeka Daily Capital*, July 30, 1958, and January 25, 1973; see also Daniel Fitzgerald, "A Bird's Eye View of Uniontown," original in Manuscript Division, KSHS.

Peterton, Osage County
1. Roger Carswell, *The Early Years of Osage County* (North Newton: Mennonite Press, n.d.), pp. 62–63.
2. Andreas, *History of Kansas*, 2:1,546.
3. Kansas State Inspector of Mines, *First Annual Report* (Topeka: Kansas State Publishing House, 1885), pp. 7–10.
4. Kansas State Inspector of Mines, *Third Annual Report* (Topeka: Kansas State Publishing House, 1888), pp. 36, 28–29.
5. Kansas State Inspector of Mines, *Fourth Annual Report* (Topeka: Kansas State Publishing House, 1891), pp. 46–59.
6. Roger Carswell and C. A. Copple, "History of Osage City and County" (n.p., 1970), pp. 94–95; see also Daniel L. Hartsock, "Coal Mining in Osage County, Kansas: Resource Development in an Economically Marginal Area" (M.A. thesis, University of Kansas, Lawrence, 1966).

Volland, Wabaunsee County
1. Wabaunsee County Historical Society, *New Branches from Old Trees* (Manhattan, Kans.: Wabaunsee County Historical Society, 1976), p. 892.
2. *Kansas City Star*, October 22, 1969.

Newbury, Wabaunsee County
1. *Topeka State Journal*, August 14, 1954.
2. Wabaunsee County Historical Society, *New Branches*, p. 846.
3. Kansas Directory Company, *Business Directory of Wabaunsee County* (Topeka: Kansas Directory Company, 1907), pp. 88–90; *Topeka State Journal*, August 14, 1954.
4. *Alma Signal*, August 27, 1892; Wabaunsee County Historical Society, *New Branches*, p. 846.

Wabaunsee, Wabaunsee County

1. Wabaunsee County Historical Society, *New Branches*, pp. 882, 883.
2. Ibid.
3. Ibid.
4. Charles Lines to the New Haven, Conn., *Daily Palladium*, June–July 1856, Manuscript Division, KSHS.
5. Ibid.
6. Ibid.
7. Ibid.
8. *Kansas City Star*, April 23, 1935.
9. Andreas, *History of Kansas*, 2:996.

Army City, Geary County

1. KSHS, comp., "Geary County Clippings," vol. 1, n.d.
2. *Topeka Daily Capital*, June 6, 1918.
3. Ibid., July 2, 1917; *Kansas City Star*, October 8, 1922.

Diamond Springs, Morris County

1. George Morehouse, "Diamond Springs: 'The Diamond of the Plains,' " *Kansas Historical Collections* 14 (1915–1918): 796.
2. Ibid., pp. 797–798.
3. Ibid., p. 801.
4. KSHS, "Diary of Samuel A. Kingman at Indian Treaty in 1865," *Kansas Historical Quarterly* 1 (1931–1932): 449–450.

CHAPTER THREE: SOUTHEAST KANSAS

Empire City, Cherokee County

1. KSHS, comp., "Cherokee County Clippings," vol. 1, 1877–1895, pp. 2–3.
2. Ibid., pp. 4–5, from unidentified article published on July 2, 1877.
3. *Topeka Daily Commonwealth*, July 2, 1877; *Empire City Mining Echo*, June 9, 1877.
4. *The New Century* (Fort Scott), August 29, 1877; *Kansas City Star*, July 10, 1907.
5. *Empire City Mining Echo*, July 6, 1877.
6. *Kansas City Star*, July 10, 1907.
7. Ibid.

Wilsonton, Labette County

1. Steven K. O'Hern, "Wilsonton—A Dream that Died," *Kanhistique Magazine* (February 1976): 2–3.
2. Ibid.
3. Ibid.

Osage Mission/St. Paul, Neosho County

1. *Topeka Daily Herald*, June 17, 1905.

2. Osage Mission Centennial, "Osage Mission" (St. Paul: Osage Mission Centennial Celebration, 1947), pp. 71–72, 18–27.

3. Ibid., pp. 71–72, 28–33.

4. A. Andreas, *History of Kansas*, 2 vols. (Chicago: Andreas, 1883), 1:829.

5. Osage Mission, "Osage," p. 13.

6. Andreas, *History of Kansas*, 1:829; Osage Mission, "Osage," pp. 76–90.

7. Osage Mission, "Osage," pp. 79–82, 90–91.

Ladore, Neosho County

1. William Elsey Connelley, "Some of the Lost Towns of Kansas," *Kansas Historical Collections* 12 (1911–1912): 450–451.

2. Genevieve Yost, "Lynchings in Kansas," *Kansas Historical Quarterly* 2 (1933): 204.

3. Connelley, "Some Lost Towns," pp. 450–451.

Octagon City, Allen County

1. KSHS, comp., "Immigration Clippings," vol. 1, n.d., p. 165.

2. KSHS, comp., "Allen County Clippings," vol. 2, 1955, p. 62.

3. Andreas, *History of Kansas,* 1:668.

4. Henry S. Clubb, in *Water Cure Journal*, clipped in the *Lawrence Herald of Freedom*, April 28, 1855.

5. Andreas, *History of Kansas,* 1:668.

6. Frank W. Blackmar, *Cyclopedia of Kansas History*, 3 vols. (Chicago: Standard Publishing Company, 1912), 2:380–381.

7. Russell Hickman, "The Vegetarian and Octagon Settlement Companies," *Kansas Historical Quarterly* 2 (1933): 377–385.

8. Ibid., pp. 382–383.

9. KSHS, "Immigration Clippings," p. 165.

10. Stewart H. Holbrook, *Dreamers of the American Dream* (Garden City, N.Y.: Doubleday & Company, 1957), pp. 48–50.

Cofachiqui, Allen County

1. Andreas, *History of Kansas*, 1:668–671.

2. "Cofachiqui," Ghost Town Files, Manuscript Division, KSHS.

3. Andreas, *History of Kansas*, 1:668–671.

4. *Humboldt Union*, May 5, 1927.

5. S. H. West, *The Life and Times of S. H. West* (Bloomington, Ill.: Pantagraph Printing & Stationery Company, 1908), p. 53.

6. Ibid.

7. *Humboldt Union*, May 5, 1927.

8. KSHS, "Allen County Clippings," 2:70; William E. Connelley, "Albert Robinson Greene," *Kansas Historical Collections* 15 (1919–1922): 2.

Mildred, Allen County

1. KSHS, comp., "Allen County Clippings," vol. 1, n.d.; John G. Clark, *Towns and*

Minerals in Southeastern Kansas—A Study in Regional Industrialization, 1890–*1930*, State Geological Survey of Kansas, Special Distribution Publication, no. 52 (Lawrence, 1970), p. 52.

Bassett, Allen County
  1. KSHS, "Allen County Clippings, 2:183.
  2. Clark, *Towns in Southeastern Kansas*, pp. 103–107.
  3. *Topeka Daily Capital*, March 27, 1915.
  4. Federal Writers' Project, *The WPA Guide to 1930s Kansas*, with a new introduction by James R. Shortridge (Lawrence: University Press of Kansas, 1984; reprint of *Kansas: A Guide to the Sunflower State* [New York, 1939]), p. 488; KSHS, "Allen County Clippings," 2:183.

Belmont, Woodson County
  1. Woodson County Historical Society, "In the Beginning," vol. 1, no. 2, 1968, p. 3.
  2. Ibid.; T. A. Holland & Company, *Holland's Kansas and Nebraska State Directory and Gazetteer*, 1866–1867 (Leavenworth: T. A. Holland & Company, 1867), p. 91.

Neosho Falls, Woodson County
  1. *Kansas City Star*, October 17, 1937.
  2. Ibid.
  3. *Kansas City Star*, October 17, 1937.
  4. Ibid.
  5. *Neosho Falls Post*, July 13, 1933. This was a letter from Frank S. Denney postmarked July 11, 1933, from Colony, Kansas.
  6. *Neosho Falls Post*, July 13, 1933. This was a letter from E. B. Moore.
  7. *Kansas City Star*, October 17, 1937.

Guilford, Wilson County
  1. L. W. Duncan, *History of Neosho and Wilson Counties, Kansas* (Fort Scott: Monitor Printing Company, 1902), pp. 917–918.
  2. *Wilson County Citizen* (Fredonia), January 19, 1950.
  3. Duncan, *History of Neosho*, pp. 917–918.
  4. *Wilson County Citizen* (Fredonia), June 12, 1874.

Cave Springs, Elk County
  1. Emporia State University, "Some Ghost Towns of Kansas," *The Heritage of Kansas Series* (Emporia: Kansas State Teachers College, 1961), pp. 14–16.
  2. *Topeka State Journal*, October 18, 1937.
  3. Emporia State University, "Some Ghost Towns," pp. 14–16.
  4. *Topeka State Journal*, October 18, 1937.

Elgin, Chautauqua County
  1. Lily-B Rozar, "Lincoln's Cousin Buried in Elgin," *Kanhistique Magazine* 4 (February 1979).

2. Ibid.
3. *Wichita Eagle-Beacon*, January 22, 1956.
4. *Topeka Daily Capital*, June 25, 1952.
5. Ibid.
6. *Wichita Eagle-Beacon*, January 22, 1956.
7. Ibid.

Midian, Butler County
1. William Green, *Midian, Kansas: History of an Oil Boom Town* (Wichita: Copycat Service Company, 1964), p. 75.
2. Ibid., pp. 70–71.
3. Jessie Stratford, *The Kingdom of Butler* (El Dorado: Butler County Historical Society, 1970), p. 117; ibid., p. 86.
4. Green, *Midian*, pp. 79–95.

Oil Hill, Butler County
1. Stratford, *Kingdom of Butler*, p. 117.
2. Ibid., pp. 117–118.

CHAPTER FOUR: NORTH CENTRAL KANSAS

Minersville, Cloud County
1. *Belleville Telescope*, March 25, 1971.
2. Agnes Tolbert, *Rock Houses of Minersville* (Chicago: Adams Press, 1963), pp. 8–14.

Agenda, Republic County
1. Elk Creek Centennial Committee, *A Gift to the Future—Our Heritage* (Elk Creek: Elk Creek Bicentennial Committee, 1976), pp. 22–71.
2. Ibid.
3. I. O. Savage, *A History of Republic County, Kansas* (Beloit: Jones & Chubbic, 1901), pp. 192–193.
4. *Agenda Times*, April 9, 1920.

Waconda, Mitchell County
1. *Topeka State Journal*, February 5, 1934.
2. Ibid.
3. *Cawker City Public Record*, October 30, 1902.
4. *Beloit Daily Call*, February 26, 1953.
5. *Cawker City Public Record*, October 30, 1902.
6. *Beloit Daily Call*, February 26, 1953; A. Andreas, *History of Kansas*, 2 vols. (Chicago: Andreas, 1883), 2:1,028.
7. Ibid.

Dispatch, Smith/Jewell Counties
  1. *Downs News*, February 16, 1961.
  2. *Beloit Daily Call*, January 23, 1951.

Webster, Rooks County
  1. *Topeka Daily Capital*, December 1, 1930.
  2. Gertrude Applegate, "The Webster Dam and a Transplanted Town," unpublished manuscript, n.d., KSHS.
  3. *Topeka Daily Capital*, December 1, 1930, and July 11, 1954.
  4. *Topeka Daily Capital*, December 1, 1930.
  5. Ibid.
  6. *Topeka Daily Capital*, July 11, 1954.

Long Island, Phillips County
  1. *Phillips County Review*, May 15, 1952.
  2. Federal Writers' Project, *The WPA Guide to 1930s Kansas*, pp. 445–446.
  3. Ibid.
  4. *Phillips County Review* (Phillipsburg), May 15, 1952.
  5. Cecil Kingery, *Phillipsburg–Phillips County Centennial, 1872–1972* (Phillipsburg: n.p., 1972), pp. 36C, 59C.
  6. *Phillips County Review*, November 16, 1972.
  7. Ibid., May 15, 1952.
  8. Kingery, *Phillipsburg*, pp. 36C, 59C.

CHAPTER FIVE: CENTRAL KANSAS

Brookville, Saline County
  1. O. P. Byers, "When Railroading Outdid the Wild West Stories," *Kansas Historical Collections* 17 (1926–1928): 342.
  2. A. Andreas, *History of Kansas*, 2 vols. (Chicago, 1883), 1:706.
  3. Ibid.
  4. *Wichita Eagle*, October 23, 1960.
  5. Kirke Mechem, ed., *Annals of Kansas, 1886–1925*, 2 vols. (Topeka: Kansas State Historical Society, 1954), 1:112.
  6. *Brookville Transcript*, February 28, 1890.
  7. *Wichita Evening Eagle*, April 25, 1952.

Sveadal, McPherson County
  1. *Lindsborg News Record*, August 29, 1963.

Beach Valley, Rice County
  1. *Lyons Daily News*, April 12, 1961.

2. Louise Barry, "Ranch at Cow Creek Crossing," *Kansas Historical Quarterly* 38 (1972): 416–444.

3. *Lyons Daily News*, April 12, 1961.

4. *Lyons Daily News*, August 17, 1946; Barry, "Ranch at Cow Creek," pp. 416–444.

5. George A. Root, "Extracts from the Diary of Captain Lambert Wolf," *Kansas Historical Quarterly* 1 (1931–1932): 201–204.

6. Barry, "Ranch at Cow Creek Crossing," p. 444.

7. Ibid.

8. *Lyons Daily News*, April 12, 1961.

Dubuque, Russell/Barton Counties

1. *Hoisington Dispatch*, November 22, 1962.

Rome, Ellis County

1. Raymond Witty, "History of Rome, Kansas," unpublished manuscript, n.d., p. 12, KSHS.

2. William Elsey Connelley, "Some of the Lost Towns of Kansas," *Kansas Historical Collections* 12 (1911–1912): 438–439.

3. Witty, "Rome," p. 12.

4. Connelley, "Some Lost Towns," p. 439.

5. Witty, "Rome," p. 12.

6. Connelley, "Some Lost Towns," p. 439.

7. Witty, "Rome," p. 12.

8. Connelley, "Some Lost Towns," p. 440.

Chetola, Ellis County

1. Rush County Historical Society, *Rush County, Kansas* (La Crosse: Rush County Historical Society, 1976), pp. 202–203.

2. *Ellis Review*, June 14, 1962.

3. *Hutchison News-Herald*, July 13, 1952.

4. Rush County Historical Society, *Rush County*, pp. 202–203.

5. *Hutchison News-Herald*, July 13, 1952.

CHAPTER SIX: SOUTH CENTRAL KANSAS

Hunnewell, Sumner County

1. *Hutchison News-Herald*, October 19, 1952.

2. A. Andreas, *History of Kansas*, 2 vols. (Chicago: Andreas, 1883), 2:1,509.

3. Jean C. Lough, "Gateway to the Promised Land," *Kansas Historical Quarterly* 25 (1959): 19.

4. Andreas, *History of Kansas* 2:1,509.

5. Ann Failing, *Shoo Fly City* (n.p.: Ann Failing, 1960), pp. 81–86.

6. *Caldwell News*, September 14, 1893.

7. Failing, *Shoo Fly*, pp. 81–86.

8. KSHS, comp., "Sumner County Clippings," vol. 2, 1921–1937, p. 62.

Runnymede, Harper County

1. Thurman Harriet, "Runnymede," unpublished manuscript, n.d., Manuscript Division, KSHS.

2. Colin Richards, *Bowler Hats and Stetsons* (New York: Ronald, Whiting & Wheaton, 1966), pp. 69–73.

3. Bernard R. Carmen, "When Runnymede Howled," *Frontier Times Magazine* (May 1963): 32–34.

4. Richards, *Bowler Hats*, pp. 69–73.

5. Harriet, "Runnymede."

6. T. A. McNeal, *When Kansas Was Young* (New York: MacMillan & Company, 1922), pp. 57–61.

7. Harriet, "Runnymede."

8. Ibid.

9. *Harper County Times*, January 1, 1908.

10. Harriet, "Runnymede."

11. Charles Seaton, "Reminiscences of Runnymede," *Kansas Historical Collections* 12 (1911–1912): 467.

Freeport, Harper County

1. *Wichita Eagle*, September 14, 1976.

2. Ibid.

3. *Hutchinson News*, July 26, 1970.

4. Gwendaline and Paul Sanders, *The Harper County Story* (Harper: n.p., 1968), p. 109.

Smallwood, Comanche County

1. McNeal, *When Kansas*, pp. 61–62.

2. *Wichita Beacon*, January 31, 1927.

3. McNeal, *When Kansas*, pp. 61–62.

4. *Wichita Beacon*, January 31, 1927.

Ash Valley, Pawnee County

1. *Larned Tiller and Toiler*, February 13, 1967.

2. Ibid.

3. Ibid.

CHAPTER SEVEN: NORTHWEST KANSAS

Nicodemus, Graham County

1. Glen Schwendemann, "Nicodemus: Negro Haven on the Solomon," *Kansas Historical Quarterly* 34 (1968): 10–31.

2. Ibid.

3. Stephen Steinberg, "My Day in Nicodemus," *Phylon: The Atlanta Review of Race and Culture* 37, 3 (1976): 243–249.

4. *Salina Journal*, February 12, 1950.

5. *Nicodemus Cyclone*, September 7, 1888.

6. *Salina Journal*, February 12, 1950.

7. Schwendemann, "Nicodemus," pp. 10–31.

8. Ibid.

9. Ibid.

10. Ibid.; see also U.S., Department of Interior, National Park Service, *Promised Land on the Solomon: Black Settlement at Nicodemus, Kansas* (Washington, D.C.: Government Printing Office, 1986), and Robert G. Athearn, *In Search of Canaan: Black Migration to Kansas, 1879–80* (Lawrence: Regents Press of Kansas, 1978).

Achilles, Rawlins County

1. G. Derek West, "The Battle of Sappa Creek," *Kansas Historical Quarterly* 34 (1968): 154–164.

2. *McDonald Standard*, July 2, 1953.

Mingo, Thomas County

1. R. I. Bruner, *Land of Windmills: Thomas County, Kansas* (Colby: Thomas County Historical Society, 1976).

2. Ibid.; Frank W. Blackmar, *Cyclopedia of Kansas History*, 3 vols. (Chicago: Standard Publishing Company, 1912), 2:289.

Voltaire, Sherman County

1. Sherman County Historical Society, *Bulletin* (Goodland: Sherman County Historical Society, August 1977).

2. *Topeka Journal*, June 5, 1920.

3. Sherman County Historical Society, *Bulletin*.

4. O. P. Byers, "Personal Recollections of the Terrible Blizzard of 1886," *Kansas Historical Collections* 12 (1911–1912): 114–115.

5. *Sherman County Herald* (Goodland), September 2, 1937.

CHAPTER EIGHT: WEST CENTRAL KANSAS

Threshing Machine Canyon/Bluffton, Trego County

1. This station is now the town of Russell in Russell County, Kansas.

2. *Topeka Daily Capital*, February 16, 1958.

3. W. A. Hill, *Historic Hays* (Hays Publishing Company, 1938), p. 54; *Topeka Daily Capital*, February 16, 1958.

4. *Topeka Daily Capital*, February 16, 1958.

5. *Hays Daily News*, May 29, 1955.

6. *Topeka Daily Capital*, February 16, 1958.

Sidney, Ness County
1. Minnie Dubbs Millbrook, *Ness, Western County, Kansas* (Detroit: Millbrook Printing Co., 1955), p. 269.
2. Ibid.; William Elsey Connelley, "Some of the Lost Towns of Kansas," *Kansas Historical Collections* 12 (1911–1912): 469.

Amy, Lane County
1. Family Heritage Society, comp., *Family Heritage Album of Lane County* (McPherson: The Compiler, 1975).
2. *Scott City News Chronicle*, January 30, 1958.
3. Family Heritage Society, *Heritage Album*.

Farnsworth, Lane County
1. *Dighton Herald*, April 14, 1954.
2. Family Heritage Society, *Heritage Album*.
3. Ibid.

Monument Station, Gove County
1. Charles R. Wetzel, "Monument Station, Gove County, " *Kansas Historical Quarterly* 26 (1960): 250–254.
2. Ibid., p. 252.
3. Ibid., pp. 253–254; Robert W. Baughman, *Kansas Post Offices* (Topeka: Kansas State Historical Society, 1961), p. 86.

McAllaster, Logan County
1. *Winona Leader*, March 21, 1985.

Russell Springs, Logan County
1. Alma Johnson, "Russell Springs: The Town that Changed," *Kanhistique Magazine* 6 (October 1980): 1.
2. *Winona Leader*, July 5, 1973.
3. Ibid.; *Topeka Daily Commonwealth*, March 27, 1887.
4. *Kansas City Star*, May 21, 1911; *Kansas City Times*, November 1, 1961.
5. *Kansas City Star*, May 21, 1911.
6. Ibid.
7. *Oakley Graphic*, November 27, 1925.
8. Ibid.
9. *Kansas City Star*, May 21, 1911.
10. *Kansas City Times*, November 1, 1961.
11. *Topeka Daily Capital*, March 24, 1937, and February 17, 1937.
12. *Topeka State Journal*, June 15, 1938.

13. *Kansas City Star*, October 23, 1960.

14. Ibid.

15. *Topeka Daily Capital*, July 11, 1963; *Kansas City Times*, August 14, 1963.

Sheridan, Logan County

1. *Harper's New Monthly Magazine*, November 1875, p. 830.

2. Wallace County Historical Society, *History of Wallace County* (Sharon Springs: Wallace County Historical Society, 1979).

3. Leslie Linville, *Visiting Historic Sites on the Central High Plains* (Osborne, Kans.: Leslie Linville, 1979), pp. 107, 124.

4. De B. Randolph Keim, *Sheridan's Troopers on the Borders* (Philadelphia: David McKay, 1885), pp. 42, 44, 45.

5. *Kansas Weekly Tribune* (Lawrence), July 30, 1868.

6. *Kansas City Commonwealth* (Topeka), August 1, 1869.

7. Editorial, *Kansas City Commonwealth* (Topeka), August 4, 1869.

8. Homer W. Wheeler, *Buffalo Days* (Indianapolis: Bobbs-Merrill, 1925), pp. 273–274.

9. *Harper's New Monthly Magazine*, November 1875, p. 835.

Wallace, Wallace County

1. KSHS, comp., "Wallace County Clippings," vol. 1, n.d., p. 7.

2. Ibid.

3. *Hays Daily News*, September 26, 1954.

4. KSHS, "Wallace County Clippings," 1:7.

5. *Oakley Graphic*, March 25, 1938.

6. *Hays Daily News*, September 26, 1954.

7. KSHS, "Wallace County Clippings," 1:7.

8. *Oakley Graphic*, March 25, 1938.

Henshaw Station, Logan County

1. "Henshaw Station," Ghost Town Files, Manuscript Division, KSHS.

2. Mrs. Frank C. Montgomery, "Fort Wallace and Its Relation to the Frontier," *Kansas Historical Collections* 17 (1926–1928): 225.

3. William E. Connelley, "Life and Adventures of George W. Brown," *Kansas Historical Collections* 17 (1926–1928): 111

4. "Henshaw Station," Ghost Town Files, Manuscript Division, KSHS.

Coronado, Wichita County

1. William Elsey Connelley, "Some of the Lost Towns of Kansas," *Kansas Historical Collections* 12 (1911–1912): 442.

2. Ibid.

3. Ibid., p. 443.

4. Ibid., p. 444.

5. Ibid., p. 445.

6. Ibid., p. 446.
7. Ibid., p. 447.
8. Ibid.

Colokan, Greeley County
1. Connor Sorenson, "Ghost Towns of Greeley County, Kansas," pamphlet, n.p., p. 11, KSHS.
2. Ibid., p. 12.
3. Ibid., pp. 13–14.
4. "Colokan," Ghost Town Files, Manuscript Division, KSHS.

CHAPTER NINE: SOUTHWEST KANSAS

Lexington, Clark County
1. John Franklin Valentine, *Lexington, 1884–1984: The History of a Kansas Community* (Ashland: Lexington Centennial Committee, 1984).
2. Ibid.

Cash City, Clark County
1. *Cash City Cashier*, October 29, 1886.
2. "Cash City," Ghost Town Files, Manuscript Division, KSHS; Frank W. Blackmar, *Cyclopedia of Kansas History*, 3 vols. (Chicago: Standard Publishing Company, 1912), 1:298–299.

Beersheba, Hodgeman County
1. *American Israelite* (Cincinnati), August 4, 1882.
2. James Rudin, "Beersheba, Kansas: 'God's Pure Air on Government Land,' " *Kansas Historical Quarterly* 34 (1968): 289.
3. Ibid., p. 295.

Ingalls, Gray County
1. William Elsey Connelley, "Some of the Lost Towns of Kansas," *Kansas Historical Collections* 12 (1911–1912): 464.
2. Ibid., pp. 465–467.

Ravanna, Finney County
1. KSHS, comp., "Finney County Clippings," vol. 1, n.d., pp. 107–108.
2. A. J. Myers, *High Plains Journal*, excerpt dated April 21, 1955.
3. Ibid.
4. KSHS, "Finney County Clippings," 1:107–108.
5. Ibid.
6. Myers, *High Plains*.
7. KSHS, "Finney County Clippings," 1:107–108.

8. Ibid.
9. *Dodge City Globe*, March 16, 1950.

Eminence, Finney County
1. *Garden City News*, November 23, 1933.
2. Leola Blanchard, *Conquest of Southwest Kansas* (Garden City: n.p., 1931), p. 213.
3. *Topeka Daily Capital*, December 3, 1933.
4. Ibid.
5. Ibid.
6. Kirke Mechem, ed., *Annals of Kansas, 1886–1925*, 2 vols. (Topeka: Kansas State Historical Society, 1954), 1:45, 46, 78, 81.
7. *Garden City News*, November 30, 1933.

Terry, Finney County
1. *Topeka Daily Capital*, April 21, 1930.
2. Blanchard, *Conquest*, pp. 181–182.

Hartland, Kearny County
1. *Ulysses News*, September 17, 1970.
2. Virginia Pierce Hicks, ed., "Sketches of Early Days in Kearny County," *Kansas Historical Quarterly* 7 (1938): 64, 77.
3. Ibid.
4. Ibid., pp. 66, 74.
5. Ibid., pp. 64, 77.
6. *Dodge City Globe*, March 26, 1934.
7. Hicks, "Sketches of Early Days," pp. 64, 77.
8. *Ulysses News*, September 17, 1970.

Chantilly, Kearny County
1. Francis L. Pierce, "Sketches of Early Days in Kearny County," *Kansas Historical Quarterly* 7 (1938): 73–75.
2. *High Plains Journal*, September 10, 1959.

Coolidge and Kendall, Hamilton County
1. *Dodge City Times*, October 4, 1883.
2. Nyle Miller and Joseph Snell, *Great Gunfighters of the Kansas Cowtowns, 1867–1886* (Lincoln: University of Nebraska Press, 1971), pp. 327–328.
3. Connelley, "Some Lost Towns," pp. 456–463.
4. Miller and Snell, *Gunfighters*, pp. 327–328.
5. Charles L. Youngblood, *A Mighty Hunter* (Boonville, Ind.: Boonville Standard Co., 1890), p. 87.
6. Connelley, "Some Lost Towns," pp. 456–463.

Trail City, Hamilton County

1. Bill Powell, "Trail City—That Was the Town That Was," *Roundup—the Denver Westerners*, vols. 20–22 (1964–1966): 3–6. Clyde Blackburn, "Trail City," *Kansas Territorial* 3 (March–April 1983): 30–31.

2. Blackburn, "Trail City," pp. 30–31; Charles Hurd, "The Story of Trail City," *Three Score and Ten: Lamar's First 70 Years on the Arkansas* (Lamar, Colo., n.p., 1956), p. 28.

3. *Coolidge Border Ruffian*, July 3, 1886.

4. Blackburn, "Trail City," pp. 30–31; Powell, "The Town That Was," pp. 3–6.

5. Powell, "The Town That Was," pp. 3–6.

6. Blackburn, "Trail City," pp. 30–31.

7. Powell, "The Town That Was," pp. 3–6.

8. *Hutchinson News-Herald*, February 3, 1952.

9. Hurd, "Story of Trail City," p. 28.

10. *Hutchinson News-Herald*, February 3, 1952; Blackburn, "Trail City," pp. 30–31.

11. Powell, "The Town That Was," pp. 3–6.

"Old" Ulysses, Grant County

1. *High Plains Journal*, April 14, 1955.

2. *Topeka Daily Capital*, September 27, 1970.

3. Emporia State University, "Some Ghost Towns of Kansas," *The Heritage of Kansas Series* (Emporia: Kansas State Teachers College, 1961), pp. 17–18.

4. *Topeka Daily Capital*, September 27, 1970.

Santa Fe, Haskell County

1. *High Plains Journal*, October 18, 1951.

2. Emporia State University, "Some Ghost Towns," p. 17.

3. *Topeka Daily Capital*, September 27, 1970.

4. Bee Jacquart, "Another Ghost Town," *The Aerend* 5, 4 (Fall 1934): 224–227.

Fargo Springs, Seward County

1. E. D. Smith, "Jedediah S. Smith and the Settlement of Kansas," *Kansas Historical Collections* 12 (1911–1912): 258–259.

2. *Liberal News*, May 2, 1935.

3. Louise Barry, "Circuit Riding in Southwest Kansas in 1885 and 1886," *Kansas Historical Quarterly* 12 (1943): 385.

4. Mechem, *Annals of Kansas*, 1: 13, 45.

5. *Fargo Springs Prairie Owl*, date of issue unrecorded.

6. *Kansas City Journal*, October 18, 1911; *Dodge City Globe*, December 26, 1922.

Springfield, Seward County

1. "Springfield," Ghost Town Files, Manuscript Division, KSHS.

2. *Seward County Courant* (Springfield), November 11, 1887.

3. Ibid.
4. *Liberal News*, January 6, 1934.
5. Ibid.
6. *Hutchinson News-Herald*, March 6, 1956.

SELECTED
BIBLIOGRAPHY

Andreas, A. *History of Kansas*. 2 vols. Chicago: Andreas, 1883. Reprint available through Atchison County Historical Society.

Athearn, Robert G. *In Search of Canaan*. Lawrence: Regents Press of Kansas, 1978.

Barry, Louise. *The Beginning of the West*. Topeka: Kansas State Historical Society, 1973.

Blackmar, Frank W. *Cyclopedia of Kansas History*. 3 vols. Chicago: Standard Publishing Company, 1912.

Emporia State University. "Some Ghost Towns of Kansas." *The Heritage of Kansas Series*. Emporia: Kansas State Teachers College, 1961.

Everts, L. H. *The Official State Atlas of Kansas*. Philadelphia: L. H. Everts & Co., 1887. Reprint available through Shawnee County (Topeka) Genealogical Society.

Federal Writers' Project, comp. *The WPA Guide to 1930s Kansas*. With a new Introduction by James R. Shortridge. Lawrence: University Press of Kansas, 1984. (Originally published as *Kansas: A Guide to the Sunflower State* [New York, 1939].)

Fitzgerald, Daniel C. *Ghost Towns of Kansas*. 3 vols. Holton: Bell Graphics, 1976–1982.

————. "Town Booming: An Economic History of Steamboat Towns along the Kansas-Missouri Border, 1840–1860." M.A. thesis, University of Kansas, Lawrence, 1983.

Ghost Town Files. Manuscript Division, Kansas State Historical Society, Topeka.

Hintz, Forrest. *Some Vanishing Towns of Kansas*. Wichita: *Wichita Eagle-Beacon*, 1982.

Kansas State Historical Society, comp. "County Clippings" volumes. Available for all Kansas counties. Kansas State Historical Society Library Division, various dates.

Kansas State Historical Society [William Elsey Connelley]. "Some of the Lost Towns of Kansas." *Kansas Historical Collections* 12 (1911–1912).

Polk, R. L. & Company. *Kansas State Gazetteer*. Detroit: R. L. Polk & Company, various dates.

Wilder, Daniel. *Annals of Kansas, 1541–1885*. Topeka: T. D. Thacher & Co., 1886.

INDEX

INDEX